MW00388489

eBay®
POWERSELLER™
MILLION DOLLAR IDEAS

Innovative Ways to Make
Your eBay Sales Soar

eBay®
POWERSELLER™
MILLION DOLLAR IDEAS

Innovative Ways to Make
Your eBay Sales Soar

Brad Schepp
Debra Schepp

McGraw-Hill
New York   Chicago   San Francisco   Lisbon
London   Madrid   Mexico City   Milan   New Delhi
San Juan   Seoul   Singapore   Sydney   Toronto

1 2 3 4 5 6 7 8 9 0   DOC/DOC   0 9 8 7 6

ISBN-13: 978-0-07-147480-1
ISBN-10:   0-07-147480-3

This publication is designed to provide accurate and authoritative information in regard to the subject matter covered. It is sold with the understanding that the publisher is not engaged in rendering legal, accounting, or other professional service. If legal advice or other expert assistance is required, the services of a competent professional person should be sought.
—*From a Declaration of Principles Jointly Adopted by a Committee of the American Bar Association and a Committee of Publishers and Associations*

McGraw-Hill books are available at special discounts to use as premiums and sales promotions, or for use in corporate training programs. For more information, please write to the Director of Special Sales, Professional Publishing, McGraw-Hill, Two Penn Plaza, New York, NY 10121-2298. Or contact your local bookstore.

This book is printed on acid-free paper.

Library of Congress Cataloging-in-Publication Data

Schepp, Brad.
  eBay powerseller million dollar ideas : innovative ways to make your eBay sales soar / by Brad Schepp and Debra Schepp.
      p. cm.
  Includes index.
  ISBN 0-07-147480-3 (pbk. : alk. paper) 1. eBay (Firm) 2. Internet auctions. 3. Selling—Computer network resources. 4. Internet marketing. 5. Internet advertising. I. Schepp, Debra. II. Title. III. Title: eBay power seller million dollar ideas.
  HF5478.S335 2006
  658.8'7—dc22
                              2006015650

To eBay's PowerSellers, who are always working, always learning, and all the while creating the life they've imagined.

CONTENTS

ACKNOWLEDGMENTS

Making a place for oneself in any community is challenging. There you are starting out in a new place. Everything can seem strange and a little intimidating. Where are the best places to shop? Who provides the best services? Who in this new community can you trust? Then, one by one, the neighbors drop by. Some leave their phone numbers. Some bring a cake, but everyone who comes to your door is interested in meeting you and willing to be friendly. (The ones who don't feel that way stay home.) Amazing as it may seem, eBay still replicates this neighborly community. You'd be surprised at how many times you can go onto the site looking for answers to your questions and have complete strangers take time from their busy lives just to help you. You'd be surprised, but we wouldn't be. We've had this experience hundreds of times now. So as we prepare to thank everyone who has helped us, first on that list will be some of the PowerSellers who have been so generous in their support.

We'll start with the go-to sellers. These are the ones who popped into our heads whenever we needed a good solid answer, quick. We're afraid they didn't quite know what they were getting into when they agreed to help us! Thanking them here will replace our buying them cocktails at eBay Live! So here's to you: Jeff and Katrina Hess of hessfine, Phil Leahy of entertainmenthouse, Lynne Baron of baronarts, Bob Buchanan and Greg Scheuer of avforsale, Christina Carr of wiccan well, Bob Kitchener of bobkitchener, Andy and Deb Mowery of debnroo, Marguerite Swope of mhswope, and Cindy Walker of superiormats.

There were also some people outside of eBay who helped us more than they'd planned. Top on this list was Debbie Levitt of As Was Incorporated at www.aswas.com, who gets paid for consulting with eBay PowerSellers but did the same for us because she's awesome. When you're ready to really get serious about your eBay business, you'll know just whom to call.

In a category of their own are our profiled sellers. These are people who gave us more than we could have asked for. They easily fit into the above category of go-to sellers, but in addition to giving us as much information as we asked for, they also agreed to have us provide you with details of their businesses and lives, including their pictures. Kevin Boyd of preferreddiscounts, Drew Friedman of whitemountaintrading, Adam Hersh of adamhershauctions, Stephanie Inge of stephintexas, Harvey Levine and Marcia Cooper of generalent, Randall Pinson of rocket-auctions, Gary Richardson of harleyglasses, Jody Rogers and Asad Bangash of beachcombers!, Robert Sachs of rosachs, and David Yaskulka of blueberryboutique. Thank you for everything you've done.

Still more PowerSellers who should get a special nod include: Ginny Bass of bamcm, Carolyn Berens of 100percenttoys, Kelvin Cook of stores.ebay.com/Fitzgeralds-Collectibles, Catherine Yeats of 4-a-little-lady, Ben Boxall of Luna Imports, Richard Chemel of IsoldIt, Rich Cseh of volcanogames, Marc DiFilippo of tailgatetickets, Garret Hebenstriet of theglowpro, Michael Kolman of parrothead88, Daniel Leff of www.theblingking.co.uk, and Mike Martyka of solidcolornecties. There are countless other wonderful sellers who were kind enough to answer our questions, but this book had a page limit so we'd better thank them collectively. We'd appreciate everything you did for us.

In the midst of our research Deb made a wonderful trip to Austin, Texas, to attend a Professional eBay Sellers Alliance (PESA) Summit. For three amazing days she was immersed in the world of eBay's Platinum and Titanium sellers, now known as Top Sellers and a world unlike any other. There she had the opportunity to actually meet people we'd only ever known through e-mail or phone calls. Her welcome was warm and friendly. Thanks so much to Tony Cicalese, one of the event organizers, who with his usual warm and loving nature encouraged her to go. Andy Mowery welcomed her when she got there and offered advice about which sessions she shouldn't miss. How cool is it to meet a friend in person? Joe Cortese, cofounder of PESA welcomed Deb. Jay Senese of jayandmarie entertained her with humorous stories of the wild life at the top of the eBay heap. David and Lucy Hardin of shoetime really took her under their wings, making sure she never ate a single meal alone. How can she ever thank them for the words, "You belong to us now, Baby Girl?"

Plenty of people representing companies that support eBay sellers were also generous with their time and expertise. Ina Steiner of AuctionBytes, Paul Lundy and Bobby Kreiner of Marketworks, Lynn Pittman of Sharpics, David Frey and Dave Popowich of Terapeak, Wayne Yaeger of Sellathon, Lisa Suttora of whatdoisell.com, Wes Clayton of Interapptive, Inc., Chris Malta and Robin Cowie of Worldwide Brands, Amanda Foley of Mpire, Bart Mowrey of i2iauction.com, Jack Reynolds of QuickDrop, Elise Wetzel and Noel Novak of IsoldIt, and Vanessa Lee of pugster.

From eBay we'd like to thank Mary Bates, Colin Rule, and Adam Nash. Their interest in our work was inspiring.

From the world of publishing, we'd like to thank the people at McGraw-Hill starting with our acquisitions editor Margie McAneny. Our new editor Dianne Wheeler stepped in and took control in the middle of the project, and we never worried about that. Sue Ray and Scott Kurtz, who took care of all the endless details deserve our appreciation. Bettina Faltermeier has kept us busy doing publicity. We've worked with a lot of publicity people, but never one better than Bettina. Kate Viotto, the sales manager does a great job, too. eBay University instructor Michael Kaiser, once again, was a great technical editor who made sure we kept the facts correct and accurate. Thank you. Bill Gladstone, our agent for this project, also deserves a nod.

Finally (yes, we mean it), we'd like to thank our family, both here at home and scattered around the country for tolerating our absence. We missed you and hope you missed us too. Now, we can actually answer the phone to chat and maybe even plan a visit if you're still speaking to us.

INTRODUCTION

We've spent the last few years immersed in a fascinating world. We've had an amazing adventure spending so much time among eBay's PowerSellers. You'll agree they are a most extraordinary group of people. They amazed us when we decided to write *eBay PowerSeller Secrets.* That's what inspired us to write it! But as we researched that book, our admiration and respect for this group of entrepreneurs grew beyond its original borders. The PowerSellers and Top Sellers (Platinum and Titanium-level PowerSellers), are among the most creative, inventive, hardworking, and interesting people we've ever met. In their own way, they truly are the pioneers of the twenty-first century.

Not only have these dedicated business owners forged new lives for themselves, but they've learned the essential details of pioneer life: adaptability and creative thinking. Those two abilities make survival possible in an ever-changing landscape that can often prove to be inhospitable at best and downright threatening at its worst. Since the publication of *eBay PowerSeller Secrets*, selling on eBay has gotten even more complicated, and earning your living this way is even harder. The landscape has changed. It's more competitive, more international in scope, and new types of fraud appear like dandelions in spring. Many eBay sellers now also sell in other venues, such as through their own independent Web stores, or through other auction sites. What worked well two years ago may no longer be viable. That would be okay if the changes were behind us. Everyone who remained successful and weathered those storms would still be happily moving forward. But the real challenge is that the changes will never be behind us! It's not enough to weather last year's storms. If you're going to have a lasting presence on eBay, you have to manage your business right now with a sharp eye on what's coming at you next week and next year. The world of e-commerce moves and changes too quickly for you to establish your good practices and leave them as they are while you happily buy and sell and collect the money. That may be fine in other venues, but it won't work on eBay.

Writers are in the idea business. They come to recognize good ideas when they find them. At least they'd better recognize them if they've gotten used to the idea of eating! That gives us something in common with eBay's PowerSellers. They are on a constant search for great ideas. The ones who really succeed don't just act like PowerSellers; they also *think* like PowerSellers. That means they are constantly evaluating everything they do to find the most efficient, cost-effective, sustainable way to run their businesses. They celebrate their successes, but they don't allow those successes to blind them to their vulnerabilities. Good practices and hard work take you a long way on eBay, but they are no guarantee for long-term success.

That brings us back to the idea behind this book of ideas you are holding in your hands. We were gratified that the sellers who worked with us to research *eBay PowerSeller Secrets* embraced it so heartily. They said that not only did we describe the issues of making your living on eBay realistically and successfully, but even more importantly, we captured what life was really like for someone who earns a living by being an eBay PowerSeller. They appreciated that we thought it was important to include that flavor of life along with advice about building the life itself. We were very gratified to discover we'd capture the essence of many of their best business practices but also the rhythms and details of their lives. The more we spoke with them and spent time among them, the more we realized that there was a nugget beyond the details of sourcing, listing, payment, and shipping. There is something within the most successful sellers that makes them look at the challenges a little differently.

The most successful eBay sellers view the challenges that come along as just that, challenges and not problems. Every new change can present a new opportunity as well as a new problem, and the success they find is based on the fact that they don't shrink from the problems; they think their way around them! Now, no one starts out on eBay with the experience and knowledge necessary to achieve this. But these sellers didn't start out that way either. They may have brought determined and hardworking personalities with them when they came to eBay, but they gained the knowledge and experience by being out there every day, constantly learning, adapting, changing, and growing. That's the way it is with pioneers.

So, when we thought about ideas for books to follow *eBay PowerSeller Secrets* we wondered, what else would sellers striving to make successful lives on eBay need to know? We'd already done a book of best practices, so we decided to turn our attention to the results of that pioneer mentality. We decided to share with readers the best ideas PowerSellers are putting into practice every day to survive and thrive in *today's* eBay environment. By sharing these ideas with you, we hope you'll learn to think like a PowerSeller and think creatively about the challenges facing you every day as an eBay seller. If you took with you the basis for an eBay business when you finished reading *eBay PowerSeller Secrets*, we hope this time you'll take with you the basis for thinking beyond the ordinary in terms of your eBay business, for never being satisfied with what's there, but instead continuing to make your spot in the world of e-commerce through creativity, imagination, and passion.

In *eBay PowerSeller Million Dollar Ideas*, you'll find we cover many of the things you need to consider when operating an eBay business. We have chapters about sourcing, listing creation, shipping, fraud, and international sales. But this time around you will also find a lot of information on selling on other venues, plus an entire chapter of ideas on how you can take your eBay experience and use it to make money through related pursuits. This may mean opening your own eBay drop-off store, or working as a trading assistant or eBay education specialist. Some of the PowerSellers we spoke with detailed how they make more money from these "sideline" businesses than they now make from their original eBay businesses. From our discussions with scores of PowerSellers we've carefully selected more than 100 individual ideas you can adapt for you own business. To make it into the book the idea had to be very creative, counterintuitive, or potentially able to help you earn significantly more money every day. For each of these ideas, we've provided some advice about how you might be able to use the idea in your own situation. Overall, you'll find hundreds of suggestions.

Not all of these ideas will be right for your individual business, and certainly not all of them will result in your earning a million dollars! We are well aware of those products being hawked to unsuspecting dreamers guaranteed to show them how to make it rich, and quickly, on eBay. We're not about to enter those ranks at this stage of the game! But the ideas that we present to you, combined, do represent the creativity and thinking of people who have earned millions of dollars on eBay. Beyond the individual ideas themselves, we hope that by reading this book, you'll come to under-stand and internalize the thinking behind the ideas. If our first eBay book captured the essence of life as a PowerSeller, we hope this one will capture the essence of thinking like a PowerSeller. Once you've gained that, you'll be on your way to a successful life, both on eBay and off.

Brad and Debra Schepp
www.bradanddeb.com

eBay®
POWERSELLER™
MILLION DOLLAR IDEAS

*Innovative Ways to Make
Your eBay Sales Soar*

CHAPTER 1

eBay Today:
It's a Whole New World

Among eBay's most successful sellers, the Nortica eBay 500 list is as important as the *Wall Street Journal* is to America's CEOs. The list is a compilation of eBay's top 500 sellers as ranked by feedback. PowerSeller Adam Hersh of AdamHershAuctions and his staff scrutinize the list monthly for ideas and inspirations. Recently Adam noticed that among the sellers on the list, there were more than a few whom eBay listed as NARU, Not a Registered User. How could a seller go from the top of the list of most successful sellers to NARU in such a brief time? How could such a successful and savvy eBay seller lose an entire business? Adam needed to know, so he and his staff interviewed 30 to 40 of these former PowerSellers. Their answers both surprised and educated him.

One of the lessons Adam learned from his interviews was that eBay is far more a world of business today than ever before. The days of "the Internet garage sale" are considered "back in the day" and are viewed with nostalgia. With more than 200 million users worldwide, eBay handles 14 percent of the world's e-commerce. More than 60 million items, found in more than 50,000 categories, are available for sale at any one time. While you can still buy Beanie Babies on eBay, collectibles are far from the site's leading revenue generator anymore. That distinction goes to eBay Motors, where cars sell at the rate of one per minute!

As eBay has grown, so have the opportunities for entrepreneurs. While in 2003, eBay estimated that 430,000 people in the United States earned all or part of their family's income through the site, by the spring of 2006, that number had jumped to an estimated 1.3 million people. In just three years, the number of eBay entrepreneurs more than tripled.

As eBay has blossomed, so have its users. Sellers are more experienced now that some of them have been selling on the site for nearly 10 years. These are people who have seen good economic times and bad. They've seen growth and slumps. They know how to survive in the face of all types of economic and business challenges. Those who don't know how to do this are no longer successful eBay entrepreneurs. Recently, Jonathan Garriss of gothamcityonline, a longtime presence on the Nortica 500 list and executive director of the Professional eBay Sellers Alliance (PESA) told a meeting of that group, "If you're still operating your business the same way you were two years ago, you've already fallen behind." That is just how quickly eBay changes and just how quickly a great business can go bad.

In addition, within the hundreds of thousands of new sellers who come to eBay each year, you'll now find yourself competing not only with other individual sellers, but also with large corporations. Wholesalers and manufacturers now use eBay to clear inventory and sell overstocked items. But there are also Fortune 500 companies in the mix such as IBM, Sears, and Best Buy. Some of the PowerSellers who worked with us for this book created their businesses with the plan that they would sell off returned merchandise for the big box stores. They are thriving.

To add to this new challenge, eBay *buyers* are sharper and more experienced than ever before, too. Internet shopping has become so mainstream that more than 627 million people worldwide have now shopped online, according to ACNielsen, a leading provider of consumer and marketplace information. These shoppers have gained a level of comfort and experience, which makes shopping online a realistic alternative to going to the store.

Of course, in any marketplace, having more shoppers is good news! However, sellers need to be prepared for how these shoppers are operating. Just a few years back, 80 percent of the people shopping on eBay browsed through categories to find what they wanted. Only 20 percent used key-word searching. By late 2005, the exact opposite was true according to Meg Whitman, eBay's president and CEO. This shows a rapid maturity among online shoppers. In a world where "Google" has become a verb, more and more people are comfortable using key-words and constructing searches. eBay sellers need to understand this fact and consider how to use it to their best advantage.

eBay sellers and buyers have grown and matured, but the selling proposition eBay offers has also changed. In January 2005, eBay announced a dramatic increase in fees for sellers, especially those sellers who were operating stores. The monthly "rent" for operating an eBay store, for example, jumped by 60 percent (from $9.95 per month to $15.95). Nonstore owners (the bulk of eBay sellers), suffered too. The Buy It Now (BIN) feature, enabling people to end auctions immediately by buying an item at the set BIN price, went from a flat $.05 to up to $.25, depending on the item's price. The widely used Gallery feature, which adds a picture alongside search listings, went from $.25 to $.35.

For smaller sellers, this may not have made much difference in their livelihoods, but large sellers saw an immediate and dramatic drop in their profit margins as their expenses skyrocketed. The dime increase for Gallery listings may seem trivial, but to PowerSellers listing thousands of items per month, that 10 cents added up very quickly. There was a great deal of talk about seller defection that didn't actually come about, but the increased fees made it necessary for all sellers to consider their business operations and how they could protect their profits in the future. The increases meant that it is now harder than ever to stay competitive on eBay and still earn a living. Still more than 1.3 million people are doing just that.

The world eBay itself occupies has also changed. If you remember the early days of television, you also remember when you had three choices of which channel you could watch: ABC, CBS, or NBC. When eBay started in 1995, online shoppers were limited to just a relatively few choices (mainly AOL, Amazon, Yahoo!, or eBay). But, just as you now have almost countless choices for TV viewing, you also have countless choices for where to shop online. To be successful in the world of e-commerce, you're going to have to know more than just a little about the world of Internet shopping *outside* of eBay.

Unfortunately, fraud has grown with equal vigor in this rapidly expanding e-commerce world, and none of us hopes to bring it into our business operations. As the market has matured, so has the sophistication of the criminals who wish to prey on that market. Of the top five "phishing" scams, Reuters recently reported that eBay scams and PayPal scams ranked one and two, respectively. Technology has made phishing even simpler than ever with look-alike e-mails sophisticated enough to catch even savvy users. You will also find criminals using spyware and keylogging to track an innocent user's travels on the Internet and keystrokes for account numbers and personal identification numbers (PINs). Some 10 million Americans are victims of identity theft every year now, according to the Federal Trade Commission, and the House Financial

Services Committee estimates that victims spent an average of 90 hours and $1,700 resolving the problem once they identified it. We'll devote Chapter 5 to an in-depth study of fraud, but no discussion of the eBay landscape today is complete without touching on this ever-troubling aspect of life online.

In the face of all these challenges, you must not grow discouraged. Many sellers now say their biggest challenges are in controlling the growth of their businesses and scaling their operations to keep pace with the rapid increase in their demands. Both of these problems fall into the category of the troubles we can all wish for!

When you decide to enter the world of eBay's top entrepreneurs, all of the problems described here will become challenges for you. Luckily, you don't have to solve them all on your own. The many PowerSellers who helped us with advice and guidance for this book are among the sharpest, smartest, most creative people you'll meet. They've been working on these issues and countless others while they've built thriving, successful, challenging lives of their own design. The tips and ideas they provide won't all be suitable for every reader's particular challenge, but they are sure to get you thinking creatively about how you can follow along on the eBay way of life. What follows now is a sample of some of the challenges eBay's most successful sellers have recognized for themselves. Of course, we'll also give you some great ideas for addressing those challenges, directly from the people most likely to know.

STAY CURRENT WITH NEW TECHNOLOGIES

Just as technology created eBay, it's also moving eBay forward. Technology and its advancement will forever alter eBay and the way people use the site both for buying and selling. We'll discuss various new technologies in great detail in Chapter 6. Here we'll look briefly at some of these new and intriguing technologies.

USE VOICE AND MUSIC IN YOUR AUCTIONS

Florida-based PowerSeller hessfine, sellers of fine jewelry and objects of art, have started using voice technology in their listings. These sellers realized that they were spending a good amount of time answering e-mails that asked questions clearly addressed in the item description. Obviously, buyers weren't bothering to read the listings all the way through. They enlisted a local singer to record a jingle to the tune of "She'll Be Comin' Round the Mountain." The entertaining ditty included details on their shipping and payment policies and encouraged listeners to read the entire listing before bidding. Katrina Hess of hessfine reports that the positive feedback they're getting from this new venture is running very near 80 percent. We can personally vouch for its ability to captivate. Our tech-savvy teenage son, who has absolutely no interest in any of his parents' projects, overheard us listening to the jingle. He stopped dead in his tracks to find out exactly what we were doing. If it can grab *his* attention, it's got to have something going for it!

LET'S GET TO WORK...

- Include a button in your listing so that listening to audio is a choice. If you have audio that starts automatically when the listing opens, be sure that button provides a quick and easy way to stop the sound. You don't want to chase away buyers who are taking a few minutes out of working in a cubicle to check eBay by announcing loudly that these folks aren't working. You'll lose a customer and probably won't see that one back again.

- Consider working on the jingle yourself. That way you'll be sure it includes all of the elements you want your buyers to know. It also makes it personal, and you might find people listen long enough to see just how your personality shines through.

- Look for local talent to do the recording and music. Do you sing like a squeaky gate? Don't worry. Every community has a local theater group. Every high school and community college has a music department. Finding local resources for this part of the task gives you easy access to talent and makes it easy to work out all the little kinks while you're developing your jingle. Hessfine, for example, hired a college student, Corey Lista, for its jingle. He has years of theater experience and was happy to branch out into a new business venture. His Web site, www.coreylista.com, lists both his accomplishments and the singing styles he can offer his customers.

- Know your audience. Some shoppers are more likely to be amused by audio than others. If you think your audience may not be in the amused category, you may want to use audio in your About Me page to personalize your business, but not in your listings.

■ ■ ■

» USE VIDEO IN YOUR LISTINGS

Just as voice technology has crept into eBay listings in the last couple of years, sellers are also starting to use video within their listings. Our friends at hessfine have also set the pace here. The 5- to 10-second videos they incorporate into select auctions allow the PowerSeller to show the workings of expensive pocket watches. With video, it became possible for the buyer to actually view the inner workings of a watch and hear any chimes. Hessfine also sold a music box for $6,500 with an auction that included video. With an expensive item such as this, the seller was certain that allowing the buyer to actually view the workings of the music box made the item far more attractive than just reading a description would have ever done.

LET'S GET TO WORK...

- Don't include video for everything you sell—consider using it only for your more expensive and complex items. It's simply not necessary to show each item in such detail, and great photos can give users all the information they might need for your less valuable items.

- Use video to show the item in perspective. For example, use video to show the item in someone's hand. Slowly rotate the item so the viewer can see all angles and appreciate the item in a clear perspective to the size of the hand.

- Keep the videos brief. You don't want to overwhelm the computer power of your customers. Keeping the videos brief and simple make it more likely that the average computer user has the technology to view them. It may seem as though everyone has broadband access these days (and certainly all eBay members should have it if it's available in their area). However, some people still use much-slower dial-up access.

■ Remember: It's likely you'll see these technologies incorporated into many eBay auctions, sooner rather than later. Don't be too intimidated to give both audio and video a chance. "They're the way of the future, so we might as well start exploring them," says Australian PowerSeller Entertainmenthouse. There is no stopping the future or the advance of technology. People will ultimately want this kind of functionality, so getting familiar with it will be ever more important.

■ ■ ■

)) REQUEST EBAY'S SALES REPORTS

Did you know you can receive data on three months' worth of your eBay sales, without paying a dime for it? Even many experienced sellers aren't aware of this fact, but eBay now offers sales reports that allow you to do some pretty sophisticated analysis of not only how well you're doing, but also how you stack up against your competition. This is a huge help to online sellers.

PowerSeller blueberryboutique uses these reports for week-to-week and month-to-month comparisons on basic data such as sales, average selling price, and items sold. They find it especially useful for evaluating their sell-through rates and their total eBay fees as a percentage of sales. They also like how the reports break down the data by time of day and by sales format (e.g., auctions are working, fixed price listings are not, and store inventory sales are down, so they need to work to bolster those). Finally, they can also review the percentage of repeat customers, and nonpaying customers.

Available to all sellers through their "My eBay pages," these reports are offered at two different levels at no charge. You can compare your activity for the past three months, and you can compare your operation against other sellers. You must take the initiative to subscribe to these new reports, even though they are free. eBay enhances and introduces features so often it can't possibly notify you of every change. Some will directly affect your business, but others may not. It's part of your job to keep track of what's going on.

■ LET'S GET TO WORK...

- ■ Whether you have a store or just use listings, eBay can provide you with this information for all of your sales.

- ■ eBay's Basic report was designed for small to medium-sized sellers and offers a high-level view of your most recent sales (i.e., over the past three months).

- ■ eBay's Basic report summarizes sales, ended listings, percentage of successful listings, your average selling price (ASP), and all of your eBay and PayPal fees.

- ■ eBay's Sales Reports Plus can be used to gain more refined information about your sales.

- ■ Sales Reports Plus provides information for nine different metrics. You'll be able to study your sales based on category *or* format (e.g., fixed price) and also category *and* format. You'll get reports by ending day or time for all formats. You'll receive buyer counts, detailed eBay fees, and unpaid item credits. You'll be able to show or hide sections of the reports, and finally, you can download all reports for use in an offline spreadsheet.

- ■ Use either form of these reports to compare yourself to other sellers in your categories. Once you see how you stack up against your competition, you can start studying their listings for ideas about what is making some of them more successful.

■ ■ ■

SELLER FEEDBACK RATING: A TOOL FOR YOU, TOO

eBay recently enhanced the search result option available to buyers by enabling them to view a seller's feedback on the Search Result page. The option can be set just once by selecting "display feedback information" when customizing search options. After that, every search you do will include this information. The tool is a real boon to buyers, because you can so easily eliminate sellers and their auctions if their feedback ratings are too low for your comfort level. You don't even have to open a single listing to narrow down your searches.

Of course, what's good news for buyers isn't necessarily good news for sellers—unless you're the kind of seller who has nothing to fear from their feedback information appearing in search results. (And, of course, that's you.) The availability of these data is just one more reason why it's getting more important every day for eBay sellers to keep their ratings high, their auctions professional and precise, and everything else about their operations up-to-the-minute. One goal of this book is to give you the ideas and motivation you need to do just that.

LET'S GET TO WORK...

- As a seller, you'll use this tool to keep track of your competition. It's important to know how the other people in your categories are doing. Once you've set this display option, every search you do will give you a quick glimpse of who your real competition is, as evidenced by feedback ratings. If you've got a great feedback rating, anyone who has less than 98 percent positive feedback is not really your competitor.

- When they use this tool, your buyers will get a quick snapshot that provides more information about you than ever before, and it's right there with their search results. Your customers are more experienced, more sophisticated, and better equipped to rate and judge your performance as a seller than they used to be.

- Although we're betting you won't need the motivation, this piece of information will keep you working hard to keep your feedback level high. You don't want to be one of those sellers who is quickly eliminated because this feature is available.

■ ■ ■

WHO ARE YOU GOING TO BE IN THIS NEW WORLD?

The world of eBay is vast and ever changing, that's true. That's all the more reason for you to take command and control your own little part of this dynamic place. Among the PowerSellers who helped us with this book, that overriding theme was apparent in every interview we conducted. Consider Marguerite Swope, a happy PowerSeller in Pennsylvania. She described a life to us that allows her to stay home with her five-year-old son. She runs an eBay business selling primarily second-hand women's apparel. This area interests her and allows her to earn back some of the second income she left when her son arrived. A talented seamstress, when we spoke she was planning her own line of ladies clothing that she will produce from her home. She's not aiming for Titanium PowerSeller status. "I don't ever need my eBay business to be more than it is," she said. "I'm perfectly happy doing just what I'm doing."

Contrast her eBay business with that of Adam Hersh's AdamHershAuctions. At the age of 27, Adam has become one of the most successful eBay sellers, employing more than 20 people in two states. He is poised to spend his whole career in e-commerce. In between these two extremes you'll find Jim Orcholski. He has established a successful eBay business selling gold, silver, and platinum coins. He could most likely take his eBay business full time and make it his career, but he happens to have a 9-to-5 job he already likes, so that's not what he wants from eBay. You'll be placing yourself somewhere on this continuum between bronze (at an average of $1,000 in sales per month) and titanium ($150,000 in sales) PowerSeller, and where you land is strictly up to you. You most likely aren't in a position to make this decision now, but as you contemplate your role, here is some advice from the sellers who have already answered it for themselves.

》 PLAN A BIG BUSINESS RIGHT FROM THE START

Many sellers think that to get off to a good start, they should start small and take baby steps that will allow them to carefully measure every time they change their business in some way. By contrast,

Adam Hersh told us that the smartest thing he ever did was to start out with the mindset of a big business. He began his eBay business while in college, and now, just a few years later, he's one of eBay's "Top Sellers" (again defined as PowerSellers at the Platinum or Titanium levels), just having passed the 100,000 feedbacks level. He sells posters, and he's not shy about buying inventory in large quantities when he comes across a good deal.

Now, we're not suggesting that you should go out now and buy all new computer equipment or rent a warehouse or otherwise overextend yourself financially as you ramp up your eBay business. But you *should* think, right from the start, about the challenges you're going to face when you no longer have a start-up company. You certainly aren't ready to address all of those challenges right now. But you'll be in a better position to address them later if you build your business with an awareness of those challenges from the start.

LET'S GET TO WORK...

- Create a business plan with a strategy for scalability. Know from the beginning how you are going to handle order fulfillment, for example. Have a plan for preparing your items to be shipped and then managing the actual shipment. But, at the same time, build that system with an eye toward what you're going to need next year and how you're going to meet those needs. Do the same with every aspect of your business from storing your goods while they sell, to creating your listings, to building your accounting system. Don't set anything new into place unless you can explain to yourself how you will expand it.

- Choose the name of your business carefully. Your hope is that it's going to become a name that your customers will remember. You want it to be something distinctive enough to describe what you do, but not so quirky that it doesn't mean anything standing alone.

- Choose a name that will help describe what you do when it comes up in Internet searches.

- Be sure you create the right URL for your Web site. A high-level PowerSeller from Connecticut told us that his first URL didn't include .com. It also was too long. Those are mistakes you can avoid.

■ ■ ■

⟩⟩ MAKE MULTICHANNEL SELLING YOUR MANTRA

This book is specifically meant to help you build your business on eBay. But eBay exists in the larger world of e-commerce, and the most successful sellers on eBay operate as part of that larger universe. As you're building your eBay business, build it across channels, so that you can expand your profitability. By across channels, we mean selling online through other auction and shopping sites (such as Amazon, Yahoo!, and Overstock) as well as through your own Web site. This may seem a little intimidating at first, since eBay makes getting started so simple. And, it's true that many eBay sellers use eBay as an incubator for their businesses. But, we've found that the most successful sellers also use other venues. A large business will require multiple sales channels to stay profitable and reach as many buyers as possible. Sellers who use multiple channels also protect their businesses from being too dependent on one source of revenue. You'll find more information on this topic in Chapter 9, but again, we can't talk about the changed world of eBay without addressing this issue here.

■ LET'S GET TO WORK...

- Building your business across channels (for example a presence on Amazon as well as your own Web site) offers your customers more options for doing business with you. You want to give your customers as many options as possible in how they reach you, so start from the beginning by thinking across the borders of eBay to the larger world of Internet commerce.

- Building your customer base across channels isn't good for just your customers. It also makes you much more attractive to your suppliers. If you can present yourself to manufacturers as having a complete strategy for marketing their products on the

Internet, you'll be that much more likely to convince them to source their product through you rather than through someone who "only" sells on eBay.

■ Be ready to move quickly to take advantage of new opportunities. Consider when Google introduced Google Base, a separate part of Google where you can upload product listings and just about any other kind of organized data (such as job listings and recipes) for free. eBay's Top Sellers jumped on it. They moved quickly to post their items on this new venue, working closely with their auction services providers to ensure they were taking full advantage of this tremendous new opportunity. "If Google came out with its own auction site, that's something I'd look at immediately," said bullion PowerSeller Jim Orcholski. With Google's deep pockets, Jim reasoned, the search engine giant would have the horsepower to market an auction site, and he wanted to be part of it as soon as it happened. As we write this, Google is about to release its own online payment system, which will provide an alternative to PayPal (at least outside of eBay). You can bet PowerSellers are on top of this!

■ ■ ■

》 FRANCHISE WITHOUT FRENCH FRIES

It is now possible for you to buy your way into an eBay business. You can buy a franchise from any one of a number of companies that supply you with everything you need to start an eBay "drop-off" store. You can also create your own eBay drop-off store, and many experienced sellers decide to go that route. But, if you don't want to do all the initial start-up yourself, you can buy a franchise and even have a complete store delivered to your chosen location, all ready for you to start selling. Starting out as a franchisee lets you take advantage of branding, software, and system operations that you'd otherwise have to create from the ground up on your own.

With a franchise, some of the biggest challenges that eBay sellers have—acquiring inventory and managing their businesses with the help of the right software tools—are taken care of for them. People with things for you to sell—all manner of things—come right to your door. And your company is likely to have systems in place for you already, so the software you need for researching and auction management is already selected for you.

■ LET'S GET TO WORK...

- ■ If you're thinking about becoming a franchisee, visit the corporate headquarters and talk to the people who you'll be working with in person.

- ■ Visit a variety of locations where people are already running the franchise so you can see what the final operation actually looks like. It will help you decide if this corporation is right for you, and it will also help you when you go about choosing your own location for your store.

- ■ Remember that becoming a franchisee drastically reduces your need to source and store products for sale.

- ■ These are not terribly expensive franchises to start. At the time of this writing, you could buy an iSold It franchise for somewhere around $100,000 to $150,000. That's still a lot of money, but in business terms it isn't a great fortune.

- ■ With some eBay drop-off store franchises, the entire store will be delivered and setup, ready for business within about 24 to 48 hours.

■ ■ ■

〉〉 EARN MORE BY GIVING MORE

PowerSeller David Yaskulka of blueberryboutique! is a strong believer in strategic philanthropy as a part of his eBay business plan. He has the numbers to back up the fact that you can do good work and also earn good money doing it. Consider the numbers MissionFish's Sean Milliken cited for an article David wrote for *AuctionBytes*. (MissionFish is eBay's partner in its Giving Works charitable program.) "Giving Works items average 40 percent higher selling prices and 50 percent higher conversion rates than like items in the eBay marketplace." eBay's Giving Works program adds further benefits to your charitable works. When you register your listings to benefit a charity within eBay's Giving Works network, you will get a special ribbon icon from eBay that will appear in the general search results and in the title bar of the listing. You'll also receive added exposure to buyers who search exclusively for Giving Works listings. For auctions that are listed with 100 percent of the proceeds going to a registered charity, eBay will also donate the listing fees and the final value fees you would have spent on the listings.

Don't discount the resulting positive publicity you'll be likely to receive by your charitable activities. Adam Hersh told *AuctionBytes* that he and his staff completed a five-month, large-scale charitable program for Big Brothers/Big Sisters. His company didn't earn any money from its efforts, but the publicity has made a big difference to it. The Korean government was so impressed by his good work that it is now one of his biggest customers.

■ LET'S GET TO WORK...

- ■ Create a program for which a percentage of all of your earnings is earmarked toward a particular charity.

- ■ Routinely schedule special auctions for charitable causes and donate all the profits from those auctions to the charity.

- ■ Get a local charity involved by offering to run a series of auctions on eBay on its behalf. This is bound to lead to some good local publicity for you and your business.

- ■ Tailor your charitable contributions to a charity that would be important to your customer base. You'll build a loyal following among people who will want to have some of the money they pay for the things they want also go to the charities they care about.

- ■ Remember to market your charitable endeavors when you are looking for new sources of product. Manufacturers may be more likely to work with you if you can tie their products to a charity they support.

■ ■ ■

REINVENT YOURSELF FOR THE NEW ENVIRONMENT

Are you frustrated that we've just completed a section about deciding who you're going to be on eBay, and now we're planning to tell you that you need to reinvent yourself? Don't be. It's the reality of life on eBay. You are never going to be finished thinking about what you're going to do next and how you're going to keep your business growing and thriving.

RECOGNIZE YOURSELF AS A PLAYER IN THE WORLD ECONOMY

That may seem like a completely ridiculous piece of advice as you sit in your home reading this book. The reality is that this is what e-commerce has done to the business world. The instant you join the world of e-commerce, you are going to be a party to and a victim of everything that happens globally.

A top-selling PowerSeller in the South was running a wildly successful eBay business in the spring of 2004, when we first met him. He had a huge warehouse with 30 full-time employees. When we spoke with him again in 2005, he'd closed the warehouse and laid off all his employees. Why? His products—shipping supplies such as bubble wrap and "peanuts"—were largely petroleum-based commodities. As the price of oil rose, his suppliers raised their prices, and he could no longer profitably sell on eBay. With the further blow of the devastation caused by hurricanes Katrina and Rita, his products just became too expensive for him to be able to turn a reasonable profit on his business. He had no choice but to pull back and regroup. He had plans for what would happen next to rebuild his business, but in the meantime, he'd had to let all of his employees go, some of whom had been with him for years. "The world economy has affected us," he noted.

LET'S GET TO WORK...

■ Stay aware of what is happening politically, economically, and environmentally in every part of the world that could affect your business.

■ If you source your products internationally, you'd better know what the problems are for the people and government living in that remote place.

■ Be aware of seasonal differences so that you are not unrealistically depending on products that can't be available to you throughout part of the year.

■ ■ ■

❯❯ CHANGE IS A GOOD THING

You are going to be operating in a rapidly changing world. You'd better be able to view change as a positive rather than negative aspect of life. If you can't be thinking about what's going to be happening next while you're busy making things happen now, you may not want to devote yourself to climbing the PowerSeller ranks. You can't allow yourself to get so devoted to any one part of your product line that you let it blind you to the realities of the marketplace.

LET'S GET TO WORK...

■ You have to constantly watch your markets to see signs of failure. You have to be ready and willing to fill your pipeline with something different quickly when those signs of failure show themselves, recommends Colorado PowerSeller debnroo.

■ Don't hold on too long to a trend even if it's been a great one. Texas-based seller, stephintexas, made a very good living by selling low-carb food items on eBay. She got in early on the whole low-carb phase and for a while she was one of only two people selling low-carb taco shells on eBay. Fortunately she was astute enough and flexible enough to recognize when the trend was starting to wind down. She was willing to walk away from it while it was still earning money so that she could begin to source other products with a longer potential future.

■ ■ ■

EDUCATE TO OPERATE

It's not enough for you to recognize you have a lot to learn about operating a successful e-commerce business. You have to also recognize that operating on eBay means operating in an environment where keeping up with the latest changes and innovations is not necessarily easy. You would think that eBay makes it very apparent when a change is taking place, but you'd be wrong. A recent example occurred when eBay changed the icon representing eBay stores. For years eBay used a little tag as the icon next to a user name to indicate that the user also had a store. Everyone knew that this icon meant, "Look for this user's store." That is, until without any forewarning, eBay changed the icon to a little door. Now, a door is not a lesser icon than a tag, but it turns out to be that way if no one knows what the door means today when everyone knew what the tag meant yesterday! It took an energetic PowerSeller, beachcombers!, to start a marketing campaign called Doors2Stores to let eBay users know the meaning of the new icon. We discuss this creative and successful campaign further in Chapter 10.

LET'S GET TO WORK...

- Don't assume you're "hearing" about everything you need to know just because you're on eBay working every day. Make it your responsibility to stay connected to eBay news and to the community at large so you'll know what's happening, and you won't miss changes as they happen. "eBay should focus more on seller retention and user education. If you want to stay on eBay and be successful, you'll have to be responsible for keeping yourself educated," says Florida-based PowerSeller tradernick. PowerSeller dealtree-auctions agrees, "Lots of eBay policies change, and you don't always get up-front information about that."

- Use the OTWA board. The Online Traders Web Alliance, founded in 1999, is the association that supports auction sellers and buyers. Its Web site offers information, resources, and community message boards to help members stay current with technological advances, legislative issues, and market conditions. Make yourself familiar with what it has to offer.

■ ■ ■

EXPANDING YOUR POTENTIAL

You may come on to eBay with a few great sources of product and everything set to run a great little business. But, if you want to run a great large business, you're going to have to continue to think of new and innovative ways to expand your potential. You've already seen how a great idea, such as selling low-carb products, can sour as the environment changes, but there's more to consider than market presence when you're trying to expand. You cannot allow yourself to depend too much on any one revenue stream, no matter how solid and lucrative it may seem. If you're here for the long run, you're going to need to continue to find new ways to make yourself profitable. Then you need to do it again and again.

OFFER YOUR SERVICES FOR FREE (SOMETIMES)

Once you've cut your eBay teeth, make yourself the local expert for eBay selling. There are still plenty of people who don't know much about buying and selling on eBay, although practically everyone has heard stories about some of the unusual things for sale. You can become a real local resource for all those people who may have something to sell or who may want some guidance in learning how to buy. Whether you charge consulting fees or simply help the people in your own neighborhood, you're sure to pop to the front of the minds of everyone who knows you just as soon as they come across something they'd like to get rid of, but simply don't feel capable of selling on eBay by themselves.

LET'S GET TO WORK...

■ Approach local businesses in your area and talk to them about selling their returns and end-of-season leftovers on eBay.

■ Target the stores and businesses that also handle the items you list and sell. You'll be able to "speak the same language." Maryland PowerSeller, whitemountaintrading, approached all the other antiques dealers in his antiques mall to offer his services. He was able to offer a business service to people who already knew and respected him.

■ Go to the local manufacturers and meet with them face to face. Even a manufacturer reluctant to sell products on eBay may feel differently when a professional e-commerce retailer approaches him in person and makes a great impression. That the person is local reduces the risks even further.

■ Every time you present yourself and your eBay expertise whether it's at the neighborhood picnic or the cocktail party for your spouse's office, you broaden your base for gathering sources and earning income. It's all about networking!

■ ■ ■

BUILD MORE THAN ONE EBAY BUSINESS

No, we're not trying to confuse you here. We mean it. Once you've gotten yourself started and have a few steady commodities to sell on eBay, consider breaking those out into more than one user ID and building more than one eBay business. This will help you to focus on each branch of your business. It will help you to streamline and target your listings, and it can help you simplify your shipping operations. You will also be able to see which product line is booming and if one of them starts to falter, you'll know that too.

LET'S GET TO WORK...

■ Tailor each user name to the specific product so that you'll have name recognition among your customers.

- Consider which of these product lines lends itself to your store listings. PowerSeller beachcombers! started on eBay the old-fashioned way, via yard and garage sales. Ultimately it kept one user name and one store for its garage-sale items and focused its Web site, all its listings, and its main store efforts on the ethnic shoes and accessories that were to become its main focus. This allowed the company to build a presence separate from its yard-sale image and focus on building its new market area, while still keeping up its original revenue stream.

- You actually earn more per item from processing sales for 100 widgets than you do by handling 1,000 of them. So, break up your widgets and sell them through smaller, more targeted businesses to keep the profit margins high.

■ ■ ■

GO TO EBAY LIVE! TO PROFIT—NOT PARTY

You probably know that every June eBay hosts the eBay Live! convention. More than 15,000 people flocked to the three-day event in 2006. That meeting was held in Las Vegas, and the next one is slated for Boston. You may not think it's worthwhile to spend the time and money to travel any distance for a meeting and convention, but in this case, you couldn't possibly be more incorrect. eBay purposely makes the convention itself inexpensive. In 2006, early registration gave three-day access to all events for $50. For procrastinators, registering the week of the event cost $70.

eBay Live! is a constant stream of classes, speeches, and meetings. Going to eBay Live! means that from early in the morning to late at night, you can immerse yourself in all things eBay. Attending the convention will push your eBay business ahead in enormous strides. You'll hear firsthand from eBay's top people what the past year has brought and forecasts for what the next year will bring. You'll be on the convention floor to see all the latest from service providers that bring you everything from auction management software, to shipping options, to the newest inventory control technologies. eBay employees, including category managers, customer support people, and PayPal staff, will also be there on the floor and staffing booths. You will be able to take classes in every subject you can imagine from sourcing products to managing employees.

■ LET'S GET TO WORK...

■ Know before you get there exactly what you want to accomplish in these three days. Research the vendors who will be there and identify which ones you most need to talk with. You will find not only the sales staff from these vendors, but also the product managers. If you're having some issues with your auction management software, for example, you'll most likely be able to talk directly to a "techie" about them. When was the last time that was possible to do face to face?

■ Go alone if you must, but better yet, go with a partner. You can split up to attend different sessions and double your exposure. You can also have someone to help you stay focused. Attending a show this big makes it easy to get distracted and scattered. If you have someone to help you anchor yourself a couple of times a day, you will be more likely not to forget to explore something you want to learn more about.

■ If you have an employee, consider taking her along. You will find that you've revved up your employee by giving her access to the energy and dynamics of this convention. You'll both go back to work with new ideas and a new burst of enthusiasm for the business.

■ Seek out your competitors. Here's a chance to meet the people who are strongest in your category. Of course, you'll know who they are before you arrive at the convention, so make it a point to introduce yourself. You'll improve your strategic position by exposing yourself to the ones who challenge you the most.

■ Don't chase the sourcing companies (e.g., drop-shippers and wholesalers) who will be on the convention floor. Everyone else there will be chasing them. Instead focus on the vendors who offer products and services to support your operations, such as auction management software. They've come to this meeting to court you, and you can talk firsthand with them about your specific issues and challenges. You won't get their attention like this once the meeting is over.

■ Provide for yourself during the event. eBay Live! is exhausting. You will spend all day in sessions and on the convention floor. Of course, you'll want to be able to take advantage of the parties and celebrations, too! The people who come to eBay Live! spend every moment of the three days talking, thinking, breathing, and eating everything eBay. For the few hours you spend back at the hotel, you're going to need to take care of yourself. Stay as close to the convention as you can. Choose the most comfortable hotel you can afford. Remember to take care of yourself as the resource you are, saving all of your energies for the work you'll be doing.

■ ■ ■

INVENT YOUR OWN PRODUCTS

Can you create or produce anything that can be sold on eBay? If you create crafts, jewelry, or artwork, it's easy to see what you might be able to sell for yourself. But don't discount dozens of other things people create that could also be sold. Only you can evaluate your abilities to produce something salable, but then only you know your market and business both inside and out. Think about a skill you have and find a way to bring that skill to the open market. If you haven't come up with one, keep thinking. We all have something we can do.

For example, PowerSeller preferreddiscounts sells pipes and cigar and tobacco accessories. He recognized that the standard leather case most pipe smokers used just wasn't adequate for carrying outdoors. Missing from the market was a durable, portable, hardcover case to carry all the accessories necessary for an avid pipe smoker. He set about filling that gap. The result is his Pipe Guardian Case. His invention includes all the accessories a pipe smoker would need. It's perfect for the smoker who is planning a weekend fishing trip. He's the only supplier, and he sells only to select distributors, so he has his little corner of the market covered.

■ LET'S GET TO WORK...

■ When you create your own unique products to sell, you're completely in the driver's seat. You determine how many of the items are in the marketplace. You determine pricing (and your profit), and you determine when (or if) other retailers may also distribute your product. Preferreddiscounts, for instance, is the only Pipe Guardian supplier, and he sells only to select distributors. He has his little corner of the market covered.

■ PowerSeller wiccan well sells new-age jewelry. She also has combined interests in writing and metaphysical studies. For now, she is offering her writings on the subject as part of her About Me page, but she is branching out to start marketing her work in addition to her jewelry. She knows her customers will be interested in the subject. She has a built-in audience, and she's going to be doing this work anyway. She has little to risk in putting her final product up for sale.

■ Do you have HTML skills? A thriving business has cropped up on eBay selling auction templates to other eBay sellers. If you have the skills, you can easily create unique, attractive templates that other sellers will gladly buy from you. Plus, you don't have to worry about shipping costs, since this product will be sent via e-mail!

■ ■ ■

⟩⟩ PROFIT WITH PARTNERS

Google, Yahoo!, and eBay all earn revenue by selling advertising space on their sites or placing ads on others. Now you can also add a revenue stream by selling advertising space for companies, too. When you enter into an affiliate relationship, you'll earn a percentage of each sale the affiliate can trace to you. The ads you include can be anything from a dynamic and colorful banner to a more subtle text ad/hyperlink. According to Harvey Levine of PowerSeller generalent, some eBay sellers "make six figures a year through these affiliate relationships."

eBay doesn't want you to litter up your listings with affiliate ads. However, there's nothing preventing you from including them on your About Me page, or, of course, your Web site. The best kind of ads don't appear to be ads at all, but rather sources for information of benefit to your buyer.

Figure 1.1 shows two affiliate ads that appear on generalent's About Me page: One is a banner ad, but the other is just a subtle text link. Each time a buyer clicks on the text link and follows through by purchasing the affiliate's product (a book), Harvey gets 50 percent of the action, or $15 in this particular case. Your commission may range from 5 percent to 50 percent of the money your affiliate earns.

· ·

FIGURE 1.1: Here are two examples of how affiliate buttons will appear on your About Me page.

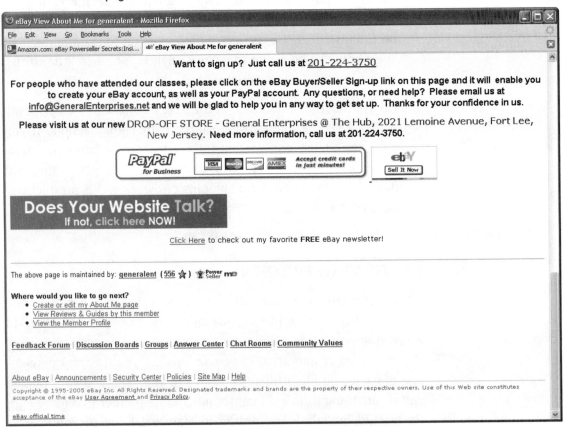

Joining affiliate programs is simple. Once you've signed up, the affiliate will provide the ad in the form of HTML code that you just paste onto your Web page. That HTML includes a number that identifies you to the affiliate, so he knows whom to credit for the lead.

Harvey screens his affiliates; he won't sign up with just anyone. "The value has to be there," he told us. "We could cram our site with hundreds of affiliates." Because they do a lot of teaching and are PowerSellers themselves, generalent wants to "give back" to their students by giving them access to the best information. Supporting select merchants through their affiliate programs is a way for them to do that. For you, it may simply be another revenue stream—one that once set up, runs by itself.

■ LET'S GET TO WORK...

■ "Affiliates are the sleeping giants," says generalent. "We're considering more avenues going into the Internet age to sell information."

■ Before you sign on with any new vendor, ask about an affiliates program. All things being equal, choose the vendor who will offer you a little something extra for helping them advertise.

■ ■ ■

THE CHALLENGE OF GROWTH IN AN EVER-EXPANDING WORLD

Now that we've filled your head with ideas of how to get your eBay business growing and booming, we're going to suggest you look at some of the problems and challenges that come with growth. You do want your business to grow, but as it's growing, you'll be facing new challenges at every stage of that growth. It's important for you to be prepared for these challenges and to be thinking of how you're going to meet them when they arise. Some of the problems you'll face will be specific to your own business and operation, but some of them are universal growing pains for eBay businesses as they expand. "eBay is a rocket, and if you're used to riding a horse, be careful when they give you controls to the rocket," warned debnroo.

DON'T GET TOO FAR AHEAD OF THE CURVE

As your eBay business expands, you'll see an expansion in your operating costs and in the day-to-day workings of your business. Be sure you're on top of the growth and not getting dragged along behind. "You will develop overhead and lease commitments. You'll feel the pressure and stress of moving a big ship. You will no longer have a little speedboat," noted debnroo. Dealtree-Auctions agrees, "From an internal standpoint, it's being able to control your costs. You have to be aware that business changes." Making changes as your business grows gets constantly more complicated.

LET'S GET TO WORK...

- Don't take on a lot of overhead until you can support it. You may feel that you need a warehouse to start housing your inventory, but before you sign a lease, make sure you have the income to support the rent and operating costs of that warehouse. It might make your life better to expand, but then it might just add a whole new set of problems to your operations. Be sure you know which outcome every move you make will bring.

- Don't bring on employees until you're sure you can consistently meet their payroll requirements. It may seem only logical, but when you know you need help getting your listings and shipping done, you may be tempted to take a step your business just can't support. An interim step may be to enlist family members or hire independent contractors as needed.

- Don't expand your business until you have the feedback level and rating to support it. For example, don't take on a midlevel store until you have enough feedback to make it practical. You'll be paying higher fees and not increasing your profits until you have the customer base to support the greater expense.

- Remember, it will be increasingly difficult to source, list, and sell successfully if you're constantly worried about meeting your monthly expenses.

■ ■ ■

Selling on eBay can be easy. Managing the business you create is not. You have to study everything you do on eBay to see if it's increasing your profitability or not. That means you should know the sell-through rate of every product you list. You should know which listing features have increased your exposure and which ones you may never pay extra for again. You should know which key words are most effective. You should study the leaders in every category you list under and know as much about their operations as you can. If you have to hold back on listing as much as you'd like, because you're spending so much time evaluating what you're doing, so be it. The business you build will be all the stronger for it, because you'll know exactly what you're doing.

LET'S GET TO WORK...

- "The biggest challenge is to be able to handle all the different aspects of business. It's running a small business, employee issues, and state laws. The selling isn't hard, but it *is* a business," noted dealtree-auctions. "We're never *not* looking at new ways to be more efficient and more productive." Start from the very beginning looking at all aspects of your business.

- Constantly evaluate your product line. Know what is most profitable. Know which items are selling well enough so that you can list them once and sell multiple items. Also know what isn't selling through at an acceptable rate and be ready to replace it with something that will move better. "I started to identify which products gave me the most profit, and then I redesigned my whole business to stress those products," said wiccan well. This seller really enjoyed the candles, bath accessories, and decorative items she was also selling. But, once she identified her profit center as jewelry, she let all the other parts of her business go and changed her focus to the area that was most profitable.

■ ■ ■

KEEP TRACK OF WHAT YOU *EARN*, NOT WHAT YOU SELL

Your eBay business will move fast. You'll be scurrying to gain profits with every step you take. But, don't forget to look at the other side of the earnings equation. It isn't just what you earn that makes you profitable. It's also what you spend. It's not enough to sell $10,000 a month on eBay if your expenses are $12,000. You may be asking yourself why we'd even bother to tell you something so obvious, but that brings us back to the story we told you as the chapter opened.

When Adam, of AdamHershAuctions, completed his interviewing of the NARU members of the Nortica 500 list, the lesson he learned was chilling. It should chill you too. Almost every one of them said the problem was in keeping track of their finances. These huge sellers were so busy selling that they weren't really looking at how much they were *earning*. Little by little, their fees were growing. PayPal money was coming in fast, but so were PayPal fees and eBay fees. Before they even realized it, these sellers were falling behind on their eBay bills. Once they became 60 days late on their fees, eBay closed their accounts, and that was the end. "I heard, over and over, 'I wish I was paying closer attention to my prices *and* my books,'" said Adam.

LET'S GET TO WORK...

- Watch every penny. Know what everything you do costs and what it brings in. Don't spend a nickel you can't profit from.

- Remember, it is always going to be easier to cut your operating costs than it is to raise your prices. You should know exactly what price you expect to get from everything you list on eBay. You can't reasonably expect to earn more than the going rate of any particular item. Therefore, your only hope of increasing your profit margin is to lower your expenses.

- Keep those fees in mind. Large sellers actually have to pay their eBay fees several times a month. That's because their total eBay fees exceed their credit limits on the credit card they used to sign on as sellers. Don't forget these details that could easily cost you everything you've built.

■ ■ ■

AND NOW, A WORD OF GOOD CHEER

Are you discouraged? Did we pound you with all the reasons why having a successful eBay business is now harder than ever? Are you contemplating where you might find that time machine to take you back to 1999, so you could get a head start on all this? None of these was our intention. We just want you to go on to the rest of the book with a sense of what lies ahead for you. Now you know for sure, we're not the "rose-colored glasses" type of eBay writers. At the same time, we love eBay. We still see it as a never-before-opportunity for having and growing your own business. We'll leave Chapter 1 with a bit of good cheer.

DON'T FORGET WHY WE'VE ALL COME HERE

There's still plenty of opportunity and fun in the world of eBay. Take this little story with you as you move on to the next chapters. PowerSeller bids4u-2 has sold a lot of unusual items. Among his most memorable was a 6-foot-tall South American rhea (stuffed, of course). He took it on consignment in his antique shop from an elderly woman who had owned it for 60 years. (Apparently, huge stuffed birds were quite fashionable in Victorian times.) This one was named "Precious," and the elderly owner wanted $800 for it. She wouldn't have parted with it, but she was on her way to an assisted-living facility, and the management said Precious couldn't come with her. bids4u-2 put it into his shop window with a price tag of $1,000. It attracted a lot of attention, but no interested buyers, even when he reduced the price all the way down to $50. He went back to his customer to ask her about listing it on eBay. It sold immediately to a collector in New Mexico for $800! Coincidentally, this fellow lived in a 2-bedroom apartment, but since he was single, there was no one to complain about his new roommate. Who knows where your next wild story will come from?

Kevin Boyd

Kevin Boyd is the PowerSeller behind preferreddiscounts. He sells collectible pipes and pipe and cigar accessories, including his own invention—the Pipe Guardian Case. Kevin came to eBay as a result of his move from Chicago to Seattle. When he left the Midwest behind, he found he'd also left life with a basement. He was forced to eliminate some of the things he wouldn't be able to store in his Seattle home. While cleaning out, he uncovered a CD of investment software with the manuals that support it. He tossed it into a trash box along with another investment CD that had no manuals. Then he got to wondering: Was there a market for this stuff? He listed the items on eBay for $1 each. The one with the manuals sold for $120 while the one without books only went for $80. He'd earned $200 from stuff he'd almost thrown away.

In 2003, he left the corporate world and started an eBay business. He started out by attending eBay University and working with the trainer as a consultant. Today he is a certified eBay instructor himself and teaches approximately six eBay classes each week. He built his eBay business by starting with products that were familiar to him. He also listened and watched friends and colleagues. He realized there was a growing interest in pipes and cigar accessories, so he started sourcing those products for sale on eBay. He also started selling marine equipment for fishing hobbyists, but when the distributor for this line faltered, he put all of his energies into his tobacco accessories. He believes the "more 'nichey' you get, the more profitable you are."

Kevin is a creative guy, an author, and an inventor. He saw a need in the market he was serving for a durable and portable case for carrying tobacco supplies, so he invented one. He says eBay is the perfect place to bring your own products to market. He encourages everyone to do that, especially writers. He's written two books about aquariums and has recently written an eBay book as well. Look for his eBay book, *eBay Answers: Answers to the Most Frequently Asked and Most Difficult Questions eBay Sellers Have During Their First 50 Listings*. The book is based on questions he receives from his students after they've taken his class, hit a roadblock, and then asked him for help. You can find his book at his Web site, www.preferreddiscounts.net.

CHAPTER 2

PowerSource Your Product Line

All eBay sellers share one eternal question: "Where will I find a steady reliable source of products to sell?" Without this steady source, your eBay business will falter quickly, and you'll find yourself among those who once sold on eBay. To make matters even more complicated, once you find such a source, you'll have to keep looking for more sources. As you've seen, the eBay market is a fickle one. You'll have to be able to adapt once the market moves on, and your great product find isn't selling as well as it once was. You'll also have to learn how to control your inventory. Finding a great source of product won't help you if you flood your market and drive your own prices down. So, you'll need to find sources and then continue to look for more sources, and it never ends.

As an added challenge, you'll be doing this research with very little help from other sellers. We've begun to joke with our PowerSeller friends that sourcing information is a lot like spy work. They might tell us about a great source they use, but then they'll have to kill us! For our own safety, we beg them not to get too specific. You won't get specifics either, but that doesn't mean we don't have great ideas for how you can effectively source products and work with other sellers. We do.

The key to sourcing for your eBay business, of course, is to find a source of products that you can purchase at a price to make your profit margins worthwhile. For the purpose of this chapter, we'll focus on your finding sources of *new* products. In our previous book, *eBay PowerSeller Secrets*, we offered recommendations for sourcing used products, too. Those sources don't change much, for example, yard sales, thrift shops, and second-hand stores. We'll share a few great new suggestions with you about finding used things, but for the most part, we'll concentrate on commodity items that you purchase new for resale.

SOURCE WHAT WILL SELL

As you're searching for those great and reliable sources, you will also have to be researching what is actually going to sell on eBay. "A good idea doesn't always make money," warns PowerSeller avforsale. "If you search [on eBay] for something you have a good supply line for and don't find any others, you've got a good idea. If you find thousands of them, you don't have such a great idea. It's too easy to do the research."

Other PowerSellers disagree that you should blaze your own path. "We've based our business model on the assumption that eBay represents the 'perfect market' at any given time for a particular product. This only works when there are many buyers and sellers. Hence my suggestion that a new seller find a product that sells a lot, not a little," advises Jay of titanium PowerSeller jayandmarie. Following this model, you should view the competitive areas of eBay as a place of great potential, not a place of deep intimidation.

Of course, to know that you're sourcing what will sell, you're going to have to learn to love research and to keep researching. The good news is that the more you think about sourcing products for your eBay business, the more sources of products you tune in to. It's a lot like getting a new car. Once you actually buy it, you see others just like it all over the road. Before you made that decision, there were just as many out there, but you weren't looking for them. Lisa Suttora, coauthor of *What to Sell on eBay and Where to Get It*, published by McGraw-Hill, calls these moments *Idea Hotspots.*™ According to Lisa, an Idea Hotspot can be almost anywhere. You might overhear a conversation while you're standing in line at the bank that makes you think of a product to sell. It could be an article you read in the paper, a trade journal, or in your favorite magazine. The more you look for them, the more Idea Hotspots you'll find.

Researching your potential product line has never been easier or more challenging. It's easier, because there are so many tools available now that did not exist even a few years ago. The maturation of e-commerce has spawned Web sites and elaborate research tools designed just to meet the needs of online sellers. It's more challenging than ever before, because there's more competition than ever before. You're going to be searching for the answers to questions lots of other people are asking too. That means you'll have to be more resourceful than ever. The ideas in this chapter will be a great place to start building your resources.

WHOLESALERS VERSUS MANUFACTURERS

We've recommended before that you aim for the manufacturers. Lots of new sellers go running toward the wholesalers. They are just so easy to find. "There are lots of wholesalers at eBay Live!," noted PowerSeller bamcm, herself a wholesaler, "People go flocking to their booths." Why would you follow that crowd? What are you going to gain that scores of others don't already have? If only sourcing were that easy!

We're not saying you can never get a great deal through a wholesaler. We're saying that the wholesaler operates for profit too. By the time she's ready to turn a product over to you, she's raised the price enough to make it worth her while. You're going to have to sell it close to retail to make your profit margin worthwhile, and that's not the way to build big on eBay. You need to find your products as close to the source as possible, without paying someone else too much in the middle. You want to find the manufacturers.

The "Catch 22" of this issue is that when you're just starting out, you won't be terribly attractive as a distribution network for manufacturers. If you want to sell DVDs for example, you can't very well approach Sony or Warner. Neither of them needs to move their movies through the likes of you. "You won't be able to start with new releases," warns entertainmenthouse. "Starting out, remember that independents are looking for distributors." That would be a better place to start trying to build your inventory. Of course, you may decide, after doing some research, that the DVD market is just too competitive for you to pursue. That decision does not represent failed sourcing research; it's the whole point of researching. You will rule out far more products than you will decide to source.

The advice to start with the smaller manufacturers is valid no matter what you're thinking of sourcing. Not only will they be more likely to need your help distributing their products, but you'll make your mistakes and gain your experience with the smaller manufacturers before you approach the larger ones. "When I started off buying from some of my distributors, they, of course, knew I was a new customer. I did not receive the best pricing that they offered for the size of the orders I was placing, Now that I have more knowledge, experience, and choices on whom to buy from, I have been able to get better pricing on my purchases from my distributors," noted PowerSeller Jim Orcholski.

As your business grows, your options for sourcing will grow also. It's not wise to start out by placing an order for $10,000 worth of merchandise. Once you can afford to buy that much inventory, you'll have the knowledge, connections, and experience you need to know where to spend your money. Your knowledge will grow just by reading the advice in this chapter. We'll share with you how some PowerSellers have been able to work out exclusive rights to their products on eBay. You'll learn how to find sources that others don't readily know about. You'll learn about sourcing for international markets and working with international suppliers. You'll even learn how to work with other PowerSellers to share the task of sourcing.

⟫ CRAFT AND EXPAND YOUR PIPELINES TILL THEY BURST!

"When I first began buying inventory, I had a single supplier which was a freight recovery business. I could walk into a backroom and cherry-pick all of the best merchandise and pay pennies on the dollar for it. My business thrived off this one supplier until they brightened up and discovered eBay themselves. I then realized the importance of developing relationships with multiple suppliers!" noted PowerSeller rocket-auctions. Consider your sources! Keep searching and expanding your pipelines at all times. Even when you believe, like this PowerSeller, that you've hit pay dirt, keep looking for more. Nothing is guaranteed except that everything you do is bound to change.

It may seem that this will make your job much harder, and the temptation is there, once you've found something great, to ease up and focus on selling as much as you can. But, that's not a long-term approach. You're not looking to make a quick buck and move on; you're working toward building a large and sustainable business. Never sit back and rest on your laurels (or anything else).

- **Sell name-brand items.** As soon as you can source them, find and sell name brands. "Selling well-advertised products makes your job easier," says PowerSeller debnroo, "There's already a general demand for your product."

- **Use brand names as key words.** Selling brand names makes it easier for your customers to find you. When we asked PowerSeller Marguerite of mhswope what she wished she'd learned sooner in her career, she replied, "Sell brand-name clothing, not just the things I like. People don't find you if you're not making a sale of a brand name." She learned that nobody searches for "ladies red shirt." Lots more customers search for "Liz Claiborne ladies red shirt."

- **Be careful with key words.** Unless you know for sure that your item is authentic, don't use key words that could result in a violation. For example, "Liz Claiborne-like ladies red shirt" will get your auction shut down for key word spamming. Only advertise the name brand if you can authenticate it.

- **Authenticate whenever you can.** Fine arts dealer and PowerSeller baronarts used to purchase her inventory at auction. Now she sticks strictly to the sales of large estates. She knows these paintings can be authenticated, and she can provide provenance (the history of the artwork) with each piece she sells. Since she sells very expensive paintings, (she sells on eBay only if the piece will bring less than $3,000) saving the more expensive works for her private Web site sales, she knows that her customers expect her to be able to verify her product authenticity. "There are far too many reproductions in the art categories on eBay. I provide a letter of authenticity with every piece I sell," reports baronarts. Other sellers who specialize in very expensive items will have their own methods of assuring their customers and their own particular preferences for sourcing precious items.

■ ■ ■

YOU PROFIT WHEN YOU BUY, NOT WHEN YOU SELL

It may surprise you, but your eBay business will profit from how you source your product, not from how you sell it. "You make your profit when you buy the item," observed generalent, a PowerSeller from suburban New Jersey. "If you buy right, you can sell right and undercut your competition," he advised. In order to do this, you're going to have to know your product area inside and out. You're going to have to keep current with the prices of things that you sell and the things that you think you might want to sell. Your knowledge base will expand as you gain experience in sourcing. In the meantime, if you think you've found a great bargain, buy a few and give them a try. As long as you don't spend too much, you're also not risking much. You'll know soon enough if your hunch was correct and if you should start looking for more and lower-cost sources of that same product.

This whole idea goes back to the "perfect market" concept Jay of jayandmarie shared with us. Once you've found an item that is selling well, Jay advised, "Devote 80 percent of your time to finding lower-cost providers for that product, and develop your profit margin that way. It is far easier to lower your costs by prudent buying, quantity buying, opportunistic buying, etc., than to get a 5 percent–better selling price on eBay."

LET'S GET TO WORK...

- Negotiate the buying price not the selling price. "Don't worry about the price it sells at," advises Jay, "You 'know' that going in because of the trading that already exists in the item at the time you buy." It is not realistic for you to expect to earn more than the item is currently bringing on eBay. You may consider it to be worth a certain amount, but the reality is it is only worth that which people will pay for it, and you know that from the current eBay sales. Your only wiggle room is in how much you pay.

- Use your buying price to undercut your competition. Once you've whittled away your buying price for your products, turn that advantage against your competition. If you can purchase an item for $25 that will sell for $55, absorb some shipping costs and undercut the final price your competitors will want for the same item. You may cut your profit margin slightly, but you'll get more sales. Lots of customers use the shipping costs as deciding points when comparing different sellers. If you can offer the same quality of shipping options, but at a lesser fee, you'll get the sale instead of the next person.

■ ■ ■

)) IF YOU CAN'T CREATE, CUSTOMIZE

In Chapter 1, we talk about creating your own products for sale on eBay. If you've been thinking about that ever since, but still can't come up with a reasonable product you can invent or make yourself, consider customizing something already manufactured. We've found PowerSellers on eBay who are supplementing and expanding their product lines by offering customization.

It's not just a matter of customizing individual products either. Think across your whole product line and see if you can't find a way to bundle items together to sell in kits. If you sell bath supplies, for example, consider adding candles to the line and creating different fragrance and mood kits to be sold together. Customizing is especially good near holidays when you can bundle several smaller items together and sell them as a more substantial gift idea. You won't be spending more per item for your inventory, but you'll be earning more as you sell the total kit for a higher price than the individual elements would bring.

LET'S GET TO WORK...

■ Customize to expand your customer base. Jody of beachcombers! is always looking for more ways to serve her customers. She sells, among other things, glass bangle bracelets from Pakistan. To increase the desirability of this popular accessory, she decided to start selling them in "spirit" sets. She will create sets of bangles to celebrate a favorite sports team or to represent the colors of an individual high school or college. Now she's opened her product line to a whole new segment of potential customers.

■ Customize to serve your market. United Kingdom–based PowerSeller blingkinguk sells custom-made belt buckles. You can find many different sellers on eBay who will sell you belt buckles of every variety, but if you want one with your own name imbedded in rhinestones, you'll have to stop by www.the-blingking.co.uk for it. Now, that's a niche market, but it's serving this PowerSeller quite well.

■ Customize within your own customer base. Once you've built a customer base, you can start to offer products that your repeat customers will want. As we saw earlier, mhswope learned early on to sell name-brand clothing, but now that she's a known and trusted seller, she's able to expand her business. She has begun designing and making her own line of clothing. A talented seamstress, she is able to produce unique clothing others will want. She couldn't build her business by selling her own creations, because she wouldn't have had any name recognition for them. But now that she is known and trusted, she can expand her eBay business to include yet another hobby she enjoys.

■ ■ ■

)) WEB SOURCING ISN'T FOR WIMPS

You're going to sell online, so you might as well learn to use the online world skillfully to help you with your sourcing. The Web is so huge and so amorphous that it's easy to get lost and spend countless unproductive hours searching for product lines and suppliers. We've searched long and hard for some great advice about how you can maximize your efforts when you're searching for online sources of products.

eBay now has a Want It Now feature shown in Figure 2.1 and available to both buyers and sellers. Buyers can use it to find specific products. Often you'll find requests for items for which a buyer was outbid on a recent auction. You can use the Want It Now feature to make sales in your categories as you fulfill the needs of such buyers, but you can also use it to figure out what buyers are shopping for. You can set up Want It Now so that every day you will receive e-mails from eBay with the results of key word searches buyers are listing. "I estimate I get 2 to 10 requests from eBay a day," reports Gary of PowerSeller harleyglasses.

Gary also lives the PowerSeller life with the motto, "Google is your friend." Of course, researching on Google or Yahoo! can be a huge time sink, too. It's too easy to wander aimlessly around on the Web and not find any reliable or dependable sources. That's when you have to harness the power of the Web with your own set of tools and expertise to bypass the extraneous and move on to the useful.

· ·

FIGURE 2.1: eBay's new Want It Now feature helps buyers and sellers find each other. You can also use it to help zero in on popular items for sourcing.

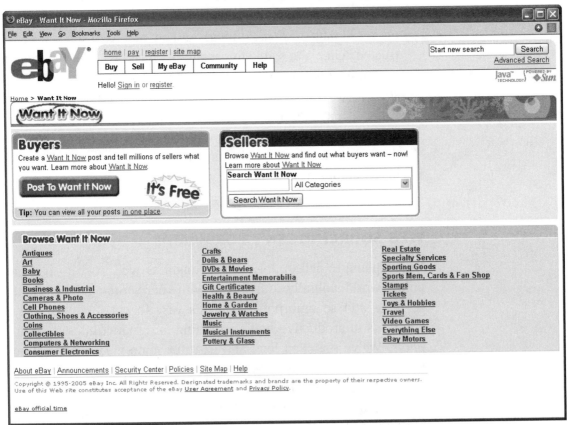

LET'S GET TO WORK...

■ Set up Google Alerts for your products (www.google.com/alerts). This is a free news feed that e-mails the latest Google items to you daily, "as-it-happens," or once a week based on the search terms you define. PowerSeller harleyglasses has set up a Google Alert for sunglasses. Every day he receives new additions to Google that relate to his subject. Through this simple setup, he was able to find a good source of MP3 sunglasses, an item that had previously eluded him through his usual "sunglasses" key word searches.

▪ Download and then use Google's own cheat sheet (www.google.com/help/cheatsheet.html). By keeping this cheat sheet handy, you'll quickly start to learn how to structure your searches for the best combinations of key words. We're all sophisticated online researchers by now, but you'd be surprised to see the extra refinements you can make to your searches when you take your advice directly from the people organizing the data.

▪ Search for your product through the image search feature. Don't be tied to just the usual search of Google through the Web tab. Also try the Image tab. Combine your search term with phrases such as "dozens" or "lots," and you'll find whole displays of the items you are searching for.

▪ Use Google to research the exhibitors at trade shows you will attend. Know before you arrive at the trade show which exhibitors you most want to approach for supply information. It's too easy for you to research them in advance and not to take advantage of this. Then, when you have your time at the show, you won't be wasting it getting to know the rudimentary facts of each potential supplier. You can arrive ready to talk business with them beyond just the basic "getting to know you" facts. Not only will you spend your trade show time more effectively, but you'll also make a better impression on a potential supplier when you show him you know more than just the basics about his business.

▪ PowerSeller beachcombers! buys shoes directly from a shoe-maker in Pakistan. Jody, co-owner of beachcombers!, actually located her source through the Internet. Now she works exclusively with this source to produce the handmade shoes she sells.

She never even spoke with him on the phone before they started working together. (For the full story, see Chapter 10.) Don't underestimate the power of diligent research conducted strictly on the Web!

■ ■ ■

PUT IT IN THE WANT ADS

You are fortunate enough to live in a world of virtual classified ads. You have the greatest opportunity ever to source your products from people all over the country. Your local newspaper may only provide a smattering of product sources, but thanks to the Web, you can easily run simultaneous want ads in New York, Los Angeles, and Chicago. And through Google Base, for example, these local ads can reach a national audience. Now that's a bit better!

Not only can you advertise for your products here, but you can also search these classifieds for promising sources, especially if you deal in vintage items. If your chosen search item fails to reveal what you want, expand your search to consider other items that might coincide with the ones you want. When you get those leads, e-mail the listing party and ask if that person has any of your type of item for sale too. "It's brought garage-saling to a whole new level!" crowed PowerSeller stephintexas, who sells vintage cowboy boots.

LET'S GET TO WORK...

■ Use Craigslist to keep ads running in major markets at all times. Set it up, and the sources will find you. "My ads are short and sweet," says stephintexas. "I use something like, 'Wanted: Cowboy boots! Paying cash (price depends on style and condition). Call today!'"

■ Consider other great placements for your ads too. stephintexas also keeps ads active at all the local college campuses. She knows that college students often need cash more than they need the latest fashions. They're also fickle, so last season's hot clothing item doesn't necessarily mean much to them now. She's found this a great source for herself, but you may have your own strategies for reaching people with desirable items to sell who need quick cash.

- Electronic classifieds are perfect, but you may also find the ads in trade magazines and journals to be good venues for your product ads. The publications that service the areas of interest that include your product offerings are bound to yield better results than more general newspapers.

- Place an ad on your About Me page. "I'm always on the lookout for new products. If you are a manufacturer or distributor and think your product may complement my line, please contact me," reads a paragraph on the About Me page of harley-glasses. eBay has become too much a cultural phenomenon not to turn up in the minds of resourceful manufacturers looking to place their products. You may be surprised to find the sources that actually come to you once you've built your eBay presence.

■ ■ ■

TERAPEAK IS UNIQUE—IT WAS BUILT FROM THE INSIDE OUT

You know that there is a wealth of information to be found by searching eBay's Completed Listings. We told you before that this is a basic first step to any sourcing decisions you might make. But searching Completed Listings can take you just so far and so deep into the mammoth database of auction information that eBay has compiled over the years. Of course, if you could only mine that data, you could learn so much more, such as which categories are hot, how competitive a given category is, when to list—you get the idea. Fortunately, eBay licenses its data to vendors such as Terapeak, who then make that information available to their subscribers. We've tried some of these auction analysis and sourcing services. The payoff just wasn't there.

But Terapeak is different. The company was founded by two eBay sellers who felt they needed more data than what was available to everyone right on the site. For a reasonable fee, starting at $9.95 per month, Terapeak provides you with access to a tremendous amount of eBay auction data that can help you with everything from product sourcing to polishing your listings.

While Terapeak does not offer a free trial of its services before you join, there are other ways you can learn about its services to assess whether it would be useful to your business. Terapeak hosts eBay Workshops, which you can "attend" live, or view the transcripts for which at any time. The site itself at http://terapeak.com/ also provides a wealth of information about what your money buys you.

We tried Terapeak for ourselves and were amazed at how, within minutes, you can start retrieving incredibly useful information. We admit we didn't even read any of the tutorials (which, by the way, are right online as pdf files, so you really have no excuse for not reading them eventually). For product sourcing, for example, Terepeak can show you in detail, what's selling on eBay (and what's been selling over the time period you designate), the best key words to use, best time to list, and provide pricing guidance. You can drill down as much as you want. For example, we started out by clicking on its Hot List button at the top of the page. That yielded 100 categories "that are doing well on eBay," which you can sort so they're ranked from 1 to 100 and from Hot to Super Hot.

We were curious about the "Super Hot" category, so we clicked on one of those links. It was for skis (not surprising, since we did this research during the ski season). But we learned much more than just that skis were hot. If you were to click on that link, you would see several charts showing things such as sales and successful listings by month as shown in Figure 2.2. You can even select up to five categories and compare their sales, etc., side by side!

LET'S GET TO WORK...

- For product sourcing ideas, you'll find the Terapeak Lite plan is sufficient and reasonable at $9.95 per month. If you discover you want more information, you can spend $16.95 a month to subscribe to Terapeak Complete, which enables you to research much more. With Terapeak Complete you'll learn where to list, how competitive your category is, which listing upgrades make sense, and who the most successful sellers are in your category ranked by variables such as market share, success rate, and listings. You can analyze these data to see which categories have "room" and you can export the data to a spreadsheet program.

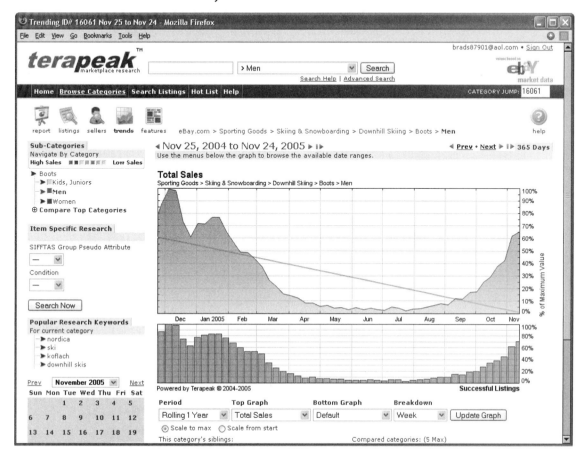

PowerSeller and wholesaler bamcm specializes in health and beauty products. She uses Terapeak every day to monitor and plan her business. She especially likes that you can see a snapshot of each sales area that goes back three months. (eBay's Completed Listings only show data from the previous two weeks.) This helps her decide which markets to pursue and also which ones to back out of. She says she sometimes decides to back out of a very competitive market for a while based on the data she gets from Terapeak. It was also these data that led her to search for a new product line of anti-aging creams. She saw that this was an area with an 84 percent sell-through rate, which meant there was still more room for her to make a profit.

- Terapeak also offers two *free* tools that can help you with your auction listings. Title Builder, http://www.terapeak.com/title-builder/ can help you choose the most effective words for your auction titles. Price Researcher, http://pages.ebay.com/sell-sportinggoods/ can help you price your sporting goods items (with data for other categories presumably on the way).

- All this sounds wonderful, and it is, but as Ina Steiner, author of *Turn eBay Data into Dollars,* warns, you must know the pitfalls of analysis as well as the benefits. When reviewing the data you should consider factors that can affect sales, such as seasonality. Also, you may see that a certain item did well (say, baseballs). But if you try to get into that product line, but don't buy the same brand as was reported on, you will not have the same results. So consider what time of year it is, and when you look at category data, plug in the brand when considering acquiring inventory. In the end, Ina reports, "People who stick with it will find using these tools worthwhile."

- If you're reluctant to make the financial commitment to Terapeak's monthly fee, you can try eBay's Marketplace Research service. It allows you to access up to 90 days' worth of data that are very similar to the information you can obtain through Terapeak. For a token $2.99, you can try it for two days. That way, you can see for yourself the benefits to be gained from this research and decide which tool you prefer.

■ ■ ■

USE WORLDWIDE BRANDS: THEY PRESCREEN FOR YOU

Worldwide Brands (www.worldwidebrands.com) is an eBay-certified solutions provider. It worked with eBay for more than three years to develop its online directories of product sourcing companies. It currently offers three different directories that, combined, represent close to 4 million products. The Drop Ship Source Directory is a great way to try out a new product area. Because you can test the market without buying a bulk of product, it makes it cost effective to use as you experiment with different product lines. The Light Bulk Wholesale Directory was designed with eBay sellers in mind. It includes only those companies willing to sell to distributors in lots of $500 or less. Both of these directories are available for a one-time fee of $69.95 each (with "lifetime" updates included).

The third directory is the WBI General Wholesale Directory. This one includes drop-shippers and wholesalers, but it doesn't distinguish between those who will sell in smaller bundles and those who require larger sales. It is part of Worldwide Brands' premium package, which includes access to all three directories and some additional tools for $197. The Market Research Wizard enables you to assess the market demand for any product you specify. It culls data from search engines to provide quantitative information on demand, competition, and current advertising. It boils all these data down to a line graph showing your chances for success with the product from 0 percent (difficult to sell) to 100 percent (best probability).

■ LET'S GET TO WORK...

- Buying the premium package gives you access to Worldwide Brands' own discount office supply store. Everything in this store is discounted from 10 to 50 percent.

- PowerSeller direct210 uses Worldwide Brands because of the screening it does for the companies that appear in its directories. Worldwide Brands has a staff of people who spend every day verifying the authenticity and legitimacy of the companies it lists in its directories. Note, all the companies who finally make it into the Light Bulk Wholesale Directory have agreed to work with smaller sellers.

- Worldwide Brands updates its directories every day, so the databases reflect constant change. If it receives a complaint about a particular provider, that company's name can be removed from the directory immediately.

- Sellers could potentially use the discount office supply store itself to source office supplies for resale on eBay.

■ ■ ■

PUT AN IMPORT AGENT TO WORK FOR YOU

PowerSeller Bob Kitchener uses an import agent, which to us sounded a bit "James Bondish" at first. Turns out, most of these agents are in large urban centers and can be tracked down on the Web or by searching under "Importing" or "Import Representatives" in directories such as Yellowpages.com. Often, they either own manufacturing companies or have deep contacts with a variety of manufacturers. You can work with them to import items from outside the United States for resale. It's a great deal for you since you can have access to imported goods without having to worry about customs and duties. Import agents will take care of all that for you. They do all the paperwork and pay import and duty fees. They also stay on top of regulatory guidelines and policies to ensure their customers are in compliance with them. Jody of beachcombers! agrees that bringing products into the United States can be a challenge. She imports everything she sells. When we asked her what one lesson she wished she'd learned sooner, she replied with one word: Customs! Jody also recommends that you use eBay's discussion boards to learn about the process before you begin.

LET'S GET TO WORK...

■ If you plan to use an import agent, find one who specializes in the types of products you want to sell. That way, you'll find one with a good source of the specific types of items you're searching for.

■ Take your time to develop a rapport with the agent you might want to use. These are important relationships that may not happen as quickly as you'd like. Ask how long he has been in business and, of course, exactly how the relationship will work.

■ For more information, start with Alibaba.com, a site for global trading information, news, and resources. Its trade forums can provide an "executive overview" of the entire field. The site, which is geared toward small and medium-sized businesses, provides online courses and seminars. You can even buy products right from the site.

■ ■ ■

MERCHANDISE BROKERS MEAN BUSINESS

As you're just starting out, it won't be reasonable for you to expect to be able to work with a merchandise broker, but many big sellers enjoy this means of product sourcing. A merchandise broker, or trading desk, works much the same way that a stockbroker does. Merchandise brokers don't own anything. They work with manufacturers or liquidators who want to move small to large quantities of product. Rather than purchase these lots themselves, they add 2 to 3 percent to the price of the merchandise and then work to sell it to other parties. PowerSeller rocket-auctions frequently works with such a broker. He's enjoyed the relationship, although it is potentially a dangerous one. "Usually, to purchase from a merchandise broker, you will need to be in a position to spend $5,000 to $10,000 in one shot. So, you need to be very selective about what deals you take a position on," he advises.

Obviously, this is not the place for you to start sourcing for your business. But, as your business grows and you gain experience, you may find this is a great option for you. Merchandise brokers often learn of manufacturers that are closing their doors. They'll have a bulk of inventory that needs to be "flipped." That's a term most commonly used in real estate, but rocket-auctions has found it useful in the surplus industry as well. "I had an independent merchandise broker tip me off to a toy company that was going out of business. I was able to buy 16 pallets of their surplus toys. The deal cost me $10,000, but in just over a year, I have easily earned five times that much."

LET'S GET TO WORK...

- Research your merchandise broker very carefully. The industry is not regulated, and it's rife with corruption. Be sure you know that merchandise actually exists, even if it means you have to travel to examine it. It's way too easy to be bilked into paying for something that simply isn't there.

- Be sure the merchandise broker you deal with can be reached in the real world. Anyone can produce a professional-looking Web site and portray himself as a broker. If brokers don't have a physical address, an office staff, or a place for you to meet in person, you'll be taking a risk by doing business with them.

■ If you're going to buy a bulk lot from a merchandise broker, be sure you can afford to sell the items *gradually*. You won't do yourself any good if you flood your own market and drive down the price of the merchandise you buy.

■ Try to stick with a merchandise broker who knows your industry. If you stay in your own market, you'll be more likely to find a reputable broker. You'll also be better able to assess the right offer, and that's vitally important.

■ ■ ■

TELL OTHER SELLERS ABOUT YOUR SOURCES

We've been telling you all along that sellers won't share their sources with you, and that's true. But, sellers are constantly looking for sources and sometimes the sources they uncover supply products they don't sell. They find far more sources of product than they find products to source. If you're willing to share what you're learning, you can actually work with other sellers who will share the sources they uncover, too. PowerSeller harleyglasses refers to this as "sharing the love."

It's a lot like the way the world works outside of eBay. "It just seems natural to share the resources with others that I don't plan to use. Like everyday life, it's reciprocal. You borrow your neighbor's weed-whacker, and he borrows your hedge trimmer. You both accomplish your tasks without duplicating resources," he said. Not only is this a good way to build your business, but it also helps the community you're joining. Most of us have found that you take out of any endeavor what you put in. If you become an active member of the eBay sellers' community, that community is more likely to respect you and support your efforts as well.

In the course of scouting sources for sunglasses, harleyglasses came across sources for Mickey Mouse Cologne, dog collars, and watches. He e-mailed the details to his friends. The fact is that sellers will share sources with you, if those sources sell products outside their own niches.

As an added bonus, once you've developed this relationship with other sellers, you're bound to also start sharing customers, too. Those sellers are likely to think of you as friends and partners. They'll add you to their favorite sellers' links in their auctions and direct buyers toward you when they can. You're building a network here for your whole business, not just for sourcing. Use eBay's discussion boards and groups to find other sellers. The more time you spend there, the more you'll know about your fellow sellers. You learn who the "sharing, cooperative" ones are. They're the ones who are willing to answer questions and offer advice. You'll also learn about their product lines and their business practices. Then you'll know whom to approach with your offers to source cooperatively.

LET'S GET TO WORK...

- When you approach other sellers to offer this cooperative sourcing, tell those sellers about yourself and your business. They will be more likely to trust you if you are open and friendly. That's only fair. How can you ask them to work with you if you approach them with a guarded and closed attitude? You will have to take that first risk.

- Once you've decided to work together, be willing to actually send samples on to the other sellers. You'll be getting samples from manufacturers and distributors for products you may want to sell. Once you decide they're not for you, go ahead and physically send them on to the next seller. That way you're sharing more than just information. The good results down the road will be worth the postage you pay.

- Use this cooperative network to expand your offerings too. Let the other sellers you work with know what you're thinking of sourcing next. Most likely those are items that fit in well with your current product line. You won't be risking a scoop by sharing your plans with other sellers on the periphery of your niche markets. They may just prove to be the supplier of your next great source!

■ ■ ■

SOURCE WHAT SELLS—ELSEWHERE

As you fine-tune your product line, you'll be able to source specifically for the international market. This is a market you may have to cultivate. Building your domestic product line can come first, but keep an eye out for international opportunities as well. As your business grows, you'll begin to learn which products sell well internationally, and then you'll learn to buy with your worldwide customer base in mind. The facts are that American brands and products are still very popular overseas. You can find some of your most profitable sales by buying with this market in mind.

How do you learn what sells overseas? How do you find suppliers? How do you work with those suppliers once you find them? You probably can guess the answer. You research, research, research, and research some more. Don't expect that you'll be able to identify your international product line from the very beginning. Give yourself time to develop strategies for communicating effectively, developing shipping and payment options, and sourcing for international buyers.

LET'S GET TO WORK...

■ "When you get a good sale from an overseas customer, do a search on eBay to see what else they have purchased or bid on and lost," advised PowerSeller wegotthebeats. "There's a wealth of free information at your fingertips if you just look for it."

■ Explore eBay's international sites to see what's selling. If you're thinking of selling in Germany, look at ebay.de. If you're thinking of the United Kingdom, look at ebay.com.uk. You'll see what's hot in those markets when you search Completed Listings in your categories of interest.

■ Once you've found a potential international supplier, see if that person can do some live chat sessions with you. "The live chat allowed me to get on-the-spot real-time answers to my questions," noted beachcombers! "This gave me more insight into the kind of person and company I was dealing with than a prewritten e-mail—a really important thing when dealing with an international company." This PowerSeller chose her source of Pakistani handmade shoes and never even spoke with her supplier until they started designing the shoes together. By live chatting she'd come to know everything she needed to know about his business practices and philosophies. She was able to trust him and his ability to provide her with the products she needed.

■ ■ ■

)) PROFIT FROM OTHERS' MISTAKES

You've probably heard that it's possible to scoop up bargains because sellers made mistakes in their listings. But you may not realize the real potential for sourcing this way and all the ways to exploit these mistakes. "It's possible to sit on eBay and have a career finding misspelled items," mused PowerSeller direct210. That's not to say you'll be doing the bulk of your sourcing through eBay's less careful sellers, but you might as well keep all your sourcing options open, and this is a rich one. Sellers make mistakes all the time, and we don't mean just spelling mistakes. Once those listings are posted, the mistakes directly affect the final prices those sellers can expect to get for their items. You can create favorite searches through eBay's "customized search options," that will keep a constant stream of mistakes coming to your attention. Then you'll be among the few eBay buyers who are able to find these treasures. You'll scoop them up for prices way below their actual value.

Because you know your product area, you'll be in a good position to figure out the most common mistakes people make when creating auctions for your products. You'll be the expert and the best one to scoop up things that others have gotten wrong either through carelessness or inexperience.

■ LET'S GET TO WORK...

■ Misspellings are the most common form of mistake you can use for your profit. Typos are another one. That seller actually knows that he's got a SHIRT not a SHRIT, but in haste, fingers move faster than brains sometimes, and you'll be surprised how many hits SHRIT will turn up. We tried it ourselves and found 67 listings for T-shrits, skirt and shrit sets, even an "awesome" Abercrobie and Fitch shrit. So start this little exercise with the most common misspellings and typos you can think of.

■ Category mistakes can also be good sources of products. Sellers who don't know as much about your product line as you do are likely to put their items in the wrong category. Of course, they won't get the same attention or traffic there, and there they sit just waiting for you to scoop them up.

■ New sellers are also a prime source of mistakes. You know that you should not sell an expensive item until you've earned the feedback rating to support it, but many new sellers don't know that. When you find a great item from a new seller, get ready to profit. "Other potential bidders may be scared they're sending money to a crook," notes PowerSeller Hendrik Sharples, "but I e-mail these people or call them on the phone. We all started with 0 feedback." According to Hendrik, this is the biggest mistake people on eBay can make, and it's also among the most profitable one for sellers.

■ ■ ■

SELL MOUNTAIN BIKES IN WINTER: USE CLEVER INVENTORY BALANCING

Now that we've neared the end of our discussion about sourcing your products, we're going to address the need for you to keep your entire inventory controlled and balanced. We've already seen that you have to be careful about not flooding your market, but does that mean you shouldn't take on a big bulk purchase of the same item when you find a great buy? Not necessarily. As long as you have the capital to invest in the bulk supply without having to turn it around quickly, you can still take the risk. That means having an inventory that is balanced between items you'll sell over the long run and items you'll turn over quickly to keep the cash flowing. As you see, it's more complicated than simply finding a great source of products you can keep on selling.

"Tell your readers not to have a closed mind about what they can sell," recommended direct210. "Be open to other things that might be an opportunity." He sold jeans for a long time, but he also found boxed mountain bikes at the end of the warm-weather season in Chicago. He discovered he could sell them for a $90 profit on eBay (listing them as Buy It Now auctions) to people who could use mountain bikes all year round. "The season had ended in Chicago, but not everywhere else." He bought some, sold them, bought more, and before long, sold all that he had purchased.

LET'S GET TO WORK ...

■ You should also keep vigilant for great deals that may be seasonal to you, but perennial to your customers. You can't necessarily build your main sources this way, but you can supplement them, and that's important.

■ "I keep a balance between my deeply stocked items and more shallowly stocked items," noted rocket-auctions. "I will often purchase large quantities of similar items if I know that I can consistently collect large profits over the item's life cycle."

■ "To keep my capital turning," continued rocket-auctions, "I also buy smaller quantities in a broad range of items. This strategy allows me to take advantage of some of the amazing 'large quantity' deals without having to worry about turning product, because I am doing that as well."

■ Work toward building a sourcing strategy, not just a source.

■ ■ ■

FORGE EXCLUSIVE DEALS WITH MANUFACTURERS

The ideal situation is for you to completely control the market. By doing so, not only can you avoid flooding it yourself, but you can also make it impossible for your competition to do the same. To that end, you'll want to work toward exclusive relationships with your suppliers. You can't expect to form these right away, but you can work toward building relationships that will lead to exclusivity. Then you will have found a great product, and you'll be the only one authorized to sell it on eBay. Sounds good, don't you agree?

But how do you do this? You have to approach each individual manufacturer and make an appeal for exclusive rights to sell on eBay. That's not going to happen for you right away. You're going to have to build your business to the point where you can assure this source you can sell in sufficient volume to make it profitable for it to provide only you with the item. But, a manufacturer who truly understands the nature of the eBay environment will also be able to see the advantage to controlling the source of her products in the market. It's a goal for you to shoot for and one that has been profitable for some of eBay's biggest sellers.

LET'S GET TO WORK...

- "Shoot for carrying a variety of licensed products," recommends titanium PowerSeller pugster. Pugster sells Italian charms for bracelets, and the company has signed exclusive selling relationships for the Curious George character, Pepsi, and Dr. Seuss's *How the Grinch Stole Christmas.* "There is a big investment in time in arranging these licensing deals, so it's better to offer a variety of items, rather than one," pugster advises.

- Approach the manufacturers with samples of what you can do for them. If they like the type of product you're offering, they'll be more likely to license their brand to you.

- Know that you'll have to make a financial commitment to them at the outset. You're going to have to guarantee the license holders a predetermined amount of money up front to get the use of the license. Then you will also have to compensate them with a percentage of each sale.

- Consider making your own product line exclusive by varying the items you sell. PowerSeller beachcombers! only authorizes her manufacturer to make 20 to 40 pairs of any one design of shoe. That way her customers know that they will continue to be able to find unique styles through her, and that they won't see exactly the same shoes wherever they go, no matter how popular the style is.

■ Because some distributors fear they will face price degradation once their items are made available on eBay, you may be able to negotiate an exclusive deal to sell their products at a minimum price. You might also offer the distributor the added service of "policing" eBay for nonauthorized sellers. This strategy may persuade an otherwise reluctant distributor to work with you exclusively.

■ ■ ■

Gary Richardson

Gary Richardson is the PowerSeller behind harley-glasses. In just under two years Gary went from an eBay skeptic to a committed PowerSeller. Gary says he avoided "eBay like the plague" at first. He considered it "scammerheaven!" Until, that is, he discovered how quickly and efficiently he could sell some of the items his family had earmarked for a yard sale. Like so many other sellers, once he'd sold everything in the garage, the hunt for new products was on. Since he's had a lifelong fascination with sunglasses, this seemed like a great place to start. As of this writing, he's listed more than 33,000 pairs on eBay. Gary doesn't pursue his eBay business full-time. His other job is as an industrial refrigeration technician. Still, in his "spare" time he's managed to build a business he, his wife, and their daughter all take pride in.

Gary does a great deal of his sourcing research on the Web, and he's also a great proponent of cooperative sourcing. He's created a network of friends and fellow eBayers who share what they find among each other. He's devoted to building the community of eBay as well as building his business. Gary is not afraid to try new things just to see what the results will be. He was quite satisfied with the results from his foray into international sales, and credits that move with really pushing his business into the "real e-commerce world."

Into the future, Gary is working on a photography method that will allow him to produce 15-frame animated gifs. This bit of programming wizardry will allow him to offer a 360-degree view of his product at a high resolution. He will include it in his listings as an optional link. We're looking forward to tracking his progress!

CHAPTER 3

Creating Sure-Fire Listings

I magine the biggest bazaar you've ever seen, one stretching for miles and miles in each direction. Countless merchants are shouting to you, imploring you to see what they're selling. Some have colorful and flashy signs; others are plainer. Some merchants seem confident and experienced, but others don't really seem to know what they're doing.

You've just envisioned eBay, of course. Because just as a merchant in your imagined bazaar gets only one chance to entice a buyer, that's all eBay sellers get as well. They must rely on their listings, their virtual storefronts, to "get people in the door." That's why it's so important to ensure that your descriptions are complete and accurate. Your pictures matter in terms of both quality and quantity. Your titles must be key word-rich so your customers can find your listings in the first place. But aside from attracting buyers, listings play a different role in your life as you move into the realm of eBay's PowerSellers and beyond to the Top Sellers. They become the face you show the eBay shopper, and they speak volumes about how you operate your business and what you know about your customers.

For the old-school eBay of the mid to late 1990s, you didn't have to sweat your listings that much. Ensuring they were merely solid, complete, and accurate was enough. You just had to get your auction listings launched and generating traffic. Fast-forward about 10 years: eBay is more competitive than ever now, and your listings must be more than just the vehicle that drives an individual sale. They have to be the vehicle that pushes your customer to see you as an eBay business, not just as someone who sells on eBay. You still need to include all the elements that make a great listing, but you also have to do it with a sense of style and professionalism that lets the eBay world know you are a significant and dedicated part of the community.

To top it all off, your listings are among the most labor-intensive part of your business. Just after finding someone to help with shipping, it is listing creation that sends busy PowerSellers looking for hired help! It's not enough to simply create a great, accurate, complete, and professional listing. You have to be able to do that over and over and over again, in a manner so efficient that you can keep your business moving along smoothly. And then you have to sustain that day after day.

In this chapter, we'll show you how to create listings that are complete, inviting, and accurate, but also appealing to the specific market you've decided to pursue. You'll learn some tricks for making your listings attractive and effective, so that your customers will not only want what you sell, but also want to buy it from *you*. We'll introduce you to some tools that will make listing your products for sale as easy and efficient as possible. Finally, we'll look at some cutting-edge technologies that will someday have you speaking directly to your customers, face to face.

⟩⟩ YOUR LISTING ADVERTISES YOUR BUSINESS, NOT JUST YOUR PRODUCT

Okay, as we've said, your listings must sell your business as well as your product! This means you'll have to watch even more carefully to ensure that every listing you put up makes the right statement about your business. Every time someone clicks out of your listings in favor of someone else's, you've lost not only the sale, but also the customer and his future business. That's why everything about your listing should speak on your behalf. From the colors you use to the language you choose, it's your first and maybe your only chance to make a great impression. "By making your templates more user-friendly and informative," says PowerSeller Randall Pinson of rocket-auctions, "you not only encourage the customer to buy the item from you, but you are also encouraging them to come back."

It's important for you to watch your tone. Keep your language friendly and inviting. "It's nothing but good vibes all the way," says PowerSeller Bob Kitchener of bobkitchener and misternailhead. "You don't want to poison the well. You want to leave people turned on to your product, not turned off. You'll never find language in my listings that threatens." You not only want to make a sale, but you also want your listings to work toward creating your image on eBay. You'll need to state your rules and policies, but be sure your language is polite and friendly. You don't want to wag a finger at someone who can potentially buy your item.

LET'S GET TO WORK...

■ Your listings are your first opportunity to show your customer service policies. Yes, your main goal is to create listings that sell, but toward that end, show your customers how much their business means to you. Keep your rules to a minimum and state them in a kind and friendly way. Consider a recent eBay search we did under "diamond rings." (Okay, so only one of us did the search. Deb was dreaming!) Checking the listings for two PowerSellers turned into an interesting exercise. One said, "Item guaranteed to be as described. No refunds." The other listing said, "You can't be sure you love it until it's on your finger. Your 100 percent satisfaction is our goal." Now, which of these sellers would you rather buy from?

■ As you can see, we believe in offering your customers a 100 percent satisfaction guarantee. That's not just our advice. It's the word of countless PowerSellers who have spoken with us on the subject. The best way to prove your sincerity and professionalism is to make it clear that you're not going to fight with your customers about their money and your product. You have plenty of time to take action if you find a bad apple, but in the meantime, you should welcome all customers with the assurance that you aren't satisfied until they are.

■ By the time you've reached PowerSeller status, some potential customers may have concerns about how quickly their orders will be processed and how much individual attention they can expect to get from you, now that you're in the "big leagues." That PowerSeller icon that you're now free to include in your listings can either work for you or against you. The language you use in your listings can go a long way to reassure bidders that they are still your main concern. So, be sure to welcome them and keep your listings friendly and inviting.

■ ■ ■

TARGET YOUR LISTINGS TO YOUR AUDIENCE

You may be tempted to design your listings around the things you find appealing and attractive, whether it's a distinctive color or overall template design. But it's more important for your customers to find your listings appealing and attractive, so it's vital that you keep your target audience in mind while you plan how those listings will look. "You're going to know what to put in your listings if you know your market," says PowerSeller consultant Debbie Levitt of As Was Consulting. "What if you were going to open a pizza parlor next to three others? How would you stand apart from the competition?" Designing your listing, choosing the language to include, creating the look your listings will have should depend directly on the market you are targeting. As an example, Debbie redesigned the look of PowerSeller tailgatetickets, as shown in Figure 3.1. Obviously, this look wouldn't work for all audiences, but for the sports enthusiasts likely to come here for venue tickets, it's a touchdown.

• •

FIGURE 3.1: This listing template for PowerSeller tailgatetickets was designed to appeal to a specific market.

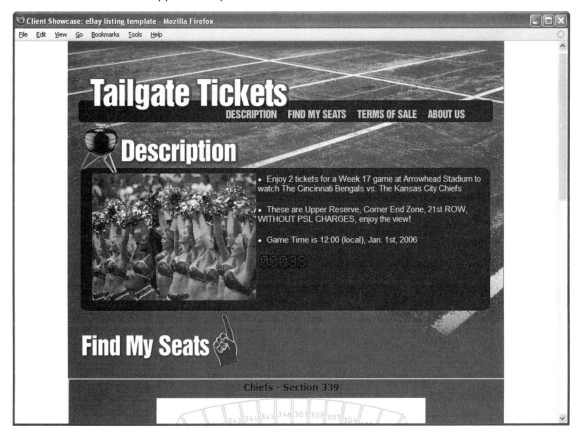

If you're selling fashion accessories, for example, you'll want the listing to appeal to the shopper with a sense of color, style, and fashion. You may show pictures of the item in different settings to suggest how the accessory could be used in a variety of ways. You may even include some of the latest fashion news. You may remember PowerSeller Christina of wiccan well, who sells jewelry and metaphysical accessories. Each of her listings includes the item's relevant properties. For example, an amethyst and amber necklace will describe the healing properties of each of these stones.

If, on the other hand, you're selling car parts, your listings should be devoid of fluff. They should be clear and concise. Your shopper isn't coming to you for a sensation or an experience. Your customer is coming to you to fulfill a specific need. That shopper doesn't want to wade through a lot of prose and read suggestions for how the product could be used. This particular type of buyer wants little more than specs, pricing, and shipping and return policies. Let your shopper get in, find the item, get out, and be back to work.

LET'S GET TO WORK...

■ The overall listing you create should be tailored to the needs of your particular customer. If you sell event tickets, for example, a seating chart will be useful to your customers. Or if you sell running shoes, details on how the shoes are constructed and how they perform under certain conditions might help seal the deal. Make sure your listings give your customers what *they* need. That's how they'll remember you, and that's how you'll become a source for them the next time they need what you've decided to sell.

■ "I have templates," explains PowerSeller Marguerite of mhswope. "I don't reinvent everything on the pages." She can use her templates for all of the repeatable information she includes in her listings, but she sells clothing, so parts of each listing must be individually prepared. "The tedious part is preparing the clothes, taking the photos, and getting the measurements," she explains. But for her market, she must include the measurements. It's going to spare her after-sale problems if her customers have this information before they buy, to determine which items will fit and which will not.

■ Sometimes, fancy is simply not better. PowerSeller Cindy Walker of superiormats sells floor mats for cars, vans, and pickup trucks. She decided to change her page designs after meeting with a design consultant at eBay Live! She went with a more "professional" look. For her business, it proved to decrease sales! "Seems the more personal our site is the better," Cindy notes. Her customers were looking for a small-time familylike seller, and the new look took her business away from that kind of image.

■ ■ ■

)) RETHINK YOUR PICTURES AND THEIR PLACEMENT

"Use a photo as if you had no description to go with it, so a person could look at the photo and understand what the product was like," advises PowerSeller Kevin Boyd. "And when writing the description, write it as if you had no photo to go with it." Although eBay isn't "old" by any means, this sounds like an old adage! It's long been a known fact that pictures matter in your listings. As eBay matures, more sellers who are looking for ways to distinguish their listings, and photos, including their quality and placement, are getting a second look.

With the new advances in digital cameras, taking great pictures has never been easier, so don't settle for anything less than great pictures. Plus, it's not just the cameras that are improving. New tools are coming to the market to make taking great shots easier than ever. Sharpics has introduced a portable photography studio that makes it easy to set up and capture clear images. Its D-Flector comes in a portfolio-type carrying case in four sizes ranging from 18 inches by 28 inches to 36 inches by 48 inches. The seamless background is white, and the images that result from using the D-Flector seem to float in space. Take a look at Figure 3.2, which shows the results of taking digital photos without the D-Flector and then with it. As you can see, the "before" shots would be much less striking against the white background of an eBay auction page than the "after" shots would be. It takes just a little practice to get the flash levels correct, but then you'll find taking great images to be a snap. Plus, because the whole unit is so light and portable, you'll be able to take it with you, to show off your skills when you visit prospective Trading Assistant clients. You'll find more product information and current pricing at www.sharpics.com. But, now that it is so much easier to take the great shots you need, you need to rethink how you place them on the pages of your listings.

· ·

FIGURE 3.2: The D-Flector from Sharpics results in product photos that seem to be floating in space, and which really pop against an eBay page's white background.

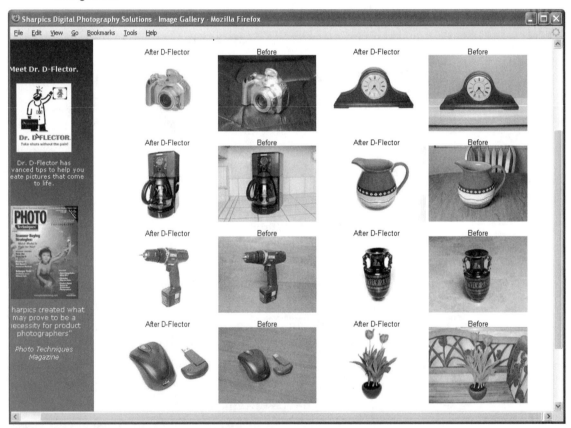

LETS' GET TO WORK...

- "If your descriptions are long and you have additional stuff you put in your auctions, side pictures are better," says PowerSeller Jeff Hess of hessfine. "People won't have to scroll down so far and for so long to see what's for sale." The old standby has been to put your picture in the center and follow it up with your description, but if you can offer more information and more images by placing the photos along the sides, that may prove to be a better choice for you.

■ Consultant Debbie Levitt prefers smaller pictures to the standard single shot in the center. "Give some thought to the size of the pictures," she advises. "Smaller ones are better, because they load quicker. Pictures are important, but they don't always need center stage!" Perhaps you will be better off with a series of smaller images rather than the one large one. It's easy enough to offer your buyers enlarged views.

■ Try eBay's Picture Show feature. This allows your buyers to flip through different views of your item like an old-time slide show. You'll need to include two or more pictures of your item to make the show work, but Picture Show comes close to letting your buyer see the item from all angles. Combine it with the Supersize feature, and there's almost no detail your customer will miss.

■ Gallery photos are often worth the $.35, unless you just list too many low-cost items to make it cost-effective. "I always use a gallery photo," says PowerSeller Kevin Boyd. "Sometimes people aren't sure what they're looking for or may just scroll down the search results." Without a gallery photo, they're not likely to click open your listing to take a closer look.

■ Select your gallery photos carefully. "Typically people use the first photo, which of course is usually a picture of the whole item," eBay University instructor Michael Kaiser told us. But that picture may not show up well in the gallery. He feels that sometimes close-ups or shots highlighting details are better. "For example, if I was selling a tie, I would use a close-up of the pattern for the gallery, not the whole tie, where you can't even see the color," he said. "Likewise, when selling shoes, a close-up of the toe as opposed to the pair would work better. This also applies to other types of items where a shot of the brand name, the close-up of a pattern, or other detail can make a gallery shot pop out."

■ ■ ■

MAYBE YOUR AUCTIONS SHOULD TALK, MOVE, OR SING

As you saw in Chapter 1, some sellers are eagerly embracing audio and video tools for their auctions. The reaction we found is truly mixed. People who love the idea swear by it, but there are still plenty of sellers who are skeptical at best, and completely averse to the idea at worst. Among the supporters, you'll find those who say the audio, for example, adds personality, allows them to "greet" their customers, and makes their listings friendlier and more alive. Among the detractors, you'll hear that anything that makes their listings load more slowly or could potentially annoy their customers is a detriment to their core goals.

In Chapter 1 we told you that audio and video are the way of the future. At some point in the past, it was the exception for eBay listings to include photos. (It sounds like ancient history now, but it's true!) Once adding pictures to your auctions became a possibility, those who had pictures had a distinct advantage over those who did not. We're obviously not there yet with audio and video, but we will be before too much longer.

Already products are available that help to eliminate some of the stumbling blocks to these new technologies. All templates that make audio possible include a quick "shut-off" button in case your customer is shopping at work. Companies are now offering video hosting, much like image hosting, that eliminates the lengthy downloads and heavy computer requirements for viewing video. For example, i2iauctions.com is an auction tool that allows you to use a microphone and webcam to create a video to include in your eBay auction listing. The video plays instantly at the click of a button and requires no downloaded files for your customer's computer. You can purchase a 30-second video for $1.99. Quantity discounts are also possible.

LET'S GET TO WORK...

- Don't just add audio or video to your listings because they're both possible. Consider where the added value will be for using them. For example, PowerSeller stephintexas includes country music in her listings for vintage cowboy boots. She has feedback that proves the women who shop for these boots actually enjoy the music. She lists the song being played just before her item description begins, in case the shopper doesn't recognize the artist. "I have a big audience in New Zealand and Australia," she says. "They really like the music, and I've seen a big bump in sales." Now, stephintexas doesn't include music when she sells stamps or books, because she has no reason to think shoppers for those items would especially appreciate the country music. It's not so much a matter of creating an atmosphere for those shoppers as it is for the ones who come for her boots.

- PowerSeller Phil of Australian-based entertainmenthouse has had great success with audio in his auctions, because of the novelty of his accent. He produced audio files that featured an Australian-accented voice and got a great reaction to them, particularly in the United Kingdom. "People said 'that's like Paul Hogan selling you DVDs,'" reports Phil. As long as you can make the audio happen without slowing the actual loading of your listings, Phil agrees it's an asset.

- Carefully chosen video can be absolutely captivating. PowerSeller dynacnc1 used a video to demonstrate a plasma router for creating metal or wooden carved signs and other items. Although most of us don't have a use for such a precise and elaborate tool, watching it automatically create beautiful designs was completely fascinating. For someone who needed such a device, the demonstration would certainly make it clear what the product's capabilities were. According to i2iauctions.com who made the video possible, using video under such circumstances, to demonstrate the capabilities of moving equipment, can increase the final selling price of the item from the typical 12 to 25 percent to a reported 200 percent increase.

- As we write this, i2iauctions.com could only provide video to eBay listings, but the company was also working on a product that would allow users to add video to any page that supported html. That would make it possible for you to create a video on your About Me page or also in your eBay store. As we said, audio and video are the way of the future, so you may just decide not to be left behind in the present!

■ ■ ■

USE MARKET RESEARCH TO DESIGN YOUR TEMPLATES

So, how will you know what appeals to your target audience? In Chapter 2 we introduced you to the Terapeak market research tool and discussed its usefulness when sourcing products. But did you know that Terapeak can also be a huge help when you are creating your listings?

In Figure 3.3 you can see how using the Terapeak service we searched eBay data going back a week, looking for listings for the popular Thumbelina doll from the 1960s. If you look at the screen shot, you'll see that this search gave us a wealth of data including the average price for which a doll was sold during this period ($69.96), the total number of listings for this item (113), number of bids they received (827), and the all-important sell-through rate (72.57 percent). The sell-through rate is simply the percentage of auctions resulting in a sale. If you look at the Listing Promotions data, you'll get a lot more information, including some that could help you if you were going to create a listing for a similar item. For example, you'll see that including a reserve probably is not a good idea since the sell-through rate of 55 percent for those auctions was lower than the average sell-through rate of 73 percent. Gallery seems a necessity, if you're going to meet or beat the average. You should also consider offering a Buy It Now (BIN) option, as the sell-through rate for those auctions was higher than average (86 vs. 73 percent). So this small amount of research gave us some invaluable advice.

It turns out our research is in keeping with what Terapeak has found for BIN auctions in general. Also, during an eBay workshop hosted by Terapeak, representatives of the compay mentioned that their research indicates that adding a reserve usually decreases an auction's chances of success. This makes sense since bidders don't generally like reserve price auctions. They don't know how high the seller has set the bar—the reserve can be reasonable to ridiculous, and some bidders will not waste their time finding out which is the case. In the same workshop, Terapeak discussed data it ran for Apple Powerbook laptops. Interestingly, it found that auctions with reserves actually had *lower* average prices than auctions without reserves. Also, the success rate for those auctions dropped from 81.36 to 70.27 percent when a reserve was used.

• •

FIGURE 3.3: A Terapeak Search Results page shows some of the useful information you can gain for creating your listings.

We are not saying that Terapeak is the only source for market data that can help you when fashioning your listings, but in our experience it's among the best.

LET'S GET TO WORK...

■ An often-overlooked source of insider research is eBay's own quarterly statements, available to all right on the site. They include information such as the percentage of sales closed with BIN. eBay instructor Michael Kaiser encourages his students to read these reports because as sellers they are part of eBay's financial picture. "As eBay goes, so goes your business," he noted.

■ You've probably searched Completed Listings on eBay, through the advanced search link that appears on most pages. Although the data provided through such a search are useful, they're only a glimpse into the universe of data that are available. Searching eBay's Completed Listings for Thumbelina in the Dolls category, for example, brings up all the auctions from the last 21 days, but you'd have to look through each one to see what features were used and so on. Considering that there were more than 250 auctions during this time period, it would take quite a while to come up with the same data Terapeak provided in minutes. Again, for more on these tools we recommend the book *Turn eBay Data into Dollars*, by Ina Steiner.

■ Aside from licensing its data to third parties, eBay has also started to provide direct access to detailed Completed Listings data through its Marketplace Research service. The data go back 90 days and include information such as average bids an item received. As you saw in Chapter 2, you can try out the service for just $2.99, which will give you access for two days. You may want to consider the $2.99 trial the next time you're planning to make an expensive purchase on the site. It's likely you'll earn your $2.99 back through the savings you'll realize by making a more informed purchase, plus you get to try out the service. If you like it, you can subscribe for $9.99 or $24.99 per month, depending on the exact services you want.

■ As we suggested, eBay's workshops can be a tremendous help when evaluating these tools. Some of the workshops Terapeak has hosted are *Find Listing Features that Work for You*, and *How Research Can Help You Make More Effective Listings*. For more information go to http://pages.ebay.com/community/workshopcalendar/index.html.

■ ■ ■

)) TEST YOUR LISTINGS

Eventually you will have the expertise and experience to know exactly how to most effectively create your listings for your target audience. While you're working toward that goal, use your listings themselves to test your thinking. As you're building your product line, try featuring the same items in different ways. Try positioning your photos in different ways within listings for the same items. If you create test listings, by changing only one element of the listing, you'll be able to see if you have a better response with one approach or another. If you use the same titles for two listings, you'll know that the presentation of the listing itself is the reason one may do better than another.

Part of the fun of operating your own business is to be free to explore different creative approaches. As you narrow down the needs of your audience, you'll have the opportunity to fine-tune the details that appeal to it. Hessfine's Jeffrey Hess ran such a test on two lots of old silver. "In one case we polished the silver, and in the other case we left it unpolished," Jeffrey told us. "We found that in the case of older silver, it's best to leave it unpolished."

▮ LET'S GET TO WORK...

■ If you're going to run tests of your auctions, ask your customers for feedback. "We may test the appearance of our photos," says Jeffrey Hess. "In one listing we may have them on the side, while in another we'll have them at the bottom. Then we'll say in the listings, 'Let us know which you prefer.'" Not only does that give him feedback, but it also encourages an interested customer to view another one of the listings!

■ "We use the questions we get to correct gaps in our listing information," says Bob Buchanan of PowerSeller avforsale. Track your e-mail for several weeks, and see if you can spot some trends. If customers are repeatedly asking for more information about specific areas, reevaluate your listings to see what you might need to add to reduce the number of questions and the size of your e-mail load.

■ These tests can help you determine which listing extras you are willing to pay for. Try different listing extras and then track them to see if one extra or another seems to generate more traffic. Don't be reluctant to try out these new features as eBay rolls them out. Test them early to assess their impact. If you find the new feature effective, you'll gain an edge over those sellers not using it yet. Just remember to test one thing at a time so you will be able to isolate the variable.

■ ■ ■

WORKING WITH THE RIGHT CONSULTANT IS A BRIGHT IDEA

We all bring our own set of skills to our work. Some of us are great businesspeople; others are better at the creative end of things, still others at scoping out great deals. Succeeding with an eBay business requires all of these skills and more, and to be truly successful, you must recognize when someone else might fill out your skill set in a way you cannot, even if it's just to set you on the right path.

Perhaps an example will help. We're going to tell you about two eBay businesses. Each has been an eBay presence for about 10 years (an eternity!). Here's how they worked together.

TheGlowPro sells glow-in-the-dark sticks and bracelets, which, if you've ever been to a nightclub or Bar Mitzvah, you've enjoyed for yourself. Although company owner Garret Hebenstreit had sold on eBay since 1997, he felt his listings could look better. What's more, he knew there were service providers out there who could create professional templates for him. To find them, he went to eBay's Solutions Directory and started to look for partners. After narrowing down his choices, he looked at samples of each company's work, finally settling on As Was, a company that's provided eBay and business consulting services for more than 10 years. "Their overall graphic design was more interesting," said Garret, "They were not just working with images, and the text and pictures were where they should be."

Garret sent an e-mail to the company and heard back from Debbie Levitt, the company's founder, within minutes. She explained the company's process, and, after checking out a few of his eBay listings, commented on what she found, noting what she liked and didn't like. "There were items that were costing me sales," Garret said. For example, Debbie didn't like the bulleted layout in bold font, which she said made his listings difficult to read. She suggested more of a graphic-intensive look.

Over the course of a weekend, As Was created a redesigned template for Garret to review. After some tweaking, As Was loaded the new template to his Marketworks (the auction management company specializing in services for eBay sellers) site for him. After that, converting existing listings to the new template took mere minutes. The bill for this and the consulting time that went along with it was $1,500.

You can see for yourself what Garret's auction template looked like before he started working with As Was (Figure 3.4) and after (Figure 3.5). The new template "has had an amazing affect on sales, absolutely," said Garret. "From June to August 2005 our sales were up 53 percent year over year and our average bids per auction jumped from 5.7 to nearly 9 this year." While his eBay key words campaign is partly responsible for this increase, he also credits the new template. Though the extra sales were great, there was even an added bonus: Many of his long-time customers e-mailed him to tell him how much they liked his new template.

■ LET'S GET TO WORK...

■ In eBay's Solutions Directory, found at solutions.ebay.com, you'll find listings for companies that provide eBay-related software and services covering many things such as Inventory Management, Photo Hosting, Sourcing, Shipping, and Listing Management. Company listings include links to each company's Web site and user ratings. You may have to look in more than one category to find the right company. As Was, for example, was listed under Business Services, and not Listing Management or Merchandising and Listing Enhancement.

■ The companies in this directory can handle other related tasks for you such as Web site design, and even creating a business plan. As Was specializes in marketing, which is extremely important as a way to distinguish your business from the countless others on eBay. Garret recognized this as part of what As

Was brought to the table. It's up to you to recognize what's needed for your business. If you're not sure where to begin, start with eBay's Solutions Finder, which suggests appropriate partners based on your business goals. Just click on GO in the box that appears on the main Solutions Directory page.

FIGURE 3.4: TheGlowPro's listings before founder Garret Hebenstreit worked with consultant Debbie Levitt of As Was.

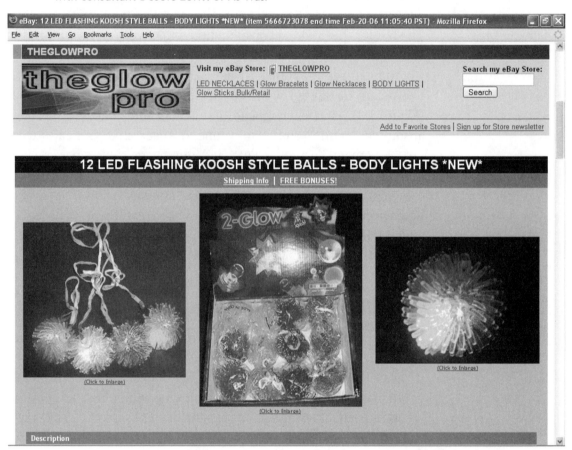

■ A redesigned template really helped Garret's business, but at about the same time he also launched an eBay key words campaign. As we have said elsewhere, with running an eBay business requiring so many balls in the air, it may be best to launch major new initiatives gradually, so you're not feeling rushed, and you can really assess the effect each new initiative is having on your business.

■ ■ ■

FIGURE 3.5: TheGlowPro's listings were far more appealing with new templates from As Was.

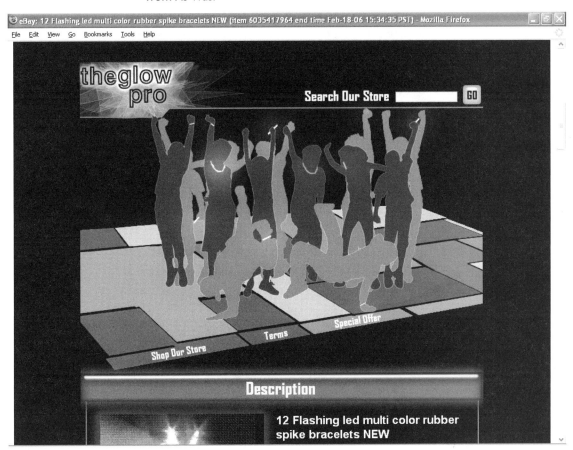

Working with a consultant isn't your only option for getting professional advice in listing design. We spoke with Bobby Krieger, creative director at Marketworks, about what that company considers important in creating effective listings. Marketworks offers a full array of auction management tools from inventory management to buyer checkout and order processing. We'll look at those in detail when we get to Chapter 6. But, in the meantime, here's what Bobby had to say about the services the company can provide to those who are looking for a more tailored and professional look for their eBay listings. Our questions are in bold type, with his answers following. See Figure 3.6 for a sample of a template Marketworks prepared for an eBay client.

. . . .

FIGURE 3.6: This eBay listing shows a Marketworks template, which shows how the company can create something that's in keeping with a client's desired image.

Who are your typical customers? Are they usually eBay PowerSellers?

Most of our customers are large-volume eBay sellers, but we also cater to emerging sellers who want to convey a credible image like some larger sellers. Since Marketworks helps sellers access customers through multiple online channels (shopping comparison sites, e-commerce Web sites, major marketplaces like eBay), we see more customers who are new to eBay and want us to create a brand for all their online sales channels.

Are your services available a la carte? For example, if someone merely wants you to design custom templates, will you do that?

We do offer marketplace-specific templates a la carte and e-commerce Web sites a la carte. The vast majority of our customers choose to brand their entire online presence, because they understand it is important to maintain the relationship and credibility with the customer at all times.

When you sit down with a client to design a template from scratch, what questions do you ask them?

We have a proprietary creative brief process that allows customers to clearly communicate their business focus, marketing strategy, mandatory design requirements, and visual design preferences. This process includes a questionnaire balancing our business leadership with their highly specific needs.

An example of a question we ask is this: *Who are your competitors? (If you include a list of your competitors, we can see why they are successful and how to make you stand out from your competition.)*

This marketing question allows our design team to quickly sort through the design and marketing techniques used by the top competitors in the category or marketplace. Since our designers do this all day every day, in a short time we can develop marketing tactics that take the best things out there and create something new, unique, and better.

What common mistakes do people make when creating their own templates?

Really that is the biggest mistake for anyone, but the top two mistakes are using scale alone (giant letters) and color (red) to establish the importance of the message. With 500 giant letters to read, they all lose importance and go unread. It's pretty frustrating to the sellers when people haven't read the terms on their template even though they are huge. It doesn't work. There are lots of ways to control where people look.

What do you try to achieve with your templates and storefronts? Are there elements that appear consistently from storefront to storefront (or template to template)?

The majority of shoppers are going to determine to buy or not based on the professional look of the merchant (especially with an off-eBay store/Web site). Our main goals are to establish the credibility of a seller with a professional design and a memorable brand. Equally important are the marketing tactics that encourage shoppers to interact with the seller's other items. We use intuitive navigation schemes and attractive visual cross-selling techniques to entice buyers.

What work should sellers do ahead of time before working with you, to help make their time with you as productive as possible?

As far as our creative services are concerned, no preparation is necessary. We make it easy for our customers to communicate their requirements and preferences because we've done this many times. We ask the key questions in a way that anyone can understand.

» OR DO IT YOURSELF. TRY EBAY'S BLACKTHORNE SOFTWARE—IT'S MORE THAN A SELLER'S ASSISTANT

We mentioned Seller's Assistant Pro in our previous book, *eBay PowerSeller Secrets*, when we suggested you consider eBay's own auction management tools. We still think that's a great idea (even better actually, as these tools improve). eBay replaced Seller's Assistant Pro (SAPro) with Blackthorne Pro. Its purpose remains the same: to allow you to create listings and manage your eBay sales offline, with a desktop-based software solution. eBay redesigned the software and improved its customization features, also making it more flexible. It costs $24.99 per month, but new subscribers can get a 30-day free trial.

PowerSeller Bob Sachs was a Blackthorne beta tester and has become a huge Blackthorne fan. When he first started using listing software, he started creating templates with Seller's Assistant Pro. "I began with basic, simple designs at first," Bob told us. Then he "moved on to designs that were more complex and involved." As he kept a watchful eye on his direct competition and other sellers also, he was inspired to experiment with headers, multicolumn formats, image placement, and image size. Around that time he also began working with Microsoft's Front Page 2000, developing new designs and features and plugging them into SAPro for listing.

But Bob says that Blackthorne has eliminated his need to use Front Page or any other editor. While it may not have all of the bells and whistles that Front Page has, it includes a very good WYSIWYG editor.

■ LET'S GET TO WORK...

■ Blackthorne's html templates are one of its best features. As we've said, a good template incorporates information you can use over and over again. "A template lets me create a single set of 'terms,'" Bob Sachs reports, "defining payments, shipping, returns, etc." This is the same for all the items he sells, so "keeping it in the template means I don't have to retype it every time."

■ The templates Bob uses through Blackthorne help ensure a consistent look and feel among his auction items and his store items. Bob's standard template, which he uses for his "primary" items, makes it simple for him to have a more unified look or style. "I can ensure that my Store, About Me, and Listings all present a similar look and feel, tying all these elements of my eBay business together."

■ Blackthorne's sales and management features are also extraordinary. Bob uses the software to track sales, payment, and shipping information. This means he always knows "how much I've sold, who I've sold it to, who's paid and who hasn't, and what needs to be shipped." He tracks sales histories for individuals or items. Finally, he creates a customized packing slip for all orders and can also create customized, personalized e-mails.

■ Lest you think Bob Sachs is Blackthorne's only fan among PowerSellers, please know that many of the other PowerSellers we interviewed for this book were either using Blackthorne already, or planning to use it soon.

■ ■ ■

⟩⟩ YOUR AUCTIONS ARE ALWAYS LIVE AND CHANGEABLE

We understand. You've gone to the trouble to create a good listing, snappy pictures, and great prose, and you think that should be enough. You've done your best, and now you're tempted to move on and let the eBay marketplace take over. However, even the busiest PowerSellers will tell you that they monitor their listings closely, when they can, throughout an auction. Adam Hersh, for example, who lists more than 100,000 eBay auctions a month, still watches some of his auctions and changes them in response to how they are doing. The lesson here is that no matter how professional looking and finely tweaked your auction template may be, there may be room to improve a given listing. With a typical seven-day eBay listing, you have the chance to revise your listing as much as you want, even changing the reserve price and adding pictures.

We can't resist telling you a personal story here. We listed a "Golden Age" *Action* comic with a starting price of $229. We thought the item was desirable, as it was in very good condition and had been professionally graded. We paid the extra $.35 for a gallery photo, and even sprung for the $1 for bold type. We took what we thought were good pictures, and we wrote a description we felt answered any questions a prospective bidder would have. Several days into the auction—nothing—no bids. We tweaked the listing, changing the title to add "Superman" since fans of the Man of Steel may use that as a search term, and not "Action Comics." We took a harder look at the pictures. Did they show the comic in the best possible light? Well maybe not, so we changed those again. Even with this extra work, however, the auction ended without a bid.

We ran it again. This time we sprung for highlighting ($5), but, to compensate for that extra cost, we raised the minimum by $10 to $239. We tweaked those pictures better than Superman himself could have. The description was now not only detailed, but it harkened back a bit to the era the comic was from—the 1940s—figuring that some of the bidders would find that appealing. What happened? This time we had several bids and sold the comic for $266. Not fantastic, but not bad either. This extra work not only resulted in a sale, but we learned some things that we can carry over to other auctions.

LET'S GET TO WORK...

- Sellers use a variety of tools to monitor, among other things, how many bidders viewed the auction (through a counter). If they subscribe to the analysis tools, they also monitor the route that traffic took to get to their auctions. And of course they monitor the bidding action.

■ In Chapter 6 we'll introduce you to eBay's OnRamp program. This puts you in touch with an eBay employee who will consult with you at no charge about your eBay business. Much of this information is marketing-related, but your consultant will also examine some of your recent listings and make suggestions there. In our experience, these tips were very helpful, so if you're ready to list, we give you permission to skip ahead to Chapter 6 now to read about the OnRamp program!

■ Don't hesitate to go onto the boards and ask for the advice of other sellers. You can request sellers to look at specific listings and provide suggestions for how you can improve what you've already done. You may not like all of the suggestions, and the sellers who respond may not necessarily be more experienced than you are, but we've found that another set of eyes can often spot things we miss in our own creations.

■ Keep your eyes open for consultants offering eBay workshops. As part of those workshops they will evaluate submitted listings. For details go to http://pages.ebay.com/community/workshopcalendar/.

■ ■ ■

Bob Sachs

Before eBay even began, Bob Sachs was selling on the Internet. He'd been buying and selling computer equipment on FIDOnet, an old electronic bulletin board system, for years when a friend mentioned eBay to him. His first trip to eBay didn't excite him much, and it wasn't until 1997 that he came back for a second look. He found that the site had "grown up some," and he started to sell odds and ends, just to get a feel for it.

When he first began as a seller, Bob was basically buying retail for resale or selling off items he himself no longer wanted. Since he built computers as a hobby, he generally had some leftover components after each upgrade. Those became part of his inventory. His next move was to buy wholesale to resell, and occasionally he'd buy bulk lots on eBay to test individual units for resale. Bob uses a spreadsheet to determine the "true cost" of a prospective item. That cost includes the price he'll have to pay, the listing expenses and PayPal fees, and even the shipping material costs. That spreadsheet helps him control the "gee that's neat" factor in sourcing for resale on eBay. Today, Bob still sells computer components on occasion, but his main focus is selling shoes consigned from the overstock inventory of a local shoe wholesaler. He also operates as a trading assistant to corporate clients to help them liquidate their inventories.

Bob explains his eBay selling philosophy in colorful terms. "You make money on eBay by either selling a lot of stuff cheap or a little stuff very dear. You can reach Bronze PowerSeller ($1,000 per month average) by selling 100 $10 widgets or 10 $100 wangles. You can sell volume or price. I'm currently doing volume." Bob estimates that about 20 percent of his business is through repeat customers, and about 30 percent of his sales are through his eBay store.

Bob has been on the beta test team for Blackthorne Pro, and he says that working with Blackthorne has given him the opportunity to continue learning every day. He notes that using Blackthorne, "Makes my life easier and frees me up to work with my customers and their inventory. The odd thing is that, if you are really 'into' the whole eBay thing, you don't notice how hard you are working! And when you get a bunch of eBay sellers together around a meal, you can lose an evening in a flash! The Blackthorne folks host a dinner each year, pre-eBay Live!, for members of the beta team, and especially those core members who have been testing for years. If the wait staff didn't remind us that the restaurant was closing, we'd probably still be talking and laughing and comparing notes when the sun came up the next morning!"

Not only is Bob a devoted husband of 25 years, a father of five, and a grandfather of six, but he's devoted to making life on eBay better for the sellers who are coming to the site long after he did. He looks forward to eBay Live! for the opportunity to meet and help the newcomers. "I've spent hours with new sellers, discussing what they are selling, how they operate, making suggestions for things to try . . . and I learn as much from them as they do from me! While I'm working to make my business a success, and I hope to someday have several sellers working for me, I never want to get so 'corporate' that I lose touch with those first-time sellers at eBay Live! That's where the fire and the passion are . . . that's what makes eBay *fun*. Otherwise eBay is just another four-letter word for work."

With Bob's spirit, enthusiasm, and devotion to eBay coupled with the fact that his eBay life frees him up to have nearly every weekend with the grandkids, we don't see him losing his fire, his passion, or his fun any time soon.

CHAPTER 4

Advertising, Incentives, Branding, and Other Ways to Make Your Mark

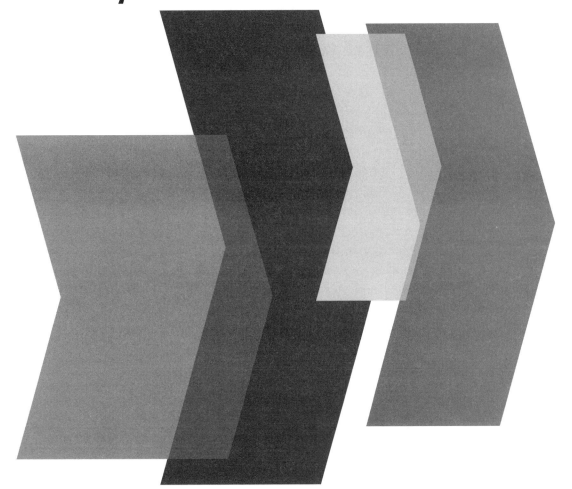

Y ou may not have spent much time thinking about how to market your eBay business as a whole. The details of setting up your operation, finding reliable sources, and just running things day to day are challenging enough. You were right to concentrate on those essentials and to think about how to create the best possible listings. But now that you've made your listings look better than ever, you're going to want to look at marketing strategies that will bring those millions of eBay users searching for great stuff to your door. So marketing your business is the next goal. Don't fret; it's all that work that will make your marketing efforts pay off. "It doesn't matter how much icing you put on a burnt cake," notes Debbie Levitt of As Was consulting. "Make sure the core is solid. Your listings should be the kind of listings that will make the sale." Of course, now they are.

Once you get a stream of customers surfing to your listings (and we'll show you how), you'll want to make sure they have reason to keep coming back for more. We have some great ideas you can use to increase the number of repeat buyers, who, after all, are the buyers you really want to have. We'll offer you some advice for creating incentives that will make you a favorite destination for your customers. We'll show you how to turn an eBay customer into a customer at your own Web site, where you keep all the profit! We'll also explore the importance of building your own brand on eBay. That's no easy task, but you can do it. Consider that a book buyer doesn't search for books by a particular publisher—one publisher is the same as the next to her (although we're partial to books by our own publisher, McGraw-Hill). Rather, she buys a book based on price, word of mouth, reviews, and, despite the adage advising against it, its cover. Similarly, eBay buyers often don't seek out a particular seller. They buy based on price, shipping, and the visceral feel they get when they view a seller's auctions.

But, it doesn't have to be that way. You *can* create a brand on eBay, and you should. One PowerSeller who is especially successful in his branding is David Yaskulka of blueberryboutique. When you view one of David's auctions, shown in Figure 4.1, you see that it's carefully branded with his logo, and it has the same look and feel as all of his other listings. That makes a clear statement. You know that you're shopping with a professional who has gone to some lengths to distinguish his auctions from the mass of eBay listings. He obviously knows what he's doing and has a long-term professional stake in ensuring his customers' satisfaction.

· ·
Figure 4.1: David Yaskulka of blueberryboutique has been very successful in creating a brand name and image for his family's eBay business.

With your incentives planned and your brand in place, you'll want to look at innovative ways you can use the Internet to direct customers to your site. New options to help you with this appear all the time. We're all familiar with the little print ads that appear along the right of Google search results and even on some eBay pages as well. We'll show you how to make the most of these. We'll take a look at how blogs (independently produced and informal information sites) can play a new role in your marketing efforts. We'll also show you some tricks for getting your business to pop up in the search results of people who are looking for information that goes along with your products. Most important, perhaps, is that we give you not only advice but tools and strategies for keeping up on these breakthroughs on your own. That way you can confidently embrace the next new and exciting way to maximize the Web to your best advantage.

After all, who knows what's coming next?

ADD YOUR REPUTATION TO YOUR BRAND FOR EXTRAORDINARY RESULTS

From your very first positive feedback, you've been building your reputation on eBay. Even more than in a brick-and-mortar business, your reputation on eBay means everything. Consider that a store can attract buyers with flashy signs, exciting décor, and attractive salespeople. You have nothing to stand behind your eBay business but your good reputation. Your customers will remember that you respond quickly to e-mail, that your packages are well produced and shipped quickly, and that your items are even better than they were described to be. However, you want to give them a little something more to remember you by as well.

That's why you will create a logo for your business. You'll also use your business name as a signature for all of your e-mails. You'll use standard colors throughout all of your operations, from listing templates to your About Me page to your invoices that you slip into every package. Your customers will quickly recognize the business they're dealing with, not just the eBay seller who sold them their latest widget. "We're in the midst of creating a template and brand for ourselves so that our listings will match our Web site which will match our business cards, so people will recognize them," says PowerSeller Harvey Levine of generalent. "You have to have a little style," added his partner Marcia Cooper. Of course, you must have the savvy business practices in place to support these efforts. Remember that all the style in the world won't help you for long if you don't deliver on the promise.

LET'S GET TO WORK...

- "Offer a 100 percent money-back guarantee," advises David Yaskulka, who learned this from his father, the owner of a flea market. Once you make this offer, you have instant credibility with your customers. It gives you an immediate competitive edge over those sellers who only sell "as is." If you find a buyer who abuses your generosity, you can always block that individual, but in the meantime you send a clear message to everyone else that you stand behind your work, and that goes a long way toward building a fine reputation.

- Build your brand through your logo, the colors you choose, and all your design elements. "The trick is to get it into the customers' minds that they didn't just buy from eBay, they bought from Blueberryboutique," says David. If you look at his listings, you'll see that David uses the same colors, the same layout, and the same terms in all his listings. You'll see he also includes his picture. You really feel as though you've entered a person's store, rather than simply come across an eBayer who may be here next week. But then again, may not.

- Build your leadership in your category. "Many people would like to buy from the Number One leader in a category," says David. There's credibility behind the leader. You won't be able to achieve this goal overnight, but neither did any of today's category leaders!

■ ■ ■

⟩⟩ USE FEEDBACK TO HELP MARKET YOUR BUSINESS

For the seller, feedback is that one last detail of every transaction. It's also among your most precious eBay possessions. Sellers understandably guard their feedback ratings and do everything they can do to keep them spotless. You can also use feedback to research the integrity and reliability of your eBay trading partners. But how many sellers have thought to use feedback as a way to market and promote their eBay businesses? Feedback, strategically worded and designed, can be your last word to the customer you've pleased and just a bit of bait to the customer who's considering shopping with you. Since you can be sure that no savvy buyer is going to bid on your listing without checking both the feedback you've received and the feedback *you've left for others*, use that little space to spread the word about what you do and how you do it.

If you use the automated feedback feature of your auction management program to leave feedback, make sure you vary it enough so that your customers will see that your operation isn't totally canned. No one will question a busy seller who uses automation, but no customer likes to feel "processed" either. So create a series of statements that randomly repeat so as not to look cold and machinelike. Your feedback statement is your last chance to thank your customer, so make it count.

LET'S GET TO WORK...

■ For every feedback you receive, leave a reply statement that highlights the item purchased. PowerSeller Drew Friedman of whitemountaintrading learned this lesson from a car seller on eBay. Now he leaves a reply that includes the item and its brand for everything he sells (see Figure 4.2). Not only does this put his entire product line up for examination, but it also provides a service to his prospective customers. If they stop by to check his feedback, they'll see the whole breadth of items he lists without having to go that extra click from the feedback page. Drew has noticed an increased sales rate for items that are featured on the first page of his feedback ratings. Also, once you have potential bidders reviewing your feedback page, they may click on the item number to which a given feedback comment refers. From the item page (the closed auction) they can easily click on a link that will take them to your items *currently* for sale.

■ In the midst of leaving your marketing message, don't forget to adequately thank your buyer!

■ Use caution if the item is of a personal nature. Be careful in describing the item if it could embarrass the buyer in any way. A seller once used this technique when a friend of ours purchased a crème to stop nail-biters from chewing their nails. The buyer was quite distraught to see a feedback statement that said something like, "Thanks for your quick payment. Great customer. From stopbitingyournails.com." The advertiser may have gotten his name out there, but he also lost a customer in the process.

▨ Include a reply statement that highlights your fast shipping, a current promotion, or a special service you offer. For example, state that gift wrapping is available or note if you have a special senior's discount on a particular day. You have an interested buyer whenever you have someone reading your feedback page, so take that moment to encourage the sale.

· ·

FIGURE 4.2: Whitemountaintrading uses feedback as an opportunity to promote its product line.

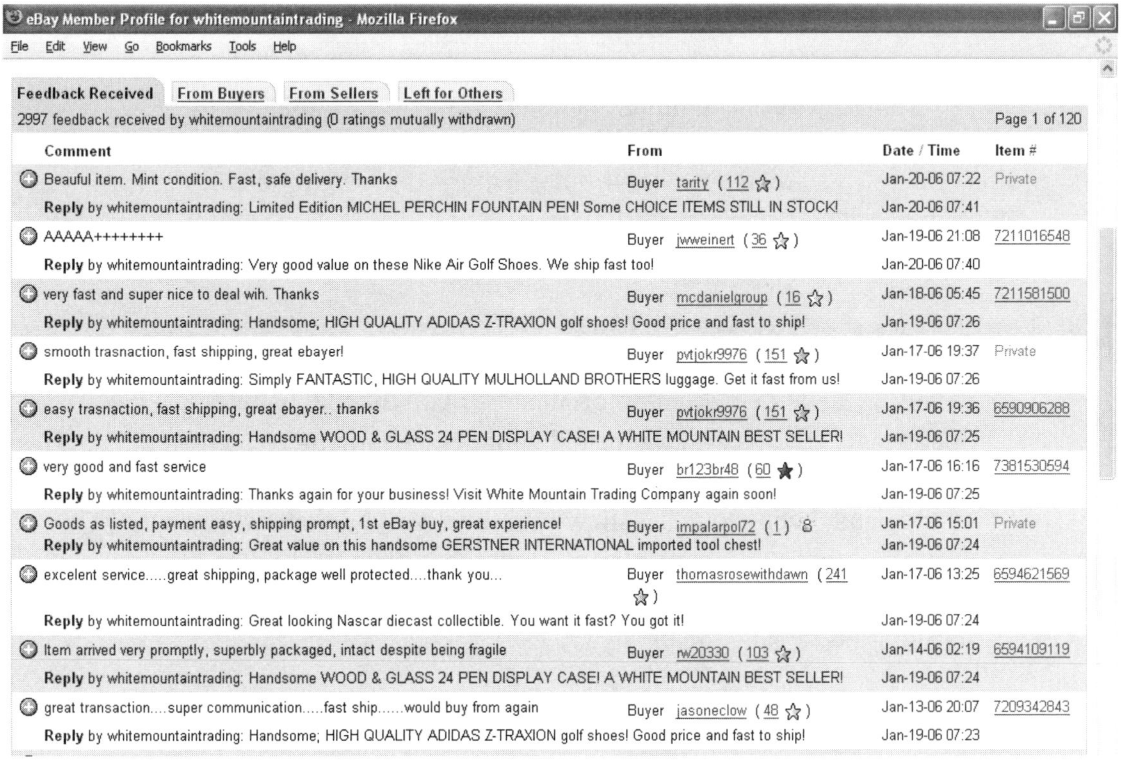

» USE "BEST OFFER" AS BAIT

When you create a Buy It Now (BIN) listing, you have the option of including a "Best Offer" feature with your listing. That means that you can invite buyers to submit to you their very best offer for the product you're selling. Those offers are binding on the buyer, so you know when you receive one that this is a person interested in owning the item you're selling. Nothing compels the buyer to offer you a reasonable price. Some of these offers will be way too low, some on the mark. At the same time, nothing compels you to sell the item listed for below your designated BIN price. As the seller you can accept the low offer, turn it down, or make a counteroffer. Best Offer allows buyers to keep alive the dream that drives eBay, the dream that they may just scoop up something great at a bargain price. But Best Offer also creates an opportunity for you to market your product line and make a sale.

Now, we're not suggesting that you bait-and-switch your buyer or engage in an off-eBay sale. Remember, we're the ones who have stressed from the very beginning that your every action on eBay be ethical, honest, and respectable. Instead, we're suggesting that you direct the interested buyer to your other listings that might be more affordable, but still satisfactory.

LET'S GET TO WORK...

- If you owned a brick-and-mortar store, you would have the opportunity to direct an interested shopper to an item he could more readily afford. If he said, "That's a little more than I wanted to spend," you wouldn't show him the door you'd show him something more in keeping with his budget. The Best Offer is the way you direct that shopper to the part of your virtual inventory that better suits his budget.

- Drew Friedman uses Best Offer to drum up sales leads. Even if he doesn't actually make the sale, he's engaged the customer. He's communicated with a prospective buyer. In this situation, you could then ask the buyer if she would mind if you contacted her when you have an item that's in her price range. You could invite her to receive a monthly newsletter, or you can offer to find an item she might like. You already have an interested party, so you should do everything possible to turn that party into a repeat customer.

■ If you decide to use Best Offer, build your inventory to include products of varying prices. If you carry an inventory that is the top of the line in its area, also stock some midlevel products that could be comparable. Use Best Offer for the more expensive item. Then, when you receive a Best Offer, you can direct that customer straight from the expensive one to something that is likely to satisfy him. You will be marketing your business, making a sale, building your product line, and creating a satisfied customer. Not bad for multitasking!

■ Best Offer can also be a way to move old inventory.

■ If you are regularly accepting Best Offer bids that are fairly far below your starting price, this may be a message that you are setting your prices too high. Remember, Best Offer prices do show up as the final price in closed listings, so be careful not to give the impression that you're routinely charging too much.

■ eBay University instructor Michael Kaiser told us that he has seen at least one seller state in the store description that buyers should consider the site in the same way they'd consider a bricks-and-mortar antiques store. It is suggested that potential customers view the prices as a jumping-off point and to feel free to make offers.

■ ■ ■

)) GIVE THEM DISCOUNTS AND CONVENIENCE

Everyone loves a discount. That's why coupons are still so popular. Plus everyone wants a little extra convenience in a world some bemoan as too complicated and fast moving. So find a way to provide both to your customers, and you're likely to keep a high percentage of the ones you find. You may have an incentive program that is as simple as offering a discount for a repeat purchase in the form of a little coupon you slip into random packages to entice that satisfied customer to come back. But discounts and incentive programs have also become more and more sophisticated among eBay sellers, and the ideas just keep coming.

David Yaskulka has started including a promotion as part of each listing whereby every buyer receives a Future Store Credit toward a purchase from his eBay store—the larger the auction purchase, the larger the store credit. Figure 4.3 shows you how that incentive chart appears within his auctions. Notice the attractive ad that draws you into reading more about the promotion. David worked with a North Carolina–based company called MyStoreCredit to create this fully automated service. As the early results of the program show here, his number of repeat eBay buyers has grown steadily since he started participating in this program.

Date	Sept. 05	Oct. 05	Nov. 05
Percentage of Repeat Buyers	24.7	29.1	34.1

David was sure to tell us that he'd done nothing else with respect to customer retention during that time that would account for this impact. David was more than pleased. "This is a big jump," he said. "My take is that MyStoreCredit moved the dial."

LET'S GET TO WORK...

■ If you want to consider alternatives to discounts, consider convenience. Beachcombers!'s Jody Rogers recently created a Gift Section for her eBay store. She sells imported bangle bracelets that are obviously popular with women, but often baffling for the men who shop for them. By creating this special Gift Section, she's making selection easy for her male customers who might be looking for gifts. They don't have to worry too much about making a mistake, because Jody has grouped together some popular items that are likely to please a customer who likes her bangles.

■ As an added convenience, Jody created a Bangle of the Month club. That makes it simple for someone to give a popular gift that will automatically arrive every month. Buyers can purchase a subscription for 3-month, 6-month, or 12-month memberships. She regularly runs auction listings for her Bangle Club, and her Gift Section is prominently featured in her eBay store.

. . . .

FIGURE 4.3: This MyStoreCredit incentive program is featured in all listings from Blueberryboutique.

If you do offer a return-customer discount, consider tying it to a positive action on your buyer's part. PowerSeller Paul Hedgecock offers special discounts to return customers. In order to get the discount, he asks the customer to click a link that will add the customer to the buyer's Favorite Sellers list and include him on Paul's e-mail list for his monthly newsletter. He gives, but he also receives.

■ ■ ■

OFFER PROMOTIONS THAT MAKE YOUR CUSTOMERS SEE THINGS YOUR WAY

There are many ways to make the promotions you offer work to your best advantage. Think of your target audience and consider what promotions might get that audience to purchase from you instead of from another seller. Perhaps you'll choose one day a week to offer free shipping, for example. Then make sure that this day is advertised in all of your e-mails and listings. Tie that day to the day you routinely put up the bulk of your listings, and your free shipping will pay for itself in volume. Bob Buchanan and Greg Scheuer of avforsale began their "$9.99 Wednesdays" several years ago. Every Wednesday, everything they list goes up on eBay at $9.99, and they make it clear that this means everything, even the most expensive audiovisual equipment they carry. "We don't list junk, just everything we'd list anyway. Last week we put up a $3,000 mixer for that. We won't be sorry, because we won't lose money on it." Of course, all of their listings and e-mails feature their $9.99 Wednesday policy, as you can see in Figure 4.4.

Sometimes promotions are tied to holidays. For example, a jewelry seller we know offers a New Year's special: Buy two (rings, earrings, bracelets) and get another free. And a seller of plastic IPod protective cases ran a promotion at that time also, offering a free case with every one purchased.

You'll be the best one to know what incentive will motivate your customers. Thinking along these lines will help you come up with your own special offering, but here are a few that proved very useful to some of the PowerSellers we spoke with.

LET'S GET TO WORK...

■ PowerSellers Harvey Levine and Marcia Cooper sell concert tickets. They offer to include a coupon for a free 2-night, 3-day stay in a motel in the city where the concert is being held. "We buy the discount coupons from a travel company out west. They believe their inducement is that if someone stays two nights, they'll be likely to stay longer. They sell us the coupons for a nominal fee with our name imprinted. Since many of our customers are college students with little money, the hotel coupon often makes it possible for them to go to the concert," says Harvey. Harvey and his partner Marcia noted that for their audience traveling to the concert site isn't a problem since college kids can usually find someone to drive if they all split the cost of the gas. The trouble is where do they stay in a strange city with very little money? These PowerSellers once traveled from New York to Arizona to check out the motel they were offering for free there. "The motels are nice, nothing fancy, but clean and nice," Marcia noted.

• •

FIGURE 4.4: If you decide on a special promotion, be sure to advertise it in all your listings and e-mails and on your About Me page.

■ Jody Rogers of beachcombers! often includes a free henna tube with her ethnic shoes or bangle bracelets. The clincher is that she doesn't include the instructions for using the henna. Instead she puts a label on the tube with instructions directing her customer to her Web site for the free instructions necessary to properly use the henna. Now her customer has to visit her Web site to use the gift, and Jody gets another chance to show off her business and products.

■ ■ ■

BLOGS MAY BE "WRITE" FOR YOU!

A blog (short for Web log) is a Web site where writers (bloggers) communicate in a conversational style about the blog's topic. Blogs can be collaborative or the creation of a single person. They range in topic from politics, science, and popular culture to business and personal accounts. Many blogs are basically online journals, but many more feature in-depth content of the kind you might find in magazines, newspapers, or trade journals. Anyone can create a blog, and they can include the same elements you'd find in a Web site such as hyperlinks and graphics.

Blogs are exciting because they are a new and underused marketing vehicle for driving traffic to your eBay listings. To learn more about how eBay sellers can use blogs, we spoke with blog expert and eBay seller Kelvin Cook.

Kelvin, who sells Navy collectibles such as T-shirts, toys, and coffee mugs had always included a lot of background information in his listings. He decided that if he was going to create all that content anyway, he should also use it for general marketing, which is how he got into blogs. Kelvin now uses several blogs to market his eBay items available through his store at http://stores.ebay.com/Fitzgeralds-Collectibles, and through other online sites. His mugs blog, for example, at http://fitzmugs.blogspot.com, is a resource to mug collectors including pictures, descriptions, and some pricing details.

Different blogs appeal to different audiences, so Kelvin tailors his content carefully to his readers. In his Navy collectibles blog he created a series of weekly posts that he called "Cruise Book in the spot light." Shown in Figure 4.5, and found at http://fitzgerald.jour-nalspace.com/?entryid = 148, each post highlights a different Navy Cruise Book from his collection. In the sidebar he links to thumbnails of his cruise books. Click on a thumbnail and you're taken to the item in his online store.

．．

FIGURE 4.5: A page from Kelvin Cook's blog shows how you can include links to your products within an informative blog page.

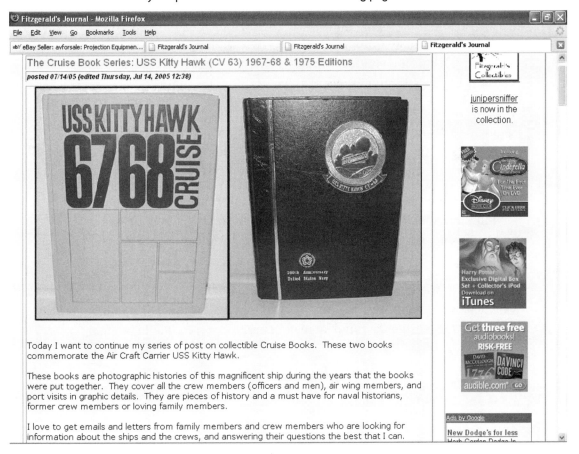

Blogs *work* as marketing vehicles. Kelvin knows he has attracted new customers through his blogs, because they've posted messages. Blogging platforms have report features, and he's noticed that the more traffic he gets to his blogs, the more sales he has. He also includes affiliate links in his blogs, and the checks he receives from those affiliate programs also prove that people are visiting him!

■ Blogs may work especially well for sellers who sell in niche markets. Prospective buyers are more eager for the specialized content you can provide there because they have relatively few sources for such information. Niche product buyers are more responsive to thumbnails and other links, and will more frequently click through to auction and store listings.

■ To get started in blogging, consider using a tool such as the free and easy-to-use "blogger" (http://www.blogger.com/start). Other platforms Kelvin recommends include type pad, movable type, journalspace, myspace, xanga, and LiveJournal.

■ Take advantage of the many tools that some blog platforms include to help you promote them, and measure how many readers and subscribers you have. Kelvin recommended Feedburner, Bloglines, My Yahoo, and My MSN.

■ Use the templates the platform offers but also spend some time thinking about how you want the blog to look. As part of this process spend time looking at other blogs. You can locate these through sites such as Technorati (http://www.technorati.com).

■ Go into blogging with your eyes open. Kelvin says it's time-intensive, it requires writing and other creative skills, and it takes some time to build a readership. However, all of your efforts will pay off.

■ ■ ■

EBAY'S REVIEWS AND GUIDES

eBay now encourages its members to post guides and reviews to the site. Reviews can be about anything—books, CDs, whatever. The guides require some explanation though. You can write a guide on any topic you think may interest other eBay members, and within that guide include links to your store and About Me page. We've written guides about whether to have your Golden Age comic books certified, how to track down items to sell on eBay, and even how to convince your boss to let you telecommute. Search engines like Google index these guides, so when searchers are looking for information on your guide's topic, your guide shows up in search results. This amounts to free advertising for you that can drive a lot of extra traffic to your listings and store. We recommend that readers write guides that are informative, choose titles that are catchy and rich in key words, and include links to their stores and About Me pages within the guides. If you write enough guides and members find them useful, you may become one of eBay's top guide writers. In that case a cool icon such as Top 5000 Reviewer appears next to your user name all over eBay. It's yet another way to establish your credibility. To learn more, just click on the Reviews & Guides link on eBay's Home Page. You'll find it in the Categories area along the left side of the page.

)) DRIVE TRAFFIC TO YOUR LISTINGS COST-EFFECTIVELY WITH EBAY KEY WORDS

Through eBay's Keyword Program you can buy small text ads or banner ads that appear at the top of eBay's search pages. (These are similar to the "paid search" ads that appear along the side on a search engine page, such as a Google page when you do a search—more on those soon.) You specify the key words you feel best reflect your product line. When someone searches using those key words, your ad appears on the Search Results page. You specify whether the ad links searchers to your listings or your store.

When you set up your campaign (online, of course) eBay will take you step by step through the process of creating effective ads. You'll see "bad," "better," "best" examples. eBay even provides a "Key word Suggestion Tool" to help you select the best key words.

You pay on a cost-per-click model, so there's a charge only if someone clicks on your ad (minimum ad cost is $.10). When setting up your campaign you specify the most you are willing to pay per click for your ad. The more you are willing to pay, the more frequently your ads appear on Search Results pages. You set up a campaign budget that you feel comfortable with (the minimum budget at this writing is $20). A variety of reports are available to help you gauge the effectiveness of your campaign.

- ■ Definitely try the program if you run a featured or anchor store. eBay will contribute money toward your campaign ($30 per month for a featured store, $100 for an anchor store), so you have little to risk, advises PowerSeller Ginny Bass of wholesaler bamcm.

- ■ Do your best to track the success of your eBay Keywords program. But, of course, the proof will be at the cash register. AVforsale has used eBay Keywords for some time and notes that their auctions have 500,000 hits a month. They feel a lot of traffic is due to the eBay Keywords program and say, "Our assumption is that it helps."

- ■ "There is a finesse with Keywords," says Ginny Bass. Not one to throw money around freely, Ginny suggests that you start small and keep the amount you bid per click in a small range of say $.20 to $.40. The fact that you can set up a do-not-exceed campaign budget makes this easy.

- ■ The Keywords program may work best for you if you sell in a small niche market that you know very well. Gary Richardson, who probably knows the Harley sunglasses market better than anyone, is a huge fan of the program. "We have excellent results with the eBay Keyword program," he says. "We dominate!" See Figure 4.6 for some examples of Gary's banner ads, which appear as part of his eBay Keyword strategy.

■ ■ ■

Robert Sachs, an eBay PowerSeller we discuss throughout this book, is one of eBay's old-timers. He's been selling shoes under the user ID rosachs since the late 1990s. One night, at two in the morning, he took the time to send us a note attesting to the effectiveness of his recent eBay Keywords campaign. He was so excited that he had positive proof his campaign worked, he had to get the message to us immediately. Here's his account.

FIGURE 4.6: These banner ads from harleyglasses appeared when we entered the key words "motorcycle sunglasses" into eBay's search box.

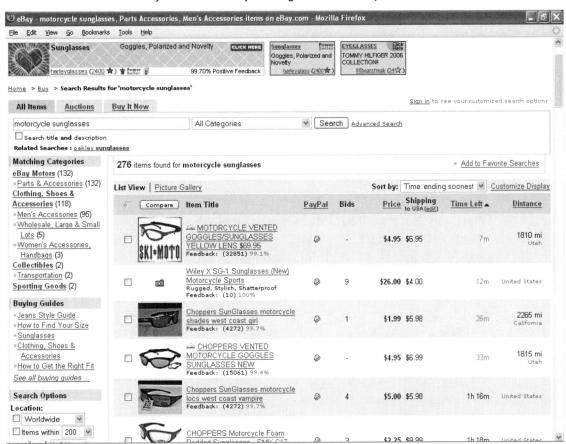

"I can now personally confirm the effectiveness of eBay Key words. I had restarted one of my ad programs in mid-December 2005, using eBay's Featured Store credit (always use free money first!), and December sales ended at $4,500 for shoes (one big single-item sale pushed my monthly total over $5,200!). January 2006 started out strong, with little slacking off from December. . . and then my funds ran out. So I decided to see just what kind of impact they really had in what is a normally slow period. Within days my sales had dropped quite noticeably—you could almost see the exact day the funds ran out just by looking at sales activity for January.

I recharged my ad campaigns (one targeted, one general) around January 14 and within a few days, sales were back on the rise. And yesterday, January 30, was the best sales day I think I've ever had! Normally Mondays are a two- to three-item sale day, maybe four. January 30 gave me nearly a dozen sales! Of course, that means I'm going to have to ship all those things eventually, but I guess you have to take the good with the really good, eh?

GOOGLE ADWORDS CAMPAIGNS CAN BE EFFECTIVE, BUT CHALLENGING TO MAKE WORK

Another example of a paid search program is Google's AdWords—the program that turned Google from the clever-little-search-engine-that-could to the mighty Internet locomotive that's rolling over everyone.

Want your piece of the action? Google AdWords campaigns are easy to create and monitor. You just designate which key words will trigger your ads to appear when someone does a Google search. You write the ad, and you monitor the results. Of course, you want to think long and hard about which key words are likely to attract your best customers to your auctions or Web site, and then write ads that will grab those prospects by their lapels and say *here—look—*and *click* on me!

You pay on a cost-per-click basis, meaning that every time someone clicks on your ads, you pay the amount you specified (from $0.01 to $100 in U.S. dollars). The more you agree to pay, the more often your ad will appear, and the better your ad's placement. You also set a daily budget.

The Google AdWords help site will provide you with all the information you will need to get you started. Go to https://adwords.google.com/select/main?cmd = Login for more information. You should know that despite Google's claims to the contrary, running a successful Google AdWords campaign is not simple; there's much to be mastered, and your budget can dry up quicker than a puddle in Tucson. You have to choose effective key words, write great ads, and carefully track your users. For more information we recommend reading *Winning Results with Google AdWords* by Andrew Goodman.

LET'S GET TO WORK...

- While a Google AdWords campaign can drive prospects to your Web site, for example, Debbie Levitt of As Was recommends that, before investing in a campaign you make sure your Web site is attractive, easy to use, and totally obvious and intuitive.

- When done effectively, a Google AdWords campaign can really boost the traffic and quality of that traffic to your Web site, thereby making you better able to compete against sites like eBay, which draw many millions of users. Lynn Baron, of baronarts, uses her Web site extensively and advertises particular pieces of fine art through Google's AdWords program. She finds this cost-effective because, "eBay is too expensive to sell good paintings. For a $5,000 painting, my fees before selling it would exceed $70." Some of the money she would normally spend on eBay fees she spends instead on AdWords campaigns. This allows her to do more volume on her Web site.

- As suggested, not all campaigns will pay off, and you must monitor your results carefully (again, this is where books like Goodman's and Google's AdWords site can really help). Over time, Drew Friedman of whitemountaintrading, dropped phrases that didn't yield measurable results and targeted his campaign more carefully to reduce "curiosity clicks." Drew suggests that you analyze your campaign results daily.

■ ■ ■

GET NOTICED AND GET PAID THROUGH SEARCH ENGINE OPTIMIZATION

You don't always have to pay for advertising that appears on Search Results pages such as Google's. Your "ad," in the form of a search result that hyperlinks to your auction or store, can appear right there among all of the search results. An example would be an eBay guide that you wrote. This kind of advertising is the result of a natural search (as opposed to a paid search).

You're quite familiar with natural searching because you probably do it every day to find information on the Internet. What you want to ensure is that when someone searches for something related to what you sell through your auctions or Web site *your* listing appears and it appears early in their search results. There are ways you can affect where your listings pop up in search engine results, and of course, on which search engines they pop up in the first place. The umbrella term for these strategies is *search engine ptimization* (SEO).

Here it is in a nutshell. Search engines are more likely to pick up your site (or guide) if:

- You've told them you exist(!).

- Other sites link to it.

- It features the kind of information that searchers are looking for.

An SEO master is Jody of beachcombers!, who, as mentioned, specializes in ethnic shoes and jewelry. Jody and her staff try to optimize for all of the search engines, with an emphasis on Google, then Yahoo! and MSN. She pays close attention to their traffic reports, including where the traffic is coming from, as well as where she shows up in searches for her most popular key words. All this work is paying off (see Figure 4.7) as Jody's store is on the first page of the major search engines for most of her key words!

As far as SEO goes, content really is king. PowerSeller and blog expert Kelvin Cook tries to build the best content he can into his blogs. His goal is to attract readers who are really interested in his content, because he believes he can sell those people something. "And if I do not sell them something, they may bookmark my blog and come back later and then buy something," said Kelvin.

LET'S GET TO WORK...

- Jody also keeps her content strong by including informational pages (both within her Web site and eBay store) that discuss her products. Her blog has many links back to the Web site and eBay store.

- Work toward getting popular sites to link to your own site. Search engines want assurance that other sites find yours to be important. Jody adds her link to "online malls, shopping sites, belly dance sites, anything that will let us add a link." You'll find that some sites will link to yours without your requesting it. As long as they are relevant to your site's content, they're helping you out by proving to the search engine that your site is relevant and important. "When I can get popular Web sites like AuctionBytes to link to me, that is the best kind of SEO that I can do," Kelvin told us.

· ·

FIGURE 4.7: Proof that SEO pays off: Although our Google search for "glass bangle bracelets" yielded 355 search results, the *first* page of results featured two links, the third and the fifth, to beachcombers!

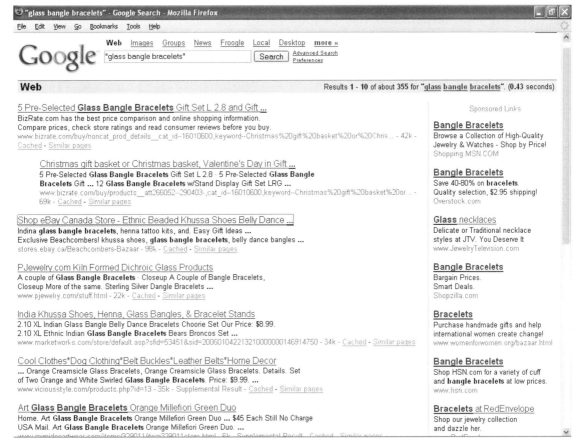

To really take advantage of SEO you're going to need to fine-tune your strategy and get familiar with terms such as "meta tags." Meta tags are descriptors that you assign to the pages of an html document that define its content. Examples of meta tags are title, author, e-mail, description, and language. "It's important to choose these carefully," says Jody, "because it's the tags that the search engines pick up and consequently show on search pages."

- Another part of SEO is search engine submission. Jody's company works with a company that submits her Web site to search engines. Even so, she also "hand submits" to engines such as DMOZ. Plus she hand submits her eBay store to some engines, "although eBay does a good job of getting it out there to the big boys." Search engine submission is a painstaking and laborious process, which is why many companies outsource it. But that doesn't mean you shouldn't become somewhat of an expert on it yourself. For example, as Jody points out, most eBay store items don't appear in standard eBay searches. But "if your store is well placed in search engines and is bringing in traffic, that's fewer auctions that you have to run, therefore lowering your eBay fees."

- Take advantage of the many great free SEO tools on the Internet such as those from the consulting firm instantposition.com (see Figure 4.8). They will enable you to check things like key word popularity and page rankings.

■ ■ ■

GET YOURSELF A SHTICK

Just because you're an eBay seller without a brick-and-mortar store, or concrete and glass for that matter, you're not absolved from the responsibility of getting known locally, especially if you are a trading assistant, or even becoming a local "personality." Some PowerSellers are even known nationally. The point of this, of course, is to generate interest and traffic to your store and auctions. How do you do this? As Rodney Dangerfield once told eBay drop-off storeowner Richard Chemel, "You got to have a shtick."

We can't all be Rodney Dangerfields, nor would we want to be (although we think it might be fun for a day or so). But you *can* develop some sort of "shtick" or characteristic personality and business presence that attracts attention (the good kind, of course).

We understand that you are more interested in devoting all of your energy to building your inventory and listings, but don't underestimate the importance of linking your name with your eBay persona. You can start that as simply as writing a regular column for your local newspaper about eBay or online commerce. Make yourself known as "that eBay guy," and take it from there. We know this is sounding more unusual as you read on, but it really is important. Perhaps some examples will shed light on this and explain how you too can "shtick" it to the competition.

. . . .

FIGURE 4.8: Instantposition.com, a provider of SEO and other Internet marketing services, offers some free SEO tools on its site.

- "You can have 1,000 items but if you don't get eyeballs they don't sell," noted Richard Chemel. So he places ads in publications such as *AuctionBytes*, but he also advertises in a site (portal) that's geared to a younger (he said "Howard Stern") market.

- If you are a trading assistant or operate an eBay drop-off store, be sure to hold special events to get yourself known in the community. Richard Chemel has a Seniors Day at his store, for example. It's about publicity and marketing, but it's also about getting people to have "a comfort level when they come into the store."

- PowerSeller Tony Cicalese of wegotthebeats.com has been traveling around the country for several years in a van with his cat, buying great CDs and selling them. Now this lifestyle isn't right for everyone, but since it is right for Tony, he makes it a point to use it in all of his promotions. He regularly updates his About Me page with tales of his travels. He even asks the question, "Is Tony a mental case?" No, he isn't. He's just an incredibly talented eBay marketer with a great shtick.

■ ■ ■

Harry Levine and Marcia Cooper

Harvey Levine and Marcia Cooper were anticipating a happy retirement when the unexpected happened to alter their plans. First one, and then the other was downsized and laid off. Now the couple, who were "sixty-ish," were faced with realizing that having to "retire" early meant they weren't quite prepared for retirement. Finding themselves on the wrong side of the optimum age for new job opportunities, the two were worried.

Then Marcia's son, Rob, a successful eBay seller asked them to help him just a bit. They were, geographically, in a better position to purchase some concert tickets he wanted to sell, so he paid them a fee to go stand in line and get the tickets. Then, he encouraged them to pursue an eBay business of their own. Marcia had never been on eBay, and Harvey had bought a few things, but neither was an expert and neither was completely at home with computers. Less than five years later, not only are Harvey and Marcia PowerSellers, but they're also trading assistants and eBay-certified Education Specialists. They report that most of their students are over 50, and they really enjoy helping the more mature newcomers to eBay find their way around.

Harvey and Marcia have not only mastered eBay, but they've learned more about the world of e-commerce and computing than they once would have dreamed they'd know. To their advantage, they both had decades' worth of business experience behind them, but neither had ever operated their own business. They've come a long way in a short time, selling not only event tickets, but also antiques, cars, and a variety of collectible items. They use audio in their listings. They incorporate venue charts to show prospective customers where their seats are located. They've found a source of views on the Internet to allow someone considering tickets for an outdoor venue to actually glimpse the view of the field from the seat they're considering. They're also very actively seeking affiliate arrangements to partner with other online vendors for mutual promotions and profits.

They learned some lessons the hard way. They found that with concert tickets they must stipulate immediate payment. Too many kids were bidding and winning only to find out that Dad would not give them the credit card, and Harvey and Marcia were stuck. In such a time-sensitive market, they quickly switched to requiring immediate payment. They also learned that they needed to increase the value of anything they took on consignment. Now they won't sell an item that's valued at less than $100. They find anything less is not worth their time or their clients'.

Both are really enjoying their roles as educators. They find at their stage of life that they enjoy giving back to the community and helping others find the freedom, excitement, and growth they've discovered. Little did either of them guess that this is what retirement would look like. "Remember, when we started this we were senior citizens," noted Marcia. "We still are!" quipped Harvey. Stop by to see their listings and enjoy some of the joy and enthusiasm they bring to their eBay lives. You'll find them on eBay at generalent or on the Web at www.generalenterprises.net.

CHAPTER 5
Fraud, Phish, and Fakes

Combating e-commerce fraud is like fighting the many-headed Hydra monster of Greek mythology. Every time Hercules thought he had slain that beast by chopping its head off (sorry for the bad pictures, but fraud is bad stuff), two more heads grew in replacement. Such is the ever-changing world of online fraud. Every time you think you've protected your business adequately from the many types of online fraud, fraudsters come up with new schemes. So rampant is online fraud, a whole new colorful vocabulary has sprung up to describe it—phishing, pharming, spoofs—you name it.

Even eBay itself is sometimes stymied by the cleverness of the attacks, as proven by a phishing attack that occurred in late 2005. Like many spoof e-mails, this one looked real enough. With a promise of revealing great tips for Christmas selling on eBay's U.K. site, the e-mail in question directed independent security consultant Richi Jennings to the Web site ebaychristmas.net, according to an IDG News Service report. Once there, the consultant was directed to enter his eBay user name and password, plus the same information for his regular e-mail account. Suspicious, the consultant sent the message onto eBay, just as eBay instructs its members to do. But eBay's fraud investigators answered by saying the message was "an official e-mail message sent to you on behalf of eBay." The consultant persisted in his claim, and eventually eBay agreed the site was phony.

So if even eBay can sometimes be blindsided by these attacks, is it any wonder that some experienced PowerSellers, who have seen it all, still suffer significant losses from fraud each year? Of course, there would be no escaping this in the brick-and-mortar world either. Just try to run a store without shoplifters, bad checks, and credit card fraud hounding you. Fraud on eBay includes those types of fraud perpetrated by buyers, but you'll also find e-mail fraud, seller fraud, and seller-to-seller fraud. Don't despair. There are some excellent strategies that PowerSellers use to keep fraud at a minimum, and we'll share those here.

E-mail fraud includes the phishing scheme described above. Just about all visitors to the online world have been warned about spoof e-mails that direct them to fake Web sites identical to the ones they generally use such as eBay, PayPal, or Amazon.com. Once at these fake Web sites, the unsuspecting visitor will be asked for user ID, password, and account number information that will then become available to the crooks behind the scenes who use the information for identity theft. Making it a hard and fast rule to never click on any link in an e-mail from someone you don't know, and to never respond to any request for identifying information, goes a long way toward foiling phishing schemes. But now, there's also pharming, which is described by the Anti-Phishing Working Group at www.antiphising.org, as phishing without the lure. Instead of coaxing you to give up your information voluntarily, pharming schemes use malicious software code to redirect your Web browser from a legitimate site to a criminal's Web site. Once you're at the fraudulent site, any personal data you enter are given to the criminal behind the scenes. As you can see, almost as quickly as users learn how to avoid a scam, a new, more insidious scam crops up to take its place.

But e-mail fraud won't be your only worry. There's also the buyer fraud that will haunt you just as the unscrupulous customers haunt your local mall. In e-commerce, the schemes may differ, but the goals are the same—to take what belongs to someone else and not pay for it. You'll find buyers who will claim that they never received your package. Some of them will return it to you broken, damaged, or replaced by an item you never sold. Still others will claim that it was damaged when they received it, and although they don't actually want to return it, they would like you to discount the price since it's not as good as they thought it would be. Some buyers will even ask you to send the package to an unconfirmed address, claiming it is a gift for a distant relative, and that will save them postage. Of course, once you ship it to an unconfirmed address, you have no recourse to claim reimbursement from PayPal if the buyer claims it never arrived. Buyers who want to rip off eBay sellers have endless imaginative ways to do it. Fortunately, although they seem to get the press, they are a distinct minority.

To complicate your fight against fraud, you'll have to deal with unscrupulous sellers who are on eBay with the intent to cheat honest buyers. Why are they your problem when you know that you're not one of them? Because they taint the entire site and make buyers wary and less likely to trust the honest sellers. They create an environment where your good customers have no reason to trust anyone who sells on eBay. They are poison to your business, and you'll want to know your category associates well enough to be your own little neighborhood watch group. Careful monitoring can go a long way toward ending the career of criminal sellers, but it takes vigilance.

Finally, you'll find sellers who are more than happy to rip off other sellers. Some of them will steal your entire listing, or even *all* your listings. Some might just take your pictures. But the worst of these will harvest your bidders. They may even approach your bidders directly, disparage your auctions, and warn them that you are untrustworthy. Of course, at the same time, they'll be ready to offer your bidders a better deal (wink, wink).

The sad reality is that all of these problems will just continue to grow, change, and evolve. Every time you think you've seen the worst and most blatant form of fraud, just give yourself a little time. It won't keep that distinction for long. Something else will come along and bump it from the top of the heap. Okay, so now that we've got your guard up, let's take a look at some of the things you can do to protect yourself out there.

DON'T ASSUME IT'S FRAUD

You must be thinking, "What, are they crazy?" Although we just assaulted you with all the ways there are to get robbed, we mean it. Don't jump to conclusions. Sometimes a situation isn't fraud so much as it is incompetence. No one wins if we all enter this arena with the attitude that I'm going to get you before you can get me! So, when you think something may be fraud, be smart and careful, but don't take to the bunkers right away.

"Some of the biggest hits we've taken from buyers were not fraud. We shipped the order, for example, and the buyer claimed he never received it. It felt like fraud at the time, but it was true," notes blueberryboutique's David Yaskulka. There's a fine line between providing excellent customer service and being ripped off. You'll have to hone your instincts in order to tell the difference, and in the meantime, you may have to give more than you'd like. No one wants to feel robbed, but it happens to all of us at one time or another.

The same can be true of other sellers taking your listing details. Of course, you know that's wrong, but as surprising as it may seem, some inexperienced sellers don't. "I found others were stealing the text and pictures from my listings," reported PowerSeller beachcombers! "I address this through e-mail. I explain to them that the material is copyrighted and remind them that eBay will end the listing if they have to and ban them from the service if they continue. I tell them I'll let it go this time, but if it happens again, I'll have to report them." Then she adds the seller to her favorites and checks back on them for a few weeks to make sure they've learned from their mistake. She's found that usually works, because these are not really criminals, they're just eBay sellers who don't know better. Now she's helped someone advance in her business instead of making her a criminal.

LET'S GET TO WORK...

- Lengthen your fuse. Once you know you'll have to deal with fraud and you won't let others defraud you with impunity, you don't have to jump every time you face a problem. Sometimes a disgruntled buyer is disgruntled legitimately, and you'll turn a bad situation into a good one, if you take a deep breath, keep your cool, and gather your facts. Then you'll be ready to address the issue, and you're likely to turn a disgruntled buyer into a loyal customer who trusts you and comes back to buy from you again.

- Remember that you're a business owner now. "Every store owner in the bricks-and-mortar world knows to expect a certain percentage of loss every year through fraud," noted Drew of PowerSeller whitemountaintrading. "It's built into the business plan. eBay sellers need to do the same. I build a percentage into my yearly outlook to cover myself for fraud. I've never come close to reaching it." Drew has a good point. If it's not possible to run a business without having some degree of loss through fraud and theft, why would you expect your eBay business to be any different?

- Know your category. Spend enough time in your category to know the major players. Watch to see who is new and who may need some education in manners and good practices. When you know the neighborhood well, you're more likely to be an effective member of the neighborhood watch team.

- Audit your auctions. Drew of whitemountaintrading audits his auctions twice a day. He enters all of his listings into eBay's search features. He searches by brand as well as by item type. Then he can see who his competitors are and what they're doing. Not only does this keep him up to date on potential fraudsters, but it also keeps him right in the forefront of his competition.

- Watch for one-day auctions. Sometimes a one-day auction can be a great way to turn something over quickly, but a one-day auction can also be a way for a criminal to make a quick strike and be gone before anyone notices. When you know your category, you'll learn to recognize suspicious one-day auctions, those offering very high-priced items, for example. If a one-day auction is set for Friday through Sunday, that can also be a warning. A scam seller will be on and off the site before anyone at eBay could possibly be available to shut the auction down. Be especially vigilant for one-day auctions that require Western Union payments or wire transfers. There really is no reason for these payment restrictions, except that they're impossible for the buyer to recover after the fact.

■ ■ ■

KEEP YOUR AUCTIONS PRIVATE

Although you won't want to make all of your auctions private, don't hesitate to use the private auction listing options with some of your listings. The high-priced items are good candidates for private auctions as are collectibles in highly competitive markets. This may seem like counterintuitive advice based solely on research numbers. Over 76 percent of the respondents to a recent survey by AuctionBytes claimed they had never used eBay's private auction option as a seller. Nearly 65 percent of them said they'd be less likely to bid on an item that was put up as a private auction. So why would you want to alienate potentially two-thirds of your likely customer base?

Private auctions protect your bidders and your business. They protect your bidders, because no one can see who is participating in the auction. That doesn't matter much if you're selling something for $24.95, but what if you're expecting to get $2,500 for your item? Or $25,000? By keeping your bidders' identities private, you're protecting the ones who come to eBay with a good deal of disposable income and an interest in buying. If you offer them privacy, unscrupulous sellers won't be able to harvest their user names and approach them with bogus offers of their own.

You're also protecting your business at the same time you're keeping the names of your bidders private from the criminals who want to prey upon them. Once a criminal knows who's bidding on your expensive item, he can approach your highest bidder or your underbidder and claim that you're selling a counterfeit. The result is that you'll lose your customers and the trust you've built by all of your honest efforts. You'll find some of your bidders are withdrawing their bids and suffering the consequences rather than risk the chance of spending a princely sum on something they no longer believe in. A customer you lose to this kind of scam is one who will be difficult to regain.

■ LET'S GET TO WORK...

■ If you decide to use a private auction, include an information box that explains to your bidders why your auction is private. You want to keep the potential criminals and scammers at bay, but you want your customers to know that you have good honest reasons for keeping their identities hidden.

■ Remind your bidders that not only are you protecting them from potential scammers, but you're also protecting them from revealing too much about their shopping habits. The markets most likely served by private auctions are subsets of eBay at large. Bidders are more likely to recognize each other, because they're interested in similar items in a relatively small market.

By keeping your auctions private, you let your bidders operate without revealing their current interests to your competitors.

■ When using private auctions, be sure to encourage bidders to contact you via e-mail, or even through a phone call, to discuss any concerns. As in all things eBay, communication is often the key to mitigating suspicion and developing good customer service.

■ Keep offering private auctions when they're appropriate. Across the whole of eBay, it may take time before the average bidder recognizes the advantages of private auctions, but that learning curve will be much smaller in the niche markets. You'll be one of the sellers helping to bring about the change in perception necessary to make private auctions more acceptable, as your bidders learn how much more protection they receive from such sales.

■ ■ ■

>> DON'T LET JUST ANYONE BID

Your ultimate goal is to bring as many bidders to your auctions as possible. Who doesn't want multiple bidders all going after a single item that just keeps increasing in its price as the bidding escalates? But that doesn't mean you shouldn't screen out bidders with whom you've had a poor experience. You will certainly encounter people who are dishonorable or unreasonable or who are some other sort of scoundrel. Those are the bidders you want to exclude and then never give them another thought.

"We have hundreds of blocked bidders," says Bob Buchanan of PowerSeller avforsale. "If you don't pay, we'll block you and leave negative feedback. We also block people who are surly or abusive." Bob makes sure each bidder has four separate opportunities to respond to payment requests before he takes this action. He believes in using the tools eBay provides, and making bad customers disappear is certainly better than having to deal with them multiple times.

"You can designate your selling preferences," notes David of PowerSeller blueberryboutique. "You can block people from certain countries, and cap the number of auctions that a zero-feedback person can buy from you. You can specify that people with a negative or neutral feedback rating or with two nonpaying bidder strikes are ineligible for your auctions." David recommends that each seller find his or her own level of comfort and stick to it.

■ LET'S GET TO WORK...

- ■ Block bidders who give you trouble from bidding on any of your future auctions when you leave them negative feedback. It may surprise you to learn that some people can be so vengeful that they will actually buy from you again for the sole purpose of flaming your feedback, but it's true. Don't give them the chance.

- ■ Don't hesitate to block someone who is currently involved in an unresolved dispute with you. Just because the problem isn't resolved, doesn't mean you should hesitate to block the person while you work out the details. If the complaint proves to be legitimate and you resolve the issue satisfactorily, you can always unblock the bidder. In the meantime, you've diminished your risk just in case you have found a criminal. You're not being rude, you're just protecting yourself.

- ■ Unfortunately blocking a bidder doesn't guarantee she's gone from your life forever. She may reappear using a different User ID, so be prepared for that possibility, for example by noting any consistencies among the bidding practices of your past and current bidders.

■ ■ ■

⟩⟩ TAKE A SECOND LOOK AT THE SECOND CHANCE

In the traditional world of auctions, second-chance offers, or bell-ringers as they're called, are good news for all the participants. "At an art auction, for example," explains Drew of whitemountaintrading, "the auctioneer will bid up a lithograph to $500, and sell it. As soon as the sale ends, he'll actually ring a bell and announce that he has good news, another identical lithograph will now be available to the next lowest bidder at $450. It's reason to celebrate. If he has more of the same thing, he'll sell them all at $450. Everyone's happy." Drew still likes second-chance offers, but a controversy has grown on eBay that puts him on the opposite side of other accomplished sellers. He understands their point of view.

A year ago we would have recommended your using a second-chance offer without any hesitation, but fraud has made us take a second look at the second chance. The problem is that fraudsters will watch auctions, especially those for high-priced items, and harvest your underbidders. They'll send fake e-mails offering to sell those underbidders the items they missed out on. They may even approach those bidders in your name, making it seem like the offer is coming from someone whom the bidder has already agreed to buy from. The problem, of course, is that the item doesn't exist. If the fraudster uses your user ID, then all the negatives come back to you. Even if he doesn't, that's an eBay buyer who once burned will be twice shy. Especially when you're dealing with high-priced items, you'll see this kind of fraud chase away, forever, just exactly the type of buyer eBay sellers most want to protect and retain.

LET'S GET TO WORK...

- If you decide to use a second-chance offer, make sure you direct your buyer to actually go to eBay.com and log in. Your second-chance offer will appear on the buyer's My eBay page, because it's legitimate. Give the buyer the instructions for doing this right in the body of the offer you send. It allows you both to use the tools eBay already provides. Never send a second-chance offer outside of eBay. It's just too risky.

- To protect yourself from people copying listings for fraudulent second-chance offers, use watermarks on photos, which make them difficult to copy. Through eBay's Picture Manager you can include such a watermark.

- If you decide not to use second-chance offers because you don't want to leave your customers open to this scam, be sure to state that very plainly in all of your listings. PowerSeller avforsale has a banner that runs across the top of all listings. It states clearly, "We do not send second-chance offers. If you receive one, it's a scam!" How long do you think a fraudster will consider running this scam on the customers who shop with this seller? A criminal will be off to the next high-priced seller in a mouse click.

■ ■ ■

DON'T TAKE YOUR OWN WORD FOR IT

Online fraud has led to a creeping skepticism among eBay buyers, so you should always be looking for ways to assure your bidders that you're an honest and knowledgeable seller. WhatsItWorthToYou.com, a Web site recommended by a top New York PowerSeller, provides online appraisals. In fact, it provides all the tools you need to learn more about your item and assure your bidders that they can depend on your descriptions and statements. Sellers can expect to see more bids and higher bids when they use these services, according to company president Erik Kafrissen, who has been providing appraisals to eBay sellers for more than five years.

WhatsItWorthToYou.com provides two types of appraisals. The classic appraisal, for $9.95, buys you an expert's opinion of what your item is worth. This includes an estimate of its fair market value (what a dealer might pay for your item), as well as its replacement cost, which is what you'd have to pay a dealer for the item. As part of the appraisal you will also receive an "online auction estimate," which is the amount the expert feels you can expect to receive for the item at auction (e.g., on eBay). A deluxe appraisal, at $19.95, gives you all the market values you'd get as a part of the classic appraisal, but you also receive more in-depth information about the item (think *Antiques Roadshow*), such as where it was manufactured, and tips for caring for it and storing it. This information would fill out your item description nicely.

As part of the process of obtaining an appraisal, you're invited to upload images as well as any other information you can provide for your item. Once you have your appraisal, you can include a link to your "appraisal certificate" within your auction listing, to boost credibility and value.

These services are very popular with new sellers, but even if you're a veteran seller, you can consider this appraisal service whenever you acquire something outside your usual area of expertise. You may find them especially useful if you take items on consignment as a trading assistant. After all, you can't be expected to be expert in every possible area of study, and offering this service to your consignees can really boost their confidence that you'll get a great price for their item.

LET'S GET TO WORK...

■ WhatsItWorthToYou.com provides *discounted* appraisals to eBay sellers. You'll pay $9.95 for a classic appraisal and $19.95 for a deluxe appraisal. For more information, surf to http://pages.ebay.com/help/community/auth-overview.html. It also has appraisal packages, where you can purchase lots of 4, 10, or 20 appraisals (classic or deluxe) at a discounted rate.

■ Its Ask an Expert service costs $2.25 and enables you to get an expert's opinion on an item; who made it, how old is it, and so on. Market value information is not included.

■ When we spoke with the company, we learned the company was planning a new service, in which one of its experts would actually write your eBay listing for you. The plans called for this to be an added service on top of one of its appraisals, for perhaps $6 to $10. (Note that if you've paid for a deluxe appraisal, most of your auction listing is done anyway.)

■ Its "Unlock the Database" service enables you to search its database of completed appraisals, by category or key word. The database includes details such as images, descriptions, date/era/period of item, grade/condition of the item, historical data, tips from the appraiser, links to relevant Web sites, date of appraisal, fair market value, replacement value, and even comments from the customer. You pay by the day, week, month, or year, and the fees range from $3.95 to $49.95.

■ ■ ■

⟩⟩ HEAD THEM OFF AT THE PASS

There is no magic bullet for preventing all possibility of fraud. You already have tools available to protect yourself from criminals. "If you're an accomplished businessperson, you'll have a level of protection for yourself and your customers already in place," noted

Drew of whitemountaintrading. Some of the best fraud protection comes from good business practices. "The problem is that 5 percent of the market will always leave themselves exposed to fraud," said Drew, "and that's all the fraudsters need to thrive." So, don't underestimate the benefit of good common sense.

An e-commerce business owner has an added level of vulnerability because of computer-based fraud, but you also have software designed to support you. "A good firewall will help you keep out a lot of bad e-mail," noted Drew. Your auction management software will also help. You can build rules into your software that alert you to potentially dangerous transactions and give you the chance to follow up on them before they're processed automatically. "We've built rules into our software, and as a result we have a low ratio of fraud," said Paul of PowerSeller dealtree. "When we do have an incident of fraud, we look at it internally to find ways to avoid it in the future."

Keep in mind that for the most part, criminals online are much like criminals in the real world. They're looking for a quick hit and to escape without getting caught. You're never going to be able to eliminate them completely, but discouraging them may be all that's necessary. They'll move on to the next, less aware and less well-prepared victim.

◼ LET'S GET TO WORK...

◼ Set your software to only ship items to confirmed addresses. Once you do this, you won't have to worry about an order slipping through and going out to an address you wouldn't choose to ship to.

◼ Set your software to flag any sale over a set amount of money. Then you can call the customer to make sure you feel secure that everything is legitimate. It won't go through automatically.

◼ Set your auction management software to file Final Value Fee refunds automatically. Not only will that recoup your lost eBay fees, but it will add the negative mark to your nonpaying bidder's eBay history that will be necessary to have his or her account suspended.

- Run a monthly spreadsheet of your PayPal account. Then you can catch any chargebacks that might slip through while you still have time to appeal them. If you allow more than 60 days to pass, you'll miss your opportunity to appeal, and it's easy, when you're busy, not to notice this detail.

- Simply including delivery confirmation with every purchase can help reduce fraud from buyers who claim they've never received your item. Build the cost of confirmation into your shipping and handling fees and don't make it an option. If someone claims not to have received your item and you have the confirmation, simply e-mailing this person the tracking number should discourage her from pursuing a false claim.

■ ■ ■

SECURITY MARK YOUR ITEMS

Isn't it infuriating when you get that new sweater home only to discover the salesperson forgot to remove the security clip that will explode with permanent ink if you tamper with it? It's bad enough that it made it through security on the way out. Now you have to take it back to the store to have it removed and go through security again on the way in! Well, of course, we all get used to the inconvenience, because we recognize that the entire shopping community works better when stores control the costs they suffer from shoplifting. If only you could find a way to secure your own items and protect yourself from buyers who switch your legitimate goods for cheap imitations. "We had a customer buy a pocket watch from us, replace the proper movement in the watch with a lesser one, and then try to return it!" reported a PowerSeller who specializes in fine jewelry.

That's how the scam works. You sell something of value, the buyer replaces it with something of lesser value, and the buyer demands a refund because the item is not as you described in your auction listing. The customer can go back to eBay and/or PayPal and claim that the item he received wasn't what you promised to send. It doesn't matter that he now has your legitimate item, which he replaced with a lesser quality fake. No one is going to know that but you and he, and he's not going to admit it. It's your word against his unless you have proof of what you sent him versus what he sent back.

- PowerSeller Richard Chemel, who operates an IsoldIt eBay drop-off store, security marks every item he ships with an ultraviolet pen. He invested a modest sum in the pen and the black light that displays the mark. When he gets a demand for a refund, he tells the customer that he'll be happy to refund the money once he receives the returned merchandise and checks for the security mark he's placed on it. The legitimate customers don't mind the extra checking, and the fraudsters drop the whole issue and go looking for an easier mark! You can find such pens complete with a black light for under $10 right on eBay.

- Make your mark something specific to your business, but simple to repeat and difficult for someone else to guess. Think of it like your PIN number. You'll strike a balance between something that is simple enough for you to remember, but complex enough to be kept private. Also make sure you can quickly and easily replicate it so that you won't add too much of an extra burden to your already hectic shipping procedures. Think of it as your own little version of those branding scenes in the old cowboy movies without feeling bad about hurting the calves!

■ ■ ■

DON'T HESITATE TO CALL THE POLICE

It may seem like you're on your own out there on the Internet, but that's not entirely true. eBay does encourage trading partners to work things out between themselves, and that's how it should be. But in some matters such as account hijacking, listing theft, and nonpaying bidders, eBay will step in. The Trust and Safety Department at eBay works continually to improve the security on the site. However, eBay and PayPal aren't your only options. If you believe you're the victim of an online criminal act, take your problem to the police.

That is certainly true if you believe you've been paid by counterfeit means. Of course, you won't be encouraging people to send you cash, but counterfeit money orders and even cashier's checks do circulate. If you suspect you've received one, take it to the police and let them investigate. You may have to work with the police in more than one jurisdiction, but these are crimes that are being committed so use your police as a resource to fight them.

Sadly, you'll also want to consider your physical safety an issue. There have been reports of sellers who were robbed or assaulted when buyers came to their locations to pick up orders. That's been a handy alternative to shipping large items in the past, but sellers now are taking a second look at the practice. A local criminal may very well be watching your listings to determine if a robbery is worthwhile. That person will have ready access to information about all the items you have for sale and possibly on the premises.

LET'S GET TO WORK...

- Educate yourself about the warning signs for counterfeit money orders and then trust your instincts. If it seems wrong, it probably is.

- Unless the money order has come from the U.S. Postal Service, hold off shipping the order for three weeks to make sure the money order clears, just as you would with a personal check. That's especially true with a payment for an expensive item. It can take that long to clear.

- State clearly in your listings that you will hold off on shipping until money orders or personal checks clear. As long as you also offer credit card payment options, you'll be giving your customers a reasonable alternative if they want faster delivery.

- Keep in mind that scammers target sellers with low feedback numbers. They're counting on you to be naive and eager to please your customers and build feedback. Be especially vigilant while you're building your feedback score.

- Train all your employees with safety in mind. Make sure they know not to click on any unknown links in e-mails and educate them to recognize potential dangers.

- If you do decide to let someone come to your location to pick up an item, make sure you're not alone when this person arrives. If you operate your business from your home, don't let people come to the house to pick items up. That's making you too vulnerable.

■ ■ ■

Drew Friedman

Drew Friedman is the president of White Mountain Trading Company, L.L.C., and he has been operating his business on eBay for more than seven years. He is a specialty dealer of fine gifts, antiquities, and, occasionally, artwork. Drew has been a businessman for many years and brings a businessman's perspective to his life on eBay. With his 99.9 percent positive feedback rating, it's clear that he knows how to please his customers. Drew is pictured here with baseball great Cal Ripkin.

Drew's interests are eclectic, and he gathers his inventory from many different sources. When he started selling on eBay, he dealt mainly in vintage and antique items he found at yard sales, auctions, and estate sales. Ultimately he offered his services to other dealers in his local antiques mall. He has gotten his ideas for inventory from sources as varied as the *Wall Street Journal* and local stores on the day after Christmas. Early in his eBay career, Drew discovered a source for a large quantity of Montblanc Writer's Series "Hemingway" Ballpoint pens for $150 that were consistently selling on eBay for $500. He said he couldn't believe it—not even after he'd looked at it "100 times!"

Well, needless to say, Drew turned his modest interest in pens into a subject in which he can now claim expert status. Drew is especially proud to sell Michel Perchin limited edition fountain and rollerball pens. These are pens created in the artistic style of Michel Perchin, the master goldsmith responsible for creating the famous Fabergé Eggs so beloved by the Russian royal family. Some of these pens are produced in such a limited number that there will only ever be 10 of them in the world! As you can imagine, they are highly prized by collectors.

Despite the fact that Drew deals with such valuable products, he doesn't feel terribly burdened by many of the buyer scams other dealers of high-priced items report. But he has been victimized by fraudulent sellers. One recent scam came from an overseas dealer who created false accounts, stole his listings, and ran one-day auctions to defraud unsuspecting buyers by offering these valuable pens at ridiculously low prices. Because Drew was so vigilant in his own category, he recognized the fraud right away. (It also helped that the pen was one of only 10 in the world, all of which Drew could account for!) Drew claims that through the years. "The harder I work the luckier I get." We think that hard work, combined with a creative mind and a great business sense, contributed mostly to this PowerSeller's success. Of course, maybe luck had a little to do with it too.

CHAPTER 6

Mind Your Business: A Seller's Toolbox

very profession has its tools of the trade. With each passing year, more and more companies are eager to offer eBay sellers indispensable tools, all touted to make the life of a PowerSeller easier, more efficient, more profitable, and more fun. There are literally hundreds of tools available to you now, but how can you tell which ones are right for you? Well, that answer, once again, is research, research, and more research. But we'll give you a head start. In this chapter we'll introduce you to a variety of products meant to help you along the road toward PowerSeller. We'll discuss an assortment of products that help you during different parts of the selling process. We're hoping you won't be disappointed to learn that this isn't a standard review of a number of auction management programs from which you can simply choose.

In *eBay PowerSeller Secrets*, we offered you just that. We selected a number of auction management products, all recommended to us by PowerSellers, and reviewed them for you. We included plenty of specifications to make it easy for you to compare products and get some ideas about which ones you might be interested in pursuing further. Well, this time we didn't want to repeat ourselves. If what you want is a detailed review of the whole field, we'll refer you to Auction Software Review at www.auctionsoftwarereview.com. This Internet newsletter is devoted exclusively to eBay-related software and solutions. That means it reviews the kind of products (e.g., auction management software) found in that chapter, as well as in some other parts of this book. We mention this newsletter because products we discuss in a book change so quickly that it's good to have a regular source you can turn to for the latest information. Other sources for updated information include the eBay Solutions Directory (discussed at length later in this chapter) and the Internet newsletter *AuctionBytes*.

Now you have a plan for further exploring specific auction management tools, and we can turn our attention to introducing you to some other types of automation PowerSellers have told us about. Not only are there tools now to manage your auctions, but you'll also find analysis tools for both eBay sales data and traffic, e-mail management tools, listing creation tools, and a variety of other gizmos and gadgets recommended to us. We'll start with some free resources available to you right on eBay. Then we'll move on to the others. We've grouped similar tools together to help you keep them clearly organized as you make your way through the chapter.

We also have some advice from PowerSellers about how to choose the tools that are right for you and how to know when you're ready to add new tools. "Automation is the only way to grow, period," says PowerSeller Bob Sachs. "No one manages hundreds of listings on paper, at least not well. I have my own personal favorite, but you need to find the solution that works for you, that fits your style and your needs. Then, push it to the max. Take advantage of every bit of leverage it can give you, and never stop asking for more." We'll introduce you to some ways that PowerSellers have done just that, and we'll give you some advice about how you can decide which tools are right for you.

"Be careful and select the one that works best with the product you are selling," advises PowerSeller Randall Pinson. Not every tool is going to be right for every application, and ultimately you will be the only one who can make the choice that's right for you. In addition to considering such things as price, features, and functionality, Randall suggests you keep your products in mind too. "Some [providers] specialize in clothing, others in music and media. Just do your homework before you settle down," he says. We'll help you get that homework underway. Evaluate every product carefully with your specific needs in mind, and be sure you're clear about what problems you're hoping to solve with each one you explore.

)) GET TO KNOW EBAY'S SOLUTIONS DIRECTORY

eBay's Solutions Directory at www.solutions.ebay.com puts hundreds of different eBay "solutions providers" together in one place for you to explore. We first introduced you to the Solutions Directory in Chapter 3, but now we'd like you to see the full range of providers offered in the Directory. Once you're there, you'll find companies and individuals providing solutions for selling and buying, and a variety of technical issues from connectivity to data analysis to creating customized software. The vast majority of the providers offer services to the seller. You can either browse the Directory or use the search engine to find specific providers.

Clicking on the hyperlinked name of the provider takes you directly to detailed information about that company. There you will get a complete description of the services each provider offers, and you can actually read ratings posted by current or former users. Each provider listing on the main directory includes a user rating on a scale of one to five. Although most of the providers had received a rating of four or five, there were more than a few with a rating of three. This rating system brings to mind the eBay Feedback score. Not all four-rated businesses can be assumed to be B students. The companies receiving a user rating of three would certainly need a second look.

LET'S GET TO WORK...

- "If people aren't sure how to move around the Solutions Directory, they should use the Solutions Finder," says Debbie Levitt, president of As Was and herself a member of the Directory. Using this Finder allows you to define the problem you're trying to solve. The Selling page of the Solutions Finder is shown in Figure 6.1. It is a great way to explore the Directory without getting sidetracked and wandering around lost.

- You can trust that the providers listed in the Directory provide services that eBay has reviewed. "There are two types of providers in the Directory," says Debbie Levitt. "There are eBay Compatible Applications and Certified Providers." According to Debbie, the eBay Compatible Applications providers usually offer software tools that eBay has thoroughly checked out. They can't receive the Compatible Application logo without going through the process put in place by eBay. Likewise, the Certified Providers have to go through a process too. Debbie noted that although both of these processes cost the provider money, it isn't possible for a company to simply "buy" its way into the Directory. If it's listed there, it has eBay's approval.

- Use caution when evaluating the user ratings. As with all user rating systems, be cautious about making your decision based on what others say. Consider the number of ratings as well as the quality of those ratings. Keep your eye on how old the ratings are and consider the source of the comment too. Does that seller have a business comparable to the one you're building? Is the remark from someone with thousands of items of feedbacks or far fewer? These answers can certainly help you see if the rating itself is skewed.

• •

FIGURE 6.1: The Solutions Finder feature of eBay's Solutions Directory makes it easy for you to ask yourself exactly what you're searching for and then move quickly to the results.

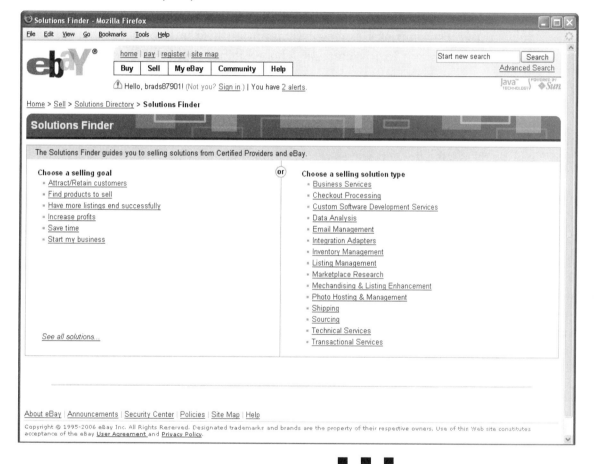

■ ■ ■

» USE EBAY'S FREE SELLER ONRAMP SERVICE TO RAMP UP YOUR BUSINESS

eBay's Seller OnRamp program, http://pages.ebay.com/startselling/ is, in our experience, a little used but tremendously helpful *free* eBay service. The program provides eBay sellers with consultation, via telephone, with a member of eBay's Marketing Department. There are two levels of help: *OnRamp* is for newer sellers or those who could benefit from basic marketing information, while *Outreach* is for sellers who have outgrown the basic OnRamp service.

We figured the best way to learn about the program was to try it for ourselves. We called the program's toll-free number —1-866-eBay (3229)—as eBay sellers, and not as your authors, and were delighted when the person who picked up the phone was ready to speak with us immediately. The basic OnRamp service was the one we tried (not realizing then there were actually two levels). We learned that OnRamp was especially helpful to those interested in basic marketing and listing creation advice including titling, item descriptions, and the overall look and feel of a listing. If we had a store, this service would have had advice there too.

Our consultant asked for our user ID and then looked up some of our previous listings. She was ready immediately with some useful pointers. She noticed we were "attaching" symbols next to key words in our listing titles. For example, we had * NEW * in the title of one of our previous listings instead of just NEW. If someone were doing a search for NEW, she pointed out, our listing wouldn't have come up because those asterisks had attached themselves to the word. We had made a similar mistake by putting a # sign next to a number. While the number is something bidders may have searched for, the # sign was not. She also told us about the things we were doing right, such as varying the font size in our descriptions, using bullets to offset important points, and using color well. Our consultant was less helpful when we asked about sourcing, but that may be because we asked about sourcing collectibles, rather than new items. There she advised using Completed Listings to get a feel for the market, checking with local antique shops, and looking for examples of eBay items where the sellers didn't realize the value of what they had. She also said they had a list of wholesalers and drop-shippers she could send, but suggested that given our product line that would not have been too helpful.

Consultants at this level will work with you until they feel they cannot help you anymore, at which point they will pass you on to the Outreach program. While this is more for PowerSellers, we were told that anyone could use it. To get started there, you call the same toll-free number to set up an appointment. To prepare for your telephone meeting, your consultant will review your listings carefully and then call you with suggestions ready.

▌ LET'S GET TO WORK...

- Don't be intimidated when you call and be ready to get to work right away if you're still at the OnRamp level. Our consultant was extremely helpful and told us to call back anytime, until they "run out of ideas." She meant it, too.

- When you're ready for more advanced advice, they're ready. PowerSeller Gary Richardson said that he and his Outreach consultant went over advanced strategies. "They did find one thing wrong and that was my key words in the store. They were causing the search engines to lower my page rank, by having too many key words repeated and a bunch of irrelevant key words," he said. Gary was happy because he fixed that problem in a day and felt he should have a "killer page rank" for his store in mere weeks. "It was just a simple thing that I had overlooked but very serious and something they pointed out in the call," he noted.

- Your consultant will likely follow up your discussions by e-mailing advice to you that's specifically related to what you discussed. Be sure to ask about this if she doesn't mention it for some reason, and to call back with any further questions. They really are there to help! Our consultant, for example, sent us a follow-up e-mail within 24 hours outlining the "next steps" we had discussed for our eBay business. She included three invaluable attachments: documents on eBay Merchandising & Listing Strategies, Advanced Listing Review, and Sourcing Supply. She also included complete contact information for her specifically.

■ ■ ■

》 TRAFFIC ANALYSIS TOOLS: FIND OUT HOW THEY FOUND YOU

It's a good thing you're already fascinated by eBay, because once you have your business up and running smoothly, you'll find that you examine every aspect of it to see where you might improve it, make it more profitable, or expand it. Traffic analysis tools will tell you where your customers are coming from, and not in a philosophical sense. They will actually tell you, among other things, where your customers were before they found you, how long they viewed your listings, how many of them went from your listings to your store, and what time of the day you had the most traffic. This can be invaluable to you as you design your listings, choose your key words, and even select your product line itself.

Two tools came up in our research over and over again: Omniture through eBay itself and Sellathon's ViewTracker. Both products will give you the traffic information you're looking for. eBay's Omniture offering is available free to anyone who owns an eBay store. Once you're signed up, you can use the tool to track traffic to your auction listings, your Fixed Price listings, your About Me page, and your Member Profile. ViewTracker will give you even more information than Omniture, but you'll pay anywhere from $4.95 per month to $24.95 per month depending upon your volume and specific needs. Sellathon does offer subscription discounts if you sign up for a year. A 30-day free trial is also available.

LET'S GET TO WORK...

- Traffic analysis will tell you not only the key words used to find your item, but also the search engine your customers used to find you, and the domain name of the site they visited before getting to you. "I'm very happy with the traffic information I get from Omniture," says David Yaskulka of blueberryboutique. "I watch to see if people are using words I don't have in my store," agrees PowerSeller Andy Mowery of debnroo. "Then I use those key words to push out to the search engines."

- Featured and anchor store subscribers can receive additional reports through Omniture that include Path Reports and Bidding and Buying Reports. Path Reports tell you where your visitor was when he entered your store and the last page he viewed before leaving. Bidding and Buying Reports tell you not just where you're customer has been, but which sites and key words led to the most actual bids and sales. They will help you determine not only your shoppers, but more importantly your buyers.

- In addition to the types of traffic reporting available to you through Omniture, ViewTracker will tell you how your shoppers sorted their search results, who is watching your auctions, and even who has registered a snipe.

- Bob Sachs is a big fan of ViewTracker. "ViewTracker is great competition for eBay's traffic tools," he said. "It's the product that's keeping eBay on its toes."

■ ■ ■

» START BUILDING YOUR "MPIRE" WITH THESE *FREE* TOOLS

In his 1966 novel, *The Moon Is a Harsh Mistress*, science fiction writer Robert A. Heinlein popularized the wise counsel: TANSTAAFL. You've probably used the full version of this acronym a thousand times—"There Ain't No Such Thing As A Free Lunch." Well, sometimes there is.

Seattle-based Mpire (www.mpire.com) has some great free services that we think are tip-worthy. Founded in 2005, Mpire prides itself on its easy-to-use auction management services and products for researching, listing, and even product sourcing (through a co-marketing deal with Worldwide Brands). It's "end-to-end auction management service," Mpire Builder, handles all the things that you've come to expect from an auction management service, such as tracking inventory, managing shipping and receiving data, and inventory management. Its pricing is simpler though than that of some other companies at a flat $29.95 per month, whether you list 5 items or 500. You can try the service free for 30 days—another plus.

But back to the free stuff, which is what we promised. Mpire's best free tool, Mpire Researcher, lets you search eBay listings going back a month, by entering item key word(s). You then pull up great data like best time/day to end, percentage of listings sold, listing upgrades that paid off, best listing type to use, and so on. This is all based on the most recent successful sales information for the item. The data come from Terapeak's mammoth database.

We compared Mpire's Researcher service to eBay's Completed Search capability. Searching for Thumbelina dolls once again, we found that Researcher's data (see Figure 6.2) went back a week further than eBay's, and was provided in a much more useful format. The search results gave us an at-a-glance snapshot of the 189 listings appearing during the previous month. We instantly learned the average selling price, percentage sold of all listings, average start price, and much more. With Completed Listings we would have had to do a lot of this same data compilation manually. Obviously, this is a much more useful tool and since the cost is the same, we recommend it. But wait, that's not all.

• •

FIGURE 6.2: Mpire's Researcher service provides a wealth of historical eBay sales data at a great price—free.

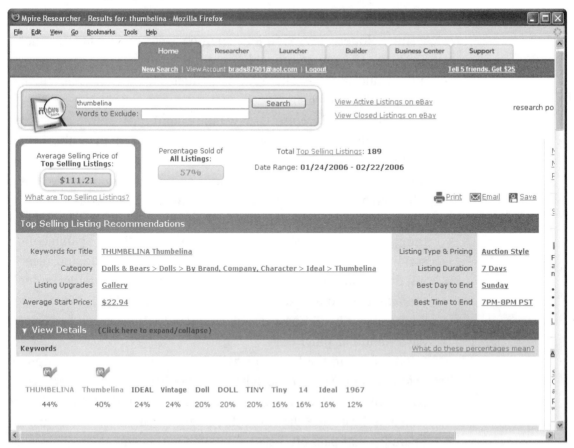

Mpire also offers a free listing tool/service known as Mpire Launcher. You can use it to schedule and create your eBay listings. It includes free design templates, plus you can also use it to remotely store (host) images. The service remains free whether you post "five listings per month or five thousand."

LET'S GET TO WORK...

- Be sure to review Mpire's Business Center, which includes eBay-related e-books and articles, a Tip of the Week, and Teleclasses that you attend via telephone. Industry experts host these classes. As with Researcher and Launcher these services are free.

- Mpire's auction management service, MpireBuilder, was very new when we were researching this book, and few of the PowerSellers we interviewed mentioned it, although some said they had heard good things about it and were waiting for it to come out of beta. It's geared toward smaller sellers, and the company claims it will serve the needs of most PowerSellers as well.

- For information on items that are currently hot on eBay, subscribe to Mpire Mpulse, a free subset of Researcher, that tracks eBay search results for things from iPods to Star Wars light sabers. It also provides data for very topical topics—when we checked it out there were searches set up for the Oscars and the Winter Olympics. Aside from these popular searches, Mpire told us sellers also were plugging in these interesting search terms: "dragon egg" (top average price is $43.79), "septic tank cleaner" (75 percent of listings sell, with a top average price of $49.11) and a "stuffed armadillo," which had a 96 percent successful sales rate and yielded a top average price of $113.68! Now there's a product niche for you.

■ ■ ■

FASHION YOUR OWN CUSTOM-TAILORED AUCTION MANAGEMENT SOLUTION

When it comes to auction management, there are as many ways for you to handle the challenge of creating and managing your listings as there are things to sell. Well maybe not that many. But you do have more than a few options. You can handle everything "manually" until you either go crazy or broke; you can use an off-the-shelf solution (including eBay's own Blackthorne), or you can bite the bullet and leave everything to a company such as Marketworks or ChannelAdvisor. We'll tell you straight out that many of eBay's largest sellers work with Marketworks or ChannelAdvisor and that each company has its loyal users. They are especially helpful if you sell through more than one online venue.

There is another alternative that may prove the most satisfying to many eBay sellers. And that's to work with an existing program, such as eBay's own Blackthorne, and have a programmer tweak it so it's custom fit to your organization. Large companies may well have their own in-house programming staffs that can handle this, but we're assuming you're not to that stage yet.

That's why the idea of working with a programming consultant may make the most sense for you. Bob Sachs feels that there's already a demand for programmers who can take a company's in-house data and make them Blackthorne compatible and savvy. To Bob, "This allows the customer the best of all worlds—they retain total control over their software and inventory, the 'solutions' are managed in-house so any custom features stay in their control and to their advantage, and they can make best use of the eBay front-end features of a solution like Blackthorne." See the sidebar for Bob's suggestions on the best way to go about hiring an eBay-savvy programmer.

LET'S GET TO WORK...

- Remember that Blackthorne, for example, is a work in progress, and functions that are not available now may well be available soon. We'll spare you the techno-babble, but in the works are add-ons to the software that will make it easier for you to "port" over your existing in-house data using commonly available database programs. So be sure you and your consultant are up on the current release's features and functionality, as well as what's soon coming down the pike, before you get too far along in the process.

■ There are other auction management tools besides eBay's and the more expensive "solutions" geared to larger-volume sellers. These include products and services from Inkfrog, Vendio, Kyozou, and SpoonFeeder. A good place to start your research is eBay's trusty Solutions Directory.

■ There's no one solution that's right for everyone. Many companies can handle your needs to some extent (as long as your business is of a modest size). You can never, however, assume you can just turn over your business to a third party and count on this party to handle things as perfectly as you would yourself 100 percent of the time. You'll have to do a fair amount of research just going into the vendor selection process, to work hard to ensure you're working with the reps who are best suited to your business and temperament, and then work with them closely, every day, to keep things running smoothly.

■ ■ ■

HOW TO HIRE AN EBAY PROGRAMMER

Programmer, PowerSeller, and all-around helpful guy Bob Sachs shares his tips for hiring a programmer to tweak off-the-shelf auction management software.

"If I were going to hire a programming consultant to integrate my in-house data with an eBay front-end, like Blackthorne, I'd work with a local search firm and be very specific about what I was looking for—an eBay consultant who can program. If I'm in a position to need a custom interface, it's quite likely I have either in-house programmers or a programming contractor on call. What I probably don't have in-house is an 'eBay person'—someone who understands the various types of listings, features, and options, and who can help ensure that what I'm pumping into eBay, and paying for, will get me results. They may not be the best results right from the start. I don't want to post hundreds of listings, however, only to find I posted in the wrong categories, didn't have Item Specifics, my shipping options were way overpriced, and didn't make sense, and my html was a mess.

"If I'm choosing to integrate with eBay via an application program like Blackthorne, then the consultant needs to know that product and be comfortable with it. If I'm thinking of working with an auction management company or ISP (Internet service provider) I need someone who can oversee that entire interface and ensure I'm getting what I'm paying for.

"I'd personally prefer someone who also sells on eBay, better yet, if they are a trading assistant. eBay 'certification' is good, but it's not the be-all/end-all. I've created applications used all over the country by businesses of all sizes, and no one ever 'certified' that I knew one bit about their business. Of course, that was back in the '80s—the 'stone age' of computers and application design."

THE SELLER SOURCEBOOK SAVES YOU MONEY AND TIME

Free is good, but so is cheap. Especially when it comes to an eBay business, which may be operating on razor-thin margins. That's why we're always glad when we can suggest a product that accomplishes so much for so little. We're talking about The Seller Sourcebook (http://sellersourcebook.com/index.html), a suite of auction sellers' tools, all available for $8 per month. Subscription plans are available that can reduce this modest cost even further to about $6 per month.

PowerSeller stephintexas first told us about how she uses The Seller Sourcebook to create her auction listings. At the time we spoke, she had been using The Seller Sourcebook for six months and had become a big fan of it, not only for its functionality but also because "everything was in one place." Not only does it handle listing creation, but it can also handle for you the things that go hand in hand with that, such as image hosting and template creation.

The Seller Sourcebook (see Figure 6.3) not only saves money but it saves time because the learning curve is modest. You don't have to learn html. However, you have more than 800 template designs to choose from, and you can store up to 200 mb of images. At an average eBay image size of 50,000 kb, that's 4,000 images!

. . . .

FIGURE 6.3: The Seller Sourcebook may be one of the best deals going in the world of eBay automation and information.

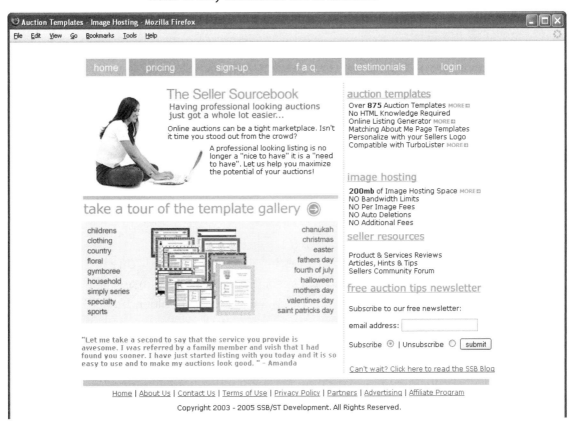

LET'S GET TO WORK...

■ To get started with The Seller Sourcebook's Listing Generator, you enter your eBay user ID and other boilerplate information such as your payment and shipping terms. Next you choose a template. Then enter your title and description and plug in your photos. This may still sound like a lot of steps, but having access to so many templates, not having to use html, and being able to retrieve any of your stored images so readily really makes it convenient.

- The Seller Sourcebook is about more than just creating listings. It's also an information source providing auction-related news and reviews of auction management products. As part of your subscription you also have access to its free library of e-books.

- You can add your business's logo to any template. While you are at it, be sure to use The Seller Sourcebook to create an About Me page that complements your business identity.

- You can't take the final step of posting your completed listing with The Seller Sourcebook. Instead it provides you with code, which you then plug into eBay's selling form. However, it's compatible with eBay's Turbo Lister and other listing software. The Seller Sourcebook is also compatible with Overstock Auctions, Yahoo Auctions, and other auction sites.

■ ■ ■

REPLY MANAGER DELIVERS AN AUTOMATED E-MAIL SOLUTION

When you were a kid, did you like getting mail? We sure did. Often when mail came for us, it was for a special occasion or because we had sent away for something fun. Of course, as you get older, mail becomes a lot more routine and sometimes even dreaded, as that mail carrier who used to bring you mostly checks and presents is now bringing you bills.

As an online merchant you'll be getting a lot of mail again, but your computer, not your mail carrier will deliver the great majority of it. Customers are a major source of e-mail, of course, but there's also e-mail from vendors and staff. Customers especially require lots of communication—the more the better from their viewpoint. There are the questions before the sale about the item itself, and perhaps about your policies (even though they may be clearly spelled out in your template). Then there are the e-mails after the sale, confirming receipt of payment and shipping, and, of course, you'll need to leave feedback.

You can easily spend way too much time sending and answering e-mail, taking valuable time away from more important tasks, like sourcing. We don't mean to downplay how important it is to quickly and, if possible, personally answer e-mail. But as your business grows, you'll need to automate that task. You'll want to be able to organize e-mail, as it comes in and goes out, and reply automatically to some e-mail.

Fortunately there are software solutions that automate routine correspondence. One solution that many PowerSellers recommend is Reply Manager, a Web-based application providing a platform for organizing incoming and outgoing mail, and providing multiple addresses so any member of your staff can access your company's e-mail. Pricing starts at $50 per month and is based on your e-mail volume. It uses a system of folders and filters, and its features include:

- SPAM and Virus Protection built-in

- Ability to accommodate multiple users and accounts

- Auto Replies and Standard Replies that you designate

- The ability to set rules for sorting incoming mail into designated folders

- Multiple users' access, with password-protected access to some accounts also possible

- Color coding of incoming e-mail so you can see immediately the source of a particular e-mail

LET'S GET TO WORK...

- While auction management software may automate some correspondence (such as the e-mails to winners of your auctions with payment details/links), services such as those from ChannelAdvisor do not *receive* e-mails, nor can they be set up to automatically reply to incoming e-mails. That's why you need a separate e-mail solution.

- Make sure that whatever e-mail manager you use can handle multiple simultaneous users from anywhere. PowerSeller Rich Cseh of volcanogames is a big fan of Reply Manager, citing its ability to handle multiple and scattered users because it is Web-based.

- You have to be 100 percent convinced of the system's reliability. Rich says he's never had a crash that resulted in "lost" e-mails since volcanogames started using Reply Manager over two years ago. "It is literally 100 percent rock-solid reliable," said Rich.

- Make sure the software can be adapted so it supplies as many different e-mail accounts as you'd ever need. Rich has set up Reply Manager so there are multiple sections with controlled access to each area. He even has his own personal e-mail coming into Reply Manager, and he's the only one with access to it.

- You'll want to make sure the software can handle any venue you're selling from. "We have multiple e-mail accounts on numerous sites," Rich told us, "and this is a one-stop shop for us! Whether we're selling on eBay, PropertyRoom, Overstock, or wherever— we manage *all* e-mails with Reply Manager."

- For further details check out Reply Manager in eBay's Solutions Directory or visit its Web site at www.replymanager.com.

- Finally, for those just starting out who are not ready to pay an additional $50 per month for a separate e-mail solution program, consider eBay's own Selling Manager Pro software. It includes e-mail automation tools and provides a good entry point. Features include the ability to generate e-mail at various points of a transaction, such as when payment is received, when the item is shipped, and even when feedback has not been left after a certain time period.

■ ■ ■

OPEN YOUR KITCHEN DRAWER AND SAVE TIME AND MONEY

We never knew a family that didn't have that "kitchen drawer." You know the one we mean. It may contain remnants of this or that, but it is also home to just the right tool when you need it. That's why you keep it in the kitchen drawer—so you'll know where to find it! Well, the same is true for your eBay toolbox. Some of the little extraneous tools we've found sellers using are more suitable to the kitchen drawer than they are to the toolbox itself. That's why we've compiled them here. You can easily scan down the list and see which ones appeal to you.

You'll find a little bit of everything here. We came across a free spreadsheet that helps one PowerSeller keep track of the actual cost of each item he sells. He uses that to determine whether a particular sourcing idea is really viable. We've found a product to help you with your search engine optimization efforts. You'll also find one that will help you if you decide if you do want to add a bit of audio and animation to your listings. Well, you get the idea. So pull open that drawer and root around a little bit.

■ eBay Sales Calculator is a nifty Excel spreadsheet tool, from eBay consultant As Was, that is specifically programmed to be an eBay sales profit and fee calculator. You can download it for free at http://www.aswas.com/everyseller.shtml. Bob Sachs, who told us about this tool, likes it because it gets new sellers thinking about the costs associated with buying and selling. And for experienced sellers, he says it's a great way to keep oneself from impulsively buying a new product line without checking out the hard numbers first. See Figure 6.4 to get a better handle on how this is set up.

■ SitePal, found at http://www.oddcast.com/sitepal/, is a tool PowerSeller parrothead88 first told us about. It allows you to add an animated character (talking cartoon heads) to your auctions, not just for fun, but to provide customer service details, product information, or perhaps something about you, the seller. The company calls these characters "Virtual Salespeople," and claims that having them at your Web store or within your auction will increase your sales. You can provide the audio, or the company can have a professional "voice talent" work with you. We're including SitePal not because we think it's a must-have tool right now, but because we think you'll be seeing a lot more of features like this to set auctions apart.

■ SmartCollector, at http://www.smartcollector.com/, is a free source of eBay sales data focusing on collectibles only. Unlike most other tools, which only provide a month or two of historical data, SmartCollector's data go back 120 days. You can do some interesting research here. For example, you can obtain a "Market Mix" report for the collectibles category of your choice, going back as far as you specify. The report can give you an idea of the supply that's available for a given product, as well as how much competition you'd face as a seller of this product.

• •

FIGURE 6.4: This free spreadsheet from eBay consultant company As Was can help you ensure that logic, not emotion, rules your eBay sourcing and listing decisions.

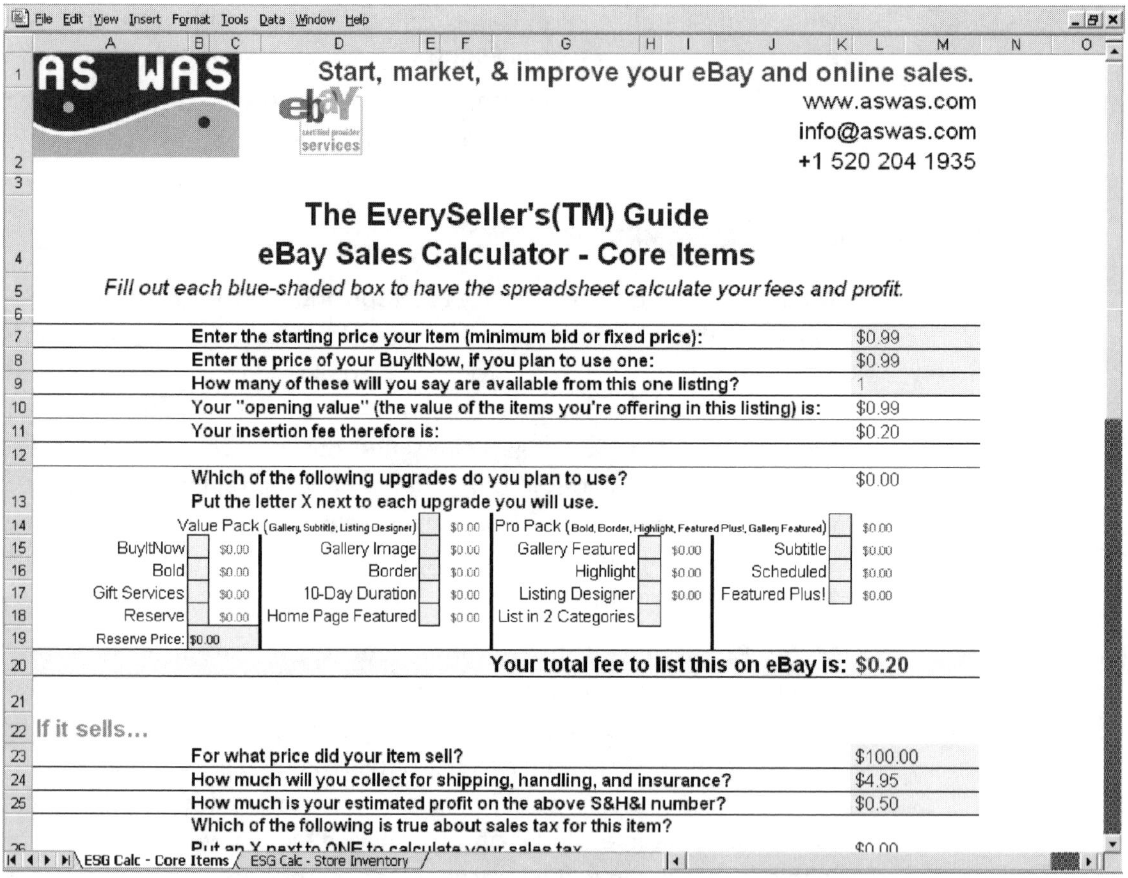

■ Vendio, at http://www.vendio.com/, provides services for eBay sellers such as image hosting and e-mail solutions and has been around what's considered forever in this business (since 1998). Here we want to highlight Vendio Gallery, which enables you to add a captivating slide show of the other products you have for sale to your auctions. Buyers can zoom in on any slide they choose to get a better look at the item. As a seller, you'll benefit because you can increase your sales by up to 18 percent by using Vendio Gallery, according to the company. Your customers will also like it because it's fun to use.

■ Wordtracker, http://www.wordtracker.com/, helps you determine which key words would be best for you to use to optimize your Web site's search engine ranking, based on how often Internet searchers use the key words you specify, and the number of Web sites that turn up when that key word is typed into a search engine. Your goal is to come up with the key words searchers enter into engines a lot, but which appear on relatively few Web pages. That will help ensure that if you use those words to optimize your site, your Web site will appear near the top of search engine results.

It may be time now to close that kitchen drawer, but your efforts to expand your eBay business and your sales are ongoing. The two appendixes at the end of the book will help you continue that research!

Randall Pinson

PowerSeller Randall Pinson started his eBay business almost by mistake. In the spring of 2000, Randall was managing a cell phone store. He came upon a large liquidation of cell phone equipment and snapped it up for a great price. He presumed it would be compatible with the service providers he was currently promoting. When he discovered the phones needed to be activated in New York and he operated the store in Utah, he had more than a little problem. A co-worker suggested he try selling a phone on eBay. When the $25 phone sold on the site for $125, Randall was interested! It wasn't long before he was selling on eBay as his full-time job, and two years later, he owned Rocket Auctions Incorporated. Today Randall operates rocket auctions on the U.S. eBay site and rockets-pockets on eBay in the United Kingdom.

Randall sells clothing, accessories, sporting goods, and toys. The company averages $45,000 in monthly sales between eBay and the other online sales channels Randall uses, which include Overstock.com. At the time of this writing, he employed one full-time and one part-time employee. Together they process an average of 50 packages a day. "I'm a minimalist when it comes to operating a business," Randall told us. "I only hired a full-time employee when I realized that I was sacrificing money-making activities by spending hours pulling orders and processing shipments myself."

Randall keeps up to date when it comes to tools that will support his business. In the summer of 2005, he started using Shipworks from Interapptive. (See Chapter 7 for more information.) Interfaced with his auction management software, Marketworks, Shipworks has greatly reduced the time it takes Randall and his staff to process their shipping tasks. He switched to Marketworks when he realized his business had outgrown eBay's Seller Assistant Pro (now Blackthorne). "This tool is significantly more expensive than the eBay branded auction management tools; however, the benefits that Marketworks has provided more than justify the expense," Randall says. He's a big supporter of using third-party providers for the tools that make a seller's life easier. "Not only are the costs justifiable," he notes "but the quality of one's life improves as well."

In November 2005, Randall wrote an article for eBay's own *Chatter Newsletter* about a trip he made with 24 other eBay PowerSellers to share their views with Congress about the Streamlined Sales Tax Project, a legislative measure that would require small sellers to collect taxes outside their own jurisdictions. According to Randall, that is the largest problem facing professional eBay sellers today. The group of 25 met with a number of representatives, both in a large group and for small group meetings. Randall had the opportunity to share his concerns in person and explain what this bill would do to the small business owner. It would mean that each seller would be required to collect taxes for 7,500 different taxing jurisdictions, keeping all the records straight and forwarding all the revenues to the correct agencies. The group was able to explain to the lawmakers why the current exemption they were considering for businesses generating $5 million or less per year was already inadequate for a large portion of sellers who depend on eBay for their livelihoods. They were also able to point out that not only are these small businesses good for the owners, but also for the communities in which they reside. They provide jobs and generate business for the U.S. Postal Service and for a variety of other businesses ranging from office supplies stores to accountants. Randall described in his article what a thrill it was to actually have a part in helping Congress research a bill and decide about legislation, opportunities that are not likely to happen to most ordinary citizens.

As for advice for other people wanting to become PowerSellers: "I would say that if you're looking to get rich quick, you better go take a real-estate seminar," Randall says. But, if you're realistic about it, you can start slowly, minimize your risks, and avoid the discouragement that many new sellers experience. As for Randall, he's built a great life for himself and his family in Utah, and who knows, we may someday get the chance to vote for him when he runs for Congress!

CHAPTER 7

Shipping: Streamline It and Make It Profitable

"The toughest thing on eBay is making the sale, but the second toughest thing is making sure it gets there," says PowerSeller and eBay trainer Harvey Levine. Of course, he means that getting your item to its final destination is second in difficulty only to selling it in the first place. Take one sale and multiply it by dozens a week, hundreds a week, or even hundreds a day, and you'll begin to get a glimpse of the realities of eBay PowerSelling.

From your very first sale, you'll be faced with the challenges of managing your shipping. As with so many other aspects of your eBay business, your shipping procedures will mature and change as your business grows. In the beginning, good practices and careful organization will go a long way toward enabling you to meet your needs. But because you're planning to have a fast-growing business, you'll have to plan early on for how you will manage the demands of shipping large volumes of packages every week. You'll need to consider everything from the space you allot for shipping to the materials you use and the carrier you hire.

Many PowerSellers find that shipping is the first part of the business that they delegate to a part-time employee or outsource entirely. Once you've established your shipping practices, it's reasonable for you to train someone to take over the production part, with you in the supervisory role. As an added benefit, once you're no longer packaging every sale for delivery, you're free to spend your time on more business-building pursuits like developing your sourcing channels and creating great listings. But whether you'll be doing your shipping yourself or hiring help, you'll need to consider your practices from every angle.

Fortunately, a good part of the shipping challenge involves good old-fashioned common sense. Experienced sellers know they must ship promptly to their buyers. They must pack carefully to create a professional-looking package, and they must label everything legibly so that their packages are likely to arrive at their intended destinations. As someone with eBay selling experience, you probably know all this. But you'll also want to consider your shipping operation as *a way to maximize your profits and promote your business*.

All eBay sellers have to develop good shipping procedures, but your shipping practices can really help you stand out from your competition. Every package you send is an opportunity to promote your business and make a statement about who you are and how you value your customer. Customers who are happy with the packages they receive from you will bring more business your way. They'll leave good feedback, which will make your business more profitable, and they may tell their friends about what a professional and accomplished eBay seller you are. Hopefully, they'll add you to their list of favorite sellers.

Not only does your shipping operation represent a great promotional opportunity, but it can also be a profit center for your business. That may not seem likely when you first consider the situation, but shipping can be transformed from a bothersome chore to a profit-making enterprise. This is possible through strategic pricing. Your shipping costs, if specified, now appear in the Results page of your customers' eBay searches. Buyers can compare your shipping fees to your competitors' as easily as they can compare prices. Using your shipping fees to your competitive advantage can help you to undercut your competition. Strategically sourcing your shipping supplies can help you keep your costs low. Working strategically with the various carriers can help you reduce your fees for transporting your goods. Finally, using smart strategies for insuring your items and tracking everything with the right software program can help you reduce your losses and diminish your vulnerability to fraud. We'll share with you some of the best strategies we've found for doing all of these things.

Before we get to the things you should do, let's discuss for a moment the things you should *not* do. (Even experienced sellers sometimes make these mistakes.) Don't state in your listings that you will not be responsible for any item that is shipped without insurance and damaged in transit. Doing this makes it seem like you're just itching for a fight. Besides, part of your responsibility as a professional seller is to make sure what you sell arrives at your buyer's address in the same condition in which it left your address. No one wants to do business in a store with a big blinking sign that screams, "You broke it! You bought it!" Think of shipping as a way to make your business more attractive than your competitors', and you won't be tempted to appear as nasty as this.

Here is another temptation you must avoid. Some sellers use their shipping practices to avoid their eBay fees, but you won't. Here's how it works. Let's say you have a flat-screen monitor to sell. Your competitors are selling similar monitors on eBay for about $250. Of course, they're paying their rightful eBay fees for every monitor they sell. You decide to list your monitor for $15 and charge your buyer $235 for shipping. That leaves you scooping up more than $200 with no Final Value or eBay listing fees and paying fees on only the $15 selling price. The problem with this is that it makes you look dishonest to your buyers and to other sellers. (That would be because it *is* dishonest.) It makes other sellers dislike you, so it alienates you from the community you're striving to succeed in. Finally, eBay is moving to crack down on this "Fee Avoidance" practice, and you'll risk losing everything you've been working to build. So, as we've said before, build your eBay business on solid ground right from the beginning. It will help you sleep at night, and it will go a long way toward making it possible for you to keep your eBay business growing and thriving. Now, let's get to the great advice we've uncovered on how you *should* be profiting from your shipping practices.

)) DOUBLE YOUR SHIPPING CHARGES

Keeping in mind that your shipping charges include more than just postage, take a look at what you charge to see if you have room to increase your fees. If, by raising your fees, you can afford to send everything through Priority mail, you'll be automatically saving in your supply costs, since Priority mail allows you to get free shipping materials. Not only will you get free materials, but you'll also be able to send your packages out with faster delivery. Buyers want fast delivery and may have no trouble at all paying the extra fee you require to provide it.

"I raised my shipping costs from $2.50 to $5 per package and haven't gotten any negative feedback from it," noted PowerSeller wiccan well. With the additional fees, she was able to hire part-time help to expedite her shipping and use higher-quality packing materials to make her packages look better. She noted that customers had started to want better packing materials, and by raising her fees, she was able to provide them with it.

LET'S GET TO WORK...

- Search your category and note how your listings stack up now that shipping fees are included on Search Results pages. See what your competitors are charging for shipping to assess whether or not you can raise your shipping fees and still stay competitive. You'll quickly see where you fit in among the pack, and don't hesitate to charge more if strategically it's a wise move.

- If charging more for your shipping makes it possible for you to provide better service and better packaging to your customers, consider it a function of customer service and don't fret about it.

- Include a link to eBay's fee schedule in some of your auction listings. That way, your customers can see what it costs you to list and sell an item on the site. Sometimes buyers forget that not every penny gets to stay in your pocket. They'll be less likely to complain about shipping costs when they see how much you actually have to pay to operate your business and provide them with the great products you offer.

- Don't forget to factor in payment for your time or the salary of your employee's time when you decide on shipping and handling charges. It's not enough to cover your expenses for the materials you'll need to complete your packages and postage costs. Your time costs you money also, and you deserve to be paid for it.

- Negotiate your best prices and buy your packing materials in bulk. Even if you only save pennies on each piece you purchase, those pennies will add up. Combining increased shipping and handling charges with decreased product expenses equals nothing but profit for you.

■ ■ ■

DON'T CHARGE ANYTHING FOR SHIPPING AND HANDLING

Once again, you might think we've gone around the bend, but not really. You are actually going to factor in your shipping and handling charges, but you're just going to make it seem to your customer that you're giving away this service for free. Here's how it works.

When you set a Fixed Priced listing, set it so that your shipping and handling charges are already figured into your profit margin. A PowerSeller from Maryland explained it like this: "If I pay $28 for an item, and I know I can ship it for $12, I may set the Buy It Now price at $65.95. That will give me an acceptable profit margin, and I can absorb the shipping fee while letting my customer feel like he's getting free shipping." This has proven to be a very successful strategy for this seller. His item comes up in search results as more than competitive when customers see he includes free shipping. Even though *we* know it's not really free, it feels free, and that's all that matters. "Free shipping is the way of the future for online sales," this PowerSeller observed. "If my customer can buy this item from Amazon.com and get free shipping, what incentive does he have to pay me to ship it to him?"

According to an ACNielsen nationwide survey of some of eBay's most successful sellers, completed in the fall of 2005, 38 percent of sellers said they would offer seasonal specials. Half of that 38 percent said they would offer free shipping as a seasonal incentive. That means approximately 20 percent of eBay's high- and mid-volume sellers already offer free shipping on a seasonal basis. Offering free shipping year round will distinguish your business even further.

LET'S GET TO WORK...

■ Don't lose money on free shipping. You have to be sure that you're covering your expenses *and* allowing for a reasonable profit margin when you offer it. You won't stay in business for long by charging less than you spend to ship your items. Remember, we're looking at the *perception* of free shipping.

- Consider free shipping only for your store items. That way you can encourage people to buy from your in-store stock items. You can still keep active shipping on your auction listings, but entice people to shop at your store for free shipping.

- Offer free shipping as an incentive to entice people to buy multiple items from you. Just as Amazon.com will throw in the shipping if you spend $25 or more, consider where your "free shipping" policy will kick in and advertise it well.

- Make "free shipping" part of your eBay identity. We know of several sellers, and at least one store manager, who include "free shipping" as part of their business names. Your goal is to make sure your customers know that free shipping is something you offer and your competitors don't.

- Don't forget to mention that not only is your shipping free, but it is also *fast*. Free shipping becomes far more powerful if you make it clear to your customers that your shipping is also fast. If you offer free shipping, but then reduce your shipping services so that it takes much longer for the item to reach your buyer, you're diminishing the service you provide. Free and fast is the one-two punch that will really make you stand out.

- By incorporating your shipping fees into the price of your items you can really gain a competitive advantage in product areas that may not seem likely at first glance. For example, eBay sellers who handle furniture are well acquainted with shipping such items. It may actually cost less to ship a couch from one coast to the other than the general public would suspect. By adding that cost to the price and bringing it to the eBay market, such savvy sellers can easily beat non-Internet competition.

■ ■ ■

MAKE YOUR CARRIERS COMPETE

You wouldn't think of walking into an auto showroom and paying the sticker price for a new car. But, how many of us would consider going to FedEx or UPS, for example, and asking what their best offer is? These carriers are enjoying a bounty from the success of eBay, and they are actually very reliable business partners. The U.S.

Postal Service is so aware of eBay's affect on its business that it offers seminars for those who want to sell on eBay. UPS helped PowerSeller avforsale locate the global insurance policy it uses to cover all its merchandise, both in its warehouse and along the delivery route. These vendors all stand to benefit from your thriving business, so don't underestimate their willingness to help your business thrive.

Different carriers will offer you different strengths, and you'll most likely find a combination of shipping options to be your best bet. The U.S. Postal Service, for example, offers the most options for international shipping, because it has the greatest number of international partners. But other factors matter as well. "The FedEx store is ten minutes from me and open until 10 p.m. so I can finish up my shipping after business hours and still get it out," says PowerSeller Jack Walters. Through a contract with DHL, PowerSeller Paul Fletcher of dealtree has automated his entire shipping process. DHL leaves a truck parked at his warehouse every morning. Every part of his shipping operation is automated and done with scanners. Every evening DHL comes for the truck loaded with Paul's daily shipments.

■ LET'S GET TO WORK...

■ Don't hesitate to meet your carrier face to face. PowerSeller Drew Friedman of whitemountaintrading took a sample of one of his most popular items into the shipping center nearest to his location. Since they were both local business owners, he addressed the carrier with the question, "What is the lowest price you can offer me to ship multiple orders of this item?" With the promise of repeat business, Drew was able to get the carrier to agree to substantially reduce his shipping charges for each item.

■ Negotiate your best deal and then take it to the largest competitor. Once you get an offer from a carrier to discount its services, go to that carrier's competitors and see if they can better the offer. Your business represents a reliable revenue stream, and you may just find you're able to initiate a price war on your behalf.

■ The larger carriers such as UPS and the U.S. Postal Service have so much experience working with eBay sellers that they can offer value beyond reduced prices. If you can get an experienced consultant to tour your operation, he or she can help you improve your shipping efficiencies. You may not actually get a reduced shipping rate, but you will save money by improving your shipping procedures and reducing your levels of waste.

■ ■ ■

APPLY TIME AND MOTION STUDIES

"eBay is all about moving as much product as you can move in the least amount of time to maximize profit," explains Michael Kolman of parrothead88. That means looking at every single movement you must make to pack, label, and ship a box. When he worked for UPS, Michael was fascinated by the studies the company did to maximize every efficiency. Did you know that the driver is more efficient if he steps out of his truck on his left foot rather than his right foot? UPS knows. It also knows how many seconds it should take to put the truck into gear and how to make sure it doesn't take a second longer.

PowerSellers need to use these same principles when they are creating their own shipping procedures. Michael noted that in the beginning he and his partner went through, "50 different ways to do 50 different things" before they hit on the most efficient way to complete their packages. A PowerSeller from Kentucky agreed, "We weighed the efficiency of having our packing table five feet away from our workstation rather than three feet away. What did having to traverse that extra two feet mean in terms of efficiency of time and space?"

LET'S GET TO WORK...

■ Build your shipping operation around those items that you ship most often and the things you need to complete those packages. Every second you save in completing these orders and getting them all ready to ship is money earned as you spend that time you save on more profitable pursuits.

■ Have supplies of all inserts and promotional materials ready to go and organized so that you can quickly pop them into the packages before they're sealed. Set aside time every week to replenish your supplies so that you never have to halt your shipping process to go make copies or search for a missing item.

■ From time to time, take a step back and evaluate every aspect of your packing operation—from the type of tape dispenser you use, to the direction in which you place the item in the box, to the dominant hand your main shipper uses. All of these things can affect the efficient flow of your operation.

■ Turn to your employees to find out how you can cut seconds off your shipping operation. Once you have hired someone to help with your shipping, make that person's input a vital part of your operation. You might find that by simply placing your items on a lower shelf, your employee can make better use of space and time. Let your employee know that you count on her experience to improve your operation and encourage her to make suggestions.

■ ■ ■

›› CARRY INSURANCE OUTSIDE YOUR CARRIER

All of the major carriers offer insurance for your packages. If you ship with UPS, your shipping fees include $100 worth of insurance. For the U.S. Postal Service, that amount of insurance will cost you an additional $2.20 per package. Multiply that by the volume of packages going out, and you'll quickly see that controlling your insurance costs is a vital part of your shipping operation. Fortunately you have some alternatives that can really add up to big savings.

PowerSellers told us of two private companies that offer to insure your packages at rates that range from 60 to 90 percent less than the fees the major carriers charge. U-PIC Insurance Services has been offering shipping insurance to its customers for more than 16 years. In addition to the online market, U-PIC insures such offline customers as Wal-Mart pharmacy services. Its main competitor, Discount Shipping Insurance (DSI) has been operating for two years, but offers steeper discounts than U-PIC. Both of these insurance companies offer simple online purchasing and claims resolution. U-PIC guarantees that it will process and pay a loss claim within seven to ten business days. You can purchase U-PIC insurance on a case-by-case basis, while DSI requires you to complete a registration process and obtain rate quotes based on how much shipping you do, the average value of your goods shipped, and your claims history.

■ LET'S GET TO WORK ...

■ When you purchase insurance outside of the carrier, you can advertise in your listings that all items are insured at no cost to your customers. That adds a level of security to your transactions and marks you as a responsible seller and shipper.

■ In considering which third-party insurance you'll purchase, consider the underwriter history of the company. Plenty of companies will sell you cheap insurance, but cheap insurance won't do you any good if the company doesn't have the capital to pay your claim should you need to file one. Make sure the insurance company you choose doesn't have a history of jumping from one underwriter to another, a sure sign that the company isn't keeping pace with its expenses.

■ Look for a third-party provider that is fully integrated with the Internet postage service you use, such as Endicia or Stamps.com.

■ Make sure you choose a third-party insurer that offers simple electronic claims form completion.

■ Include an icon in your listings trumpeting your third-party insurance. (Your insurer can supply this.) Viewing the icon will allow auction browsers to quickly see that you offer "free" insurance. It can be a competitive edge that everything you ship is insured at no additional cost to them. Figure 7.1 is an example of a possible icon.

FIGURE 7.1: This icon from DSI shows your customer that your auctions include insured shipping.

Keep in mind that all of the private insurance companies have specified countries that they exclude from their insurance plans. Be sure you know which countries cannot be included before you ship internationally.

■ ■ ■

INSURE YOURSELF

One of the simplest ways to safeguard your shipping and simplify the whole subject of insurance is to just "insure yourself." This is a major point of discussion among PowerSellers and one place that many claim to achieve real operational savings. Insuring yourself is simply accepting the financial responsibility for everything you ship. You never actually buy insurance, either from your carrier or from a third party, yet everything you ship is insured.

A New York–based PowerSeller explained it like this: Suppose you ship 1,000 items this month, and they all have a value of $100. In order to insure them through the U.S. Postal Service, you will spend $2,200, or $2.20 for each package you ship. Now, factor in how many claims you are likely to have this month on lost or damaged goods. If you think you'll lose 22 packages, then you'll be breaking even if you pay for insurance. Of course, 22 packages over four weeks is a pretty high rate of loss. If you are losing that many packages, maybe you should be taking a better look at your packing and shipping procedures. If, on the other hand, you're more likely to lose one or two packages a week, (still a relatively high loss rate for that number of shipments), you'll be better off just covering that loss out of your own pocket. You would then save all that money you would have spent on insurance to settle your claims for yourself.

■ Keep careful track for a few months to determine how much you spend on insurance versus how much you actually lose. You may be paying a very high rate to provide yourself with more protection than you actually need. This may be an area where you'll be better off taking the risk.

■ Set aside a portion of your earnings as a hedge against future loss. Start out by paying yourself the rate you'd pay for postal insurance. Before too long, you'll have enough set aside to repay your customer for a lost package, and you'll still be ahead.

■ Insuring yourself makes it possible for you to settle claims quickly without having your customer wait until the paperwork is processed. That can go a long way toward smoothing the rough edges of a transaction that's gone bad and regaining a customer.

■ Just as with a third-party insurer, you may want to advertise that all of your items are insured at no cost to the buyer, but here's a word of caution for the self-insured. If you do this, keep careful track of those customers who claim damaged or missing goods. Insuring yourself leaves you vulnerable to fraud since you won't have the resources of a large corporation behind you if you need to dispute a claim. Be prepared to block buyers who make more claims than you think are reasonable.

■ ■ ■

UP-SELL AND CROSS-SELL THROUGH SHIPPING

When your customer opens your box, for just a moment, you have her undivided attention. Your auction listings compete with countless others. Your eBay store resides in a virtual mall. But, when the tape comes off and your item is revealed, it's just you and your buyer. Make the most of this magical moment, and you'll be able to sell to this customer again. Consider your product line and look for an inexpensive item that complements each item you sell. That's what you're going to give to each customer as an incentive and reward. You already saw, in Chapter 4, how to market your business and Web site through promotional giveaways, but you can also turn one sale into multiple sales that way, too.

"When I sold taco shells, I sent a packet of taco seasoning with my shipment," says Stephanie Inge of stephintexas. "I knew it was good and unusual. It wasn't something you could buy in just any supermarket in the United States. I also knew my customer was buying taco shells, so I could assume he would be interested in the taco seasoning." Now, she's made a sale, and offered a sample to a proven customer. It cost her very little to buy the taco seasoning in bulk, nothing to add it to the shipment, and she's likely to have created a repeat buyer because of it.

LET'S GET TO WORK...

- Offer an additional service with each purchase. Offer to add a gift card with a handwritten message. Offer to wrap the item as a gift. "Many buyers will gladly pay for gift wrapping. I offer to wrap a gift for an additional $2," says PowerSeller Adam Hersh. "It's a nice little profit booster for me."

- Use your congratulatory e-mail to showcase your other items. "I offer to combine shipping with each of my congratulatory e-mails," says stephintexas. "I also include a thumbnail image of another item I'm selling that will go well with the purchased item. If I sell a pair of boots, I'll send an image of a belt that would go well with them." As long as you have your customer wanting one of your items, use this as the moment to get them to want another too.

- Encourage repeat business by offering a discount certificate for repeat buyers. You've already proven yourself to be a great eBay seller, so include a discount certificate to encourage that buyer to shop with you again. Date the certificate so that the buyer has a period of time to redeem your coupon before it expires. You'll be able to see how effective a marketing tool this is when you see how often the certificate is redeemed.

■ ■ ■

)) SHIPPING AS ADVERTISING

Every package you send out is a little emissary into the world from your business. eBay and the U.S. Postal Service now offer Priority mail boxes that are branded with eBay's logo. They're free, and that's good. But, why should you promote eBay when you could be promoting yourself? Yes, your customer can have a good feeling when he receives your item and it's packaged in an eBay box, but just think of the great impression your package will make when it arrives and it's packed with your own logo and brand! Now, that makes a professional impression.

eBay prides itself on the idea of a "level playing field." "The little guy on eBay can have as much credibility as Sears," says PowerSeller Ben Boxall. So take that credibility and extend it to your shipping operations. So many sellers on eBay scrimp with shipping, but when you think of it as the one moment you really get to "touch" your customer, you'll see that spending what you need to create great packages is worth the money. When you brand everything with your own advertising, you're increasing the likelihood that you'll earn back some of what you spend.

LET'S GET TO WORK...

- Customizing packages should be part of an overall strategy to present a professional image. A side benefit is that packages that are completed with attention to neatness and a professional appearance may arrive more quickly with fewer chances of a delivery mistake. eBay introduced its Get It Fast feature because many buyers told the company they didn't consider buying items they needed quickly on eBay. So offering safe, professional, and efficient packaging and shipping is one way to assure customers that their items will arrive quickly in good condition.

- Include your logo and Web site on each label and box you ship. "I've had postal workers come shop with me," says Jody of beachcombers! "They saw my label and were curious about what my Web site was about!" You never know where your next customer will come from.

- Have a stamp made with your logo and Web site address. Then be sure to stamp each of your boxes so that everyone who handles them, from the carrier to the customer, will see your branding information. You can purchase a customized stamp on eBay for under $25.

■ ■ ■

GET SHIP-SHAPE WITH SHIPWORKS— A POWERSELLER FAVORITE

Shipping is one of the biggest "pain points" for people doing online commerce, according to Wes Clayton, president of Interapptive, Inc. But you didn't need for Wes to tell you that. Interapptive manufactures ShipWorks, a desktop-based tool that greatly streamlines the shipping process. ShipWorks offers a direct connection between your business and UPS, Endicia, FedEx, and the U.S. Postal Service. All of your necessary information, from addresses to shipping options, gets keyed once and never again. ShipWorks streamlines printing shipping labels and invoices, and providing tracking data to your customers. Of course, there are other programs that can do these things, but PowerSellers mentioned ShipWorks especially, because it offers some advantages over other programs and services (including eBay's).

Specifically, because ShipWorks is a desktop-based system, rather than Web-based, you don't have to worry about the service being unavailable or slow due to problems on the vendor's end. It also means that the user interface can be more streamlined and easier to work with. In fact, "pure simplicity" is one of Interapptive's selling points. With ShipWorks, you can process orders in bulk, something that eBay's shipping services do not handle. You can also use ShipWorks for inventory control as it will notify you when your supply of a particular item begins to run low.

LET'S GET TO WORK...

- You pay for ShipWorks monthly, based on how much shipping you do. For 1 to 99 packages, you'll pay $15. The rate for 100 to 999 packages is $30, and any number above 1,000 costs $50.

- This price "auto flexes" each month based on your usage, so if you are a seasonal seller, you're not locked in to a rate that doesn't reflect your level of business for a given month.

- The ShipWorks staff will work with you to customize the software for your particular application. Ben Boxall was quite pleased with ShipWorks' staff, and its willingness to go the extra mile and even write custom macros to make his operation smoother.

- Use ShipWorks to automate your customer communications. The software can be set to automatically send your customers notices when their items are shipped. These e-mails will automatically include tracking information. A titanium PowerSeller told us that ShipWorks reduced the number of customer inquiries he receives tenfold.

- Using ShipWorks has proven efficiencies. "This program has cut my order/shipment processing time from 3 to 4 hours a day to about 45 minutes," says Randall of rocket-auctions.

■ ■ ■

WEATHERIZE YOUR SHIPMENTS

You'll have to strike a balance between streamlining your shipping operations and also creating packages that safeguard your items on their way to their new homes. How you actually accomplish this will vary depending upon how breakable your items are. Most of us consider packing the item carefully and then imagine that it's going to be carried from one part of its trip to the next. Umm, that's not always the case. Packages get tossed, dropped, and misused in many ways on their journeys, and you have to pack for a tough trip, no matter where your item is going.

One aspect of shipping that often gets overlooked is the weather. In winter your item may be subjected to cold temperatures, sleet, and snow. You'll need to consider how to keep the object dry even if the package gets wet. In the summer, you'll have to plan for extended periods of heat exposure. Your package may withstand its trip in the back of a truck on a day when the temperature is 95 degrees, but what if that truck has a flat tire? Will your package withstand the inside temperature while the truck is left on the side of the road for several hours? eBay seller Catherine Yeats of 4-a-little-lady has some great advice for weatherizing your shipments, some of which we share below. Since she operates her business from her home in Wyoming, she should know!

■ LET'S GET TO WORK...

- ■ Wrap your item in plastic if you're sending it in a cardboard box or mailer. Bubble mailers, although they're great for cushioning, aren't waterproof. Actually, they absorb moisture if they get wet, which can actually cause more damage to the item inside.

- ■ In the winter, tape your box as you normally would, but then add one single piece of tape that wraps around the entire box covering the flaps on the box bottom and ending at the beginning point on the box top. Now if your box gets wet, that tape will actually help hold it together. It's not meant to seal the box, simply reinforce it.

- ■ Include the shipping and invoice information in a sealed plastic bag inside the package. You can't be sure that your paperwork won't be destroyed in a dampened box. This way your customer will have all the necessary information safely delivered in plastic.

- ■ Finally, don't forget to put an extra layer of packing tape over your label. That's not to keep the label in place, but it's quick and easy plastic protection to safeguard your label from running and smearing if it gets wet. Just note, however, the U.S. Postal Service asks that you *not* tape over the bar code if your label includes one.

■ ■ ■

)) DON'T DROP YOUR DROP-SHIPPER

If you want to start a fight at a PowerSeller's gathering, make a strong statement either for or against the use of drop-shippers! Just when we thought it was safe to boldly advise you against ever using a drop-shipper, we met PowerSellers who have built substantial parts of their businesses around them and wouldn't consider cutting back. These sellers like the convenience and reliability of the shippers they use. They appreciate that they can expand the products they offer their customers without having to expand their warehouses. But even the PowerSellers who love working with drop-shippers agree that a great deal of your success with a drop-shipper hinges on your finding the right company to work with.

That's the challenge. How do you find a drop-shipper you can depend on? If you enter into an agreement with an unreliable drop-shipper, you may find yourself in a situation where you will be selling a product that you physically can't deliver. As you can imagine, that does nothing for your reputation as a seller, which is why so many PowerSellers dislike using drop-shippers. In Chapter 2 we recommended using Worldwide Brands for researching your product sources. As you may remember, they offer a drop-shipper directory and verify each company listing before it appears, to ensure that the company will work with small-volume sellers. You can also run your own tests on potential drop-shippers. PowerSellers who use them note that they've researched them carefully before they've risked doing business with them.

LET'S GET TO WORK...

- Communicate with your drop-shipper often, just as you would with any other valued member of your team. When you're just starting to work with a new drop-shipper, talk to your representative often. Make sure you feel confident about the professional level of services the company provides before you entrust your company's reputation to it.

- Purchase a small supply of all inventory items you plan to drop-ship, and keep these at the ready in case your drop-shipper runs out or for some other reason cannot fulfill your orders. You may eventually trust your drop-shipper completely, but being able to step in and complete an order for an out-of-stock item from your own inventory will go a long way toward easing your anxiety in turning over control of at least part of your order fulfillment to others.

- Drop-shipping is a good way to try out a *new* area, because you don't have the same risks. Should your market test work out, you can then try to find cheaper sources of the product to improve your margins.

- Remember that if your drop-shipper operates outside of your own state, you'll have to charge sales tax to customers both from your own state and the state in which your drop-shipper is based. Be sure to state that in your auction listings or you will be the one who has to pay state taxes to your drop-shipper's state.

- You can eliminate the need to pay dual sales tax if your drop-shipper will use your own label, according to McGraw-Hill author, Cliff Ennico. Many drop-shippers won't be willing to replace their label with yours—it's an added step that leads to confusion and potential mistakes, and drop-shippers will generally insist on having their merchandise returned to them in the event that it can't be delivered. Still, if you can get yours to agree, you'll have only the sales tax to pay for customers in your own state.

■ ■ ■

Stephanie Inge

Stephanie Inge is known on eBay as stephintexas. You'll go a long way before you find a friendlier, happier eBay seller. Stephanie has been selling on eBay for more than six years, and even though her specialty is selling vintage cowboy boots, she'll sell a little bit of everything that strikes her fancy. She describes her business as a "one-girl shows" and although she runs it herself without help, she also finds time to teach eBay classes as a Certified eBay Educational Specialist. Her students know her as Dr. eBay!

Stephanie started selling on eBay years ago to help boost the sales at her antique booth. She and a friend operated a little booth in an antiques mall, and she had a little pitcher that just wasn't selling. Since she was only asking $4.90 for it, she thought there'd be little risk in putting it up for sale on eBay to see what would happen. When she sold it for $17, she was hooked! She sold through the inventory of her booth and never looked back.

For a time Stephanie was selling low-carb taco shells. She was one of only two sellers on eBay to carry this product, and she was riding the crest of the low-carb craze. Although it was a great revenue stream for her, Stephanie began to see that the craze was ending, and she moved out of the low-carb market before the bottom dropped. "When you're not listing, you better be educating yourself about what's selling," Stephanie told us. It takes real willpower and self-confidence to walk away from a product line that's still selling, but Stephanie proved it was the right move for her. Today she happily specializes in vintage cowboy boots.

Stephanie wraps each boot individually to protect it from damage. She prides herself on trying to be "the quickest shipper on eBay." Keeping that goal in mind helps her to always strive to move her products out quickly, whether or not she can actually prove that she's the quickest. She includes a handwritten note with each package, and she calls her customers by name on every e-mail. She also includes delivery confirmation with every package she sends.

Stephanie recently vowed to become more involved in the eBay community. She founded an eBay sellers group in Dallas, which is a sister group to the one in Atlanta. She is also working on establishing an eBay Walk of Fame. Her goal is to give back to the community she feels has given her so much. Stephanie wants to "make a living, but also enjoy living" through eBay. She offers friendly, warm, reliable service to her customers, and solid, well-proven advice to the students who take her classes. Stop by her auctions or send her an e-mail, and you'll experience good old Texas hospitality firsthand!

CHAPTER 8

Selling Internationally: Around the World with eBay

Throughout this book we've been telling you about the rapidly changing world of e-commerce. Well, it is still just that: a world. You can operate your eBay business only in the United States, but making that decision is consciously limiting your growth and potential. It's no longer a question of *if* you should sell internationally, but rather when and how. "International sales are mission critical," says PowerSeller blueberryboutique, and we couldn't agree more. It may be possible to build a big eBay business without expanding your borders, but why would you want to build a business knowing that you're turning away the vast majority of the world's inhabitants? If you make the decision not to sell internationally, at least you'd better understand why and exactly what you're walking away from. Oh, and don't worry There will be plenty of other eBay sellers who will be happy to take your place at the international table.

As we write this, international sales are growing faster on eBay than are domestic sales. eBay's net revenues for international sales now *consistently* grow at a higher percentage than do domestic sales. Already eBay is the eighth-largest global retailer in the world, with an estimated $43 billion in revenues for 2005. There is a lot of money to be spent overseas, and sellers who serve those customers can expect to see their businesses grow.

PowerSellers support this statement. "I'm singing 'O Canada' right now!" exclaimed Gary Richardson from harleyglasses when we asked him how he felt about international sales. "It's the best move we ever made. It will really launch us into the e-commerce world." "That's simple: SALE!" responded PowerSeller Stephen Ganus of eagleauctionsUSA, when asked the same question. "I've been selling overseas for four years or more and have never had a problem, other than that shipping does tend to be a bit slow in some countries," he said. Both of these sellers have seen their revenues jump with international expansion.

But what about the scary stories people like to swap about international customers? "Our international customers are some of the most polite customers we have and the quickest to pay," said Jody of beachcombers! "Customs can be a challenge, but for the most part, they're among our favorites!" There can certainly be some added challenges and some additional risks involved with selling internationally, but that's why we've gathered some great advice for you here in this chapter. Not only will you find many challenges are overcome with some experience, but you'll find the opportunities may very well outstrip any challenge you'll have to face. Some U.S. brands and products are actually more in demand overseas than they are here, and savvy sellers who can recognize those items will position themselves to see their profits soar.

International selling is not for rookie eBay sellers. You'll want to be sure you have the feedback score and experience necessary to bolster you as you take this next step. "Make your mistakes domestically," recommends Kevin Boyd of PowerSeller preferreddiscounts. "New sellers are bound to make mistakes, and you should make them here before you branch out internationally." Kevin estimates that 20 to 30 percent of his sales are international, so he certainly sees the potential in this marketplace. He recommends that you complete approximately 25 domestic sales before you pursue the international market, but he definitely advises you to pursue it. Adam Hersh agrees, "Initially selling internationally seemed like a problem, then it seemed like an obstacle, then it seemed like it's not bad," he reminisced. As you gain more experience, you gain more confidence in dealing with potential problems. "You will have some additional challenges," noted PowerSeller Bob Kitchener. "I estimate that out of 100 packages sent overseas, I have trouble with three or four of them. With domestic sales that may be only one out of 100." Still the additional work is worth the reward it brings, and Bob will continue to sell internationally.

Remember that when you sell internationally, you're offering your products to another country, not another planet! "Within English-speaking countries you can sell as easily to Perth as you can to Peoria. An e-mail is an e-mail," notes debnroo's Andy Mowery. But even if your customer doesn't come from an English-speaking country, you can overcome the difficulties of language and culture with a bit of education, patience, and experience. "Don't appear afraid of this unusual situation," advises Tony of wegotthebeats.com. "Sales with international customers should appear to the customer as seamless and routine as those with U.S. customers." Tony should know. A full 50 percent of his sales are to overseas customers. Now let's get to the tips that will help you feel as comfortable selling internationally as these PowerSellers do.

A POWERSELLER'S TOP 10 COUNTRIES

PowerSeller Adam Hersh of AdamHershAuctions was generous enough to share this list of his top 10 international markets based on actual sales. Adam has received more than 150,000 positive feedbacks and is a trend-setter among PowerSellers. This list represents sales made through his eBay.com accounts only. His accounts on eBay's international sites would naturally vary.

United Kingdom	France
Canada	Italy
Australia	Ireland
China	The Netherlands
Germany	Spain

» MAKE SHIPPING EXPENSIVE

International buyers aren't different from domestic buyers in that they'd like to save some money whenever possible. Although we'd advise you to use your shipping charges as a marketing tool to keep your auctions priced competitively, that's not true for international sales. Packages sent via the less expensive methods of shipping naturally take longer to arrive at their destinations. That's going to add to the challenge of selling internationally. You will already have to factor in the time it will take your package to pass through customs. You have little control over that, but charging more to ship your item by the most expeditious way will help shorten the time between your hands and your customer's. That is bound to help the overall flow of your sale.

"Buyers generally choose to ship with uninsured shipping that's not trackable," said a Florida PowerSeller. "But we encourage them to take more expensive shipping with tracking and signature delivery." Everyone wants to save money, but we go further than this PowerSeller to advise you not to just encourage your buyers to go with the more expensive route, but to offer *only* the more expensive shipping options. It's your best protection against keeping your shipping open-ended with no way to know what you can expect.

■ LET'S GET TO WORK...

- When it makes sense based on the value of your item, use Global Express Guaranteed. This is the premium international service from the U.S. Postal Service. In alliance with FedEx, the U.S. Postal Service offers service guarantees to meet destination delivery standards or the postage fees are refunded. Shipping only from specific Zip Codes (although even our little town is included on the list), this service includes up to $100 of insurance for packages that weigh less than 70 pounds. If you ship a 10-pound package to Great Britain, for example, you'll spend $95 for it to go through Global Express Guaranteed as opposed to $32.75 through Economy Mail Parcel Post, but the difference in time and safety may make it worthwhile, again if the value of the item supports it.

- Use the Global Priority flat rate envelopes if you can. The larger of these envelopes measures 9.5 by 12.5 inches. That will accommodate some of your smaller items such as CDs. Then for a flat rate of $9 you can ship the item to specified countries in Western Europe, the Caribbean, Central and South America, the Pacific Rim, the Middle East, and Africa.

- In spite of the fact that you may be charging more for premium shipping, still offer your international customers reduced shipping for multiple sales. You'll encourage them to buy more, and you'll be able to help them offset the greater expense of the premium shipping charges. Remember that experienced international eBay buyers are aware of and accustomed to higher shipping costs.

- Be sure to inform your international buyers that you use extra care in preparing their packages. Double-box every item and use the most durable packing materials available. You and your customer both know that the journey is going to be a long and potentially difficult one. Everyone will feel better knowing that extra care was put into preparing the package for overseas travel.

- Keep your international sales in your active file for longer than you would your domestic sales. "I keep my international sales in an active status for about two weeks," says Texas PowerSeller stephintexas. "Then I send a quick e-mail telling that customer I'm planning to leave positive feedback for him. If he hasn't received his item then, I'll hear back and know that I need to follow-up on this." If you consider the sale finished when you ship the item, you may not know that a problem is looming. Keeping track of it through this seller's simple method makes it easy to see if trouble is ahead.

■ ■ ■

KNOW WHEN NOT TO MAKE THE SALE

You will want to make it clear to your international buyers that they must contact you for shipping information *before* they bid. This gives you the perfect opportunity to decide whether or not you want to do business with a particular international customer. Yes, this is going to require a little extra work on your part, but you know that about international selling when you start, and the extra trouble can certainly prove to be worth the effort. By requiring your prospective buyer to contact you for shipping information before bidding, you're giving yourself the information you'll need to pre-screen this international customer. You can then check his feedback rating and the details of the country in which he resides.

Not only will this allow you to turn down a sale from a customer who doesn't meet your standards (for example, a low feedback score or a troubled history), but it also gives you the opportunity to verify that the item for sale is one that can be shipped to the country in question. Every country has restrictions about what can cross its borders, and sometimes they're surprising. Eventually, you'll know which of your products are restricted in which areas, but in the meantime, use this extra step to help you learn and to forestall problems before they exist.

■ LET'S GET TO WORK...

■ The U.S. Postal Service Web site has a complete list of restricted items by country. Eventually, you'll learn what applies to you, but this handy resource is always available to you.

■ Be aware of some surprising restrictions. Some of the restrictions you'll find are political and economic. "I learned I can't ship products made in China into Mexico," reported Carlos Paris of PowerSeller elvibora. That's not a restriction you'd know about intuitively, so don't assume everything is okay just because the product to be shipped seems innocuous.

■ Sometimes your international restrictions will alter your product line. Just as international opportunities will expand your product line, they can also cause you to pull back on some items. "I knew I couldn't ship a decorative knife to all countries, but I decided to stop selling *Life* magazine covers when I encountered some trouble with sales in Germany," reported PowerSeller Jack Walters of bids4u-2. Jack discovered the restrictions for selling anything in Germany with images of the Third Reich. He decided to simply drop this part of his product line to maximize his German sales opportunities.

■ ■ ■

〉〉 MAKE HONESTY YOUR CUSTOM(S)

We're all vulnerable to peer pressure, especially when our peers seem to be getting away with something. But, just in case your mom never asked you what you would do if all of your friends were jumping off a bridge, we thought we would. Here's what we mean: Often in response to buyer requests, sellers declare their international packages as gifts to avoid the duty fees countries charge. You see, there are no duties charged for gifts. Likewise, sellers will undervalue the items shipped for the same purpose, again, often at the recipient's request. Most of them seem to get away with it. But, it's not a good idea, because doing this is a violation of federal law.

You aren't responsible for the duties charged; they're for your customer to pay. But if you lie on your customs form, that is your responsibility. If you're discovered (and packages *are* randomly opened), you will be the one to be fined and charged. Now plenty of sellers will tell you that's true, but you aren't likely to be found out. That's also true. But if you are found out, you are sure to be in trouble, so don't do it.

Aside from the potential of getting caught and punished, you'll know that you're operating part of your business dishonestly. We've always encouraged the people who build eBay businesses to do so with integrity. It's still the cornerstone of the eBay model, even if that model has now been tainted with ever-increasing episodes of fraud. A wise person once said, "If you want people to think you're honest, don't lie to them." We still think it's good advice.

LET'S GET TO WORK...

■ State clearly in your listings that international customers are responsible for all duties and charges imposed by their own countries. That way, they won't be surprised, and no one can claim you have any reason to contribute to this additional expense.

■ Some sellers go one step further with their listings and state that they are aware that international customers may be subject to additional taxes. They encourage those buyers to take that into account in their final bid.

■ You can rest assured that sellers report that even when an international customer has asked for the gift designation, they almost always back down and agree to the proper designation to make the purchase.

■ Remember that your customs form is a binding document. It's not a simple shipping label. It's a document that you verify to be truthful when you sign it.

■ Keep in mind that if your customer asks you to falsify your customs form, you are expected to report that to eBay as a violation. You may want to handle it personally and not turn in your customer, or you may feel that this is a trust and safety issue worthy of reporting. You'll have to decide. It may be that your customer doesn't understand the rules, and you can gently educate him. That may be especially true if he's worked with other sellers who are willing to falsify the forms for him.

■ ■ ■

FIND A "LOCAL" INTERNATIONAL PARTNER THOUSANDS OF MILES AWAY

There's no doubt about it, some things are just easier when kept inside borders. As you build your business, look for partners in countries where your current customers, or a large pool of prospective customers, reside. You may find a company with a warehouse in England that will be happy to fulfill your orders for your British customers. You may also link yourself to other eBay sellers who are based in other countries. That way you can offer to help them fulfill their orders in the United States while they help you fulfill your orders in their countries. It's all about maximizing the world community in which your eBay business will reside.

By building these international relationships, you'll completely eliminate the greatest challenges to your international sales. You'll be better able to track the packages that are shipped within the country you're selling in. You'll be able to eliminate the duties your customers are charged, and your shipping times will be greatly reduced. It's an arrangement that can work for everyone involved.

How do you make such arrangements and with whom? Your fellow eBay sellers, located in countries in which you would like to establish beachheads, may be your best bet. Andy Mowery of debnroo met Phil Leahy, one of Australia's top eBay sellers, at a meeting of the Professional eBay Sellers Alliance (PESA). Before long they had formed a partnership whereby Phil agreed to store and ship products earmarked for Andy's Australian customers.

Phil says he's now meeting a lot of American sellers who are trying to expand, and he's looking to help them. Another seller he is working with, for example, is PowerSeller laptopbrokers. As with debnroo, laptopbrokers had customers in Australia and wanted to expand there further. Rather than send laptops out one by one, they sent inventory to Phil, who handles local fulfillment for them.

■ Sure you should look to build relationships outside your country, but you have to get your domestic business up and running first, with inventory moving well, and with sufficient cash flow.

■ The key to forming these relationships is keeping your eyes and ears open to these kinds of opportunities. That may start with your mining the eBay seller community for possible partners. You may want to begin with foreign-based sellers outside your own product category. Ask if they have warehouses, and if they would be interested in shipping your orders for you.

■ Some of your customers may help you forge local relationships. If you have regular, dependable customers in countries in which you're looking to expand, let them know about your intentions. Ask if they know of any local companies that may be interested in warehousing your products and also handling fulfillment.

■ An added benefit of establishing these foreign relationships is that you may get to travel more (and create even more opportunities and strategies for sourcing for and servicing foreign customers). Andy Mowery told us that he had always wanted to go Australia, and now because of his relationship with Phil he may be able to go there on business and have some of the costs paid for.

■ Finally, forming local partnerships is one model, of course, for how you can do business internationally. Remember though that international trading is more about being proactive online and shipping from where you are.

■ ■ ■

READ THE FOREIGN PRESS

eBay is a worldwide phenomenon, and it's not just the press in the United States that offers stories and information about the life of eBay selling. You probably already know about the online newsletter, *AuctionBytes*, one of the best sources for information not only about eBay, but about the online auction world at large. Did you know there are *AuctionBytes*-type newsletters specific to other countries?

The UK's *eMarketBytes* is a fantastic reference and is the one we'll describe here in depth. But there are also newsletters covering Canada's auction industry (for example, *CDNauction* at www.cdnauction.com), and China has *ChinaTechNews.com*.

Aside from these auction-centric resources, foreign newspapers can provide insights into international buying trends. Of course the business sections of these papers will tell you about what's going on in the commercial world, but the other sections of the paper will also give you a feel for what the population is thinking about. You'll even be able to spot fads and trends by keeping up to date with what the local press is emphasizing. So if you're regularly selling into France, for example, you may want to read *Expatica France* (yes, some of these newspapers are in English). A good site for locating foreign newspapers is onlinenewspapers.com.

LET'S GET TO WORK...

- To begin your research, try *eMarketBytes*, based in the United Kingdom. This is a newsletter that offers eBay news, updates, and events. You will also find the U.K. perspective on other online sales venues including Froogle, Amazon, and others less well known in the United States such as Kelkoo, and QXL. Just reading the news articles provides a great education about what is currently on the minds of British online sellers. "*eMarketBytes* is another great source of an international e-commerce view. I've been reading it daily along with my other favorites," notes Adam Hersh.

- *eMarketBytes* also has forums where you can communicate with other sellers. Through them you can actually get to know sellers based in the United Kingdom. This would be a great opportunity to start forging relationships for the mutual advancement of your businesses. To post on the forums, you must be a registered user, but registration is free, so that's not a problem.

- The site also has All About Guides that cover such subjects as selling on eBay, eBay UK, and frequently searched key words on eBay. These will be especially helpful as you seek to discover what issues are of interest to the eBay community in the United Kingdom.

■ The site is run by experienced eBay sellers with over 20,000 eBay transactions among them so that you can be sure they know the issues that concern the eBay community at large, and the community in the United Kingdom specifically.

■ ■ ■

SPEAK THE LANGUAGE, EVEN WHEN YOU DON'T

eBay sellers in the United States have a decided advantage over their counterparts in other countries, because more people from overseas have a smattering of English knowledge than Americans have of languages other than English. Many of the sellers you encounter will likely have studied at least a little bit of English. Plus, with the exposure to the culture of the United States, these customers are more likely to have some basic understanding of your products, branding, and cultural background than you will for theirs.

Your challenge is to stay sensitive to the fact that the world is bigger than the United States. "Your international customers are not stupid or trying to insult you," says Tony from PowerSeller wegot-thebeats.com. It's very easy for someone trying to communicate with you to make a mistake by choosing the wrong word or phrase. "Don't take each word literally and use context tools when you are trying to figure out what someone is saying," advises Tony. "English is a complex language." You only have to try to communicate with buyers who don't speak English. You don't have to be an expert. These buyers, if they use eBay routinely, are accustomed to dealing with sellers who don't know their languages. The point is buying on eBay is a little more difficult for them. If you can prove yourself to be a competent, approachable, friendly seller, they're more likely to stick with you than to branch out in search of your competition. You'll make a long-term customer and provide a valuable service at the same time.

■ LET'S GET TO WORK...

■ Hire people who *do* speak the language. If you are branching out into specific markets, for example Germany, France, and Spain, search for local people who are fluent in those languages and contract with them to help you with your communications. "You can use this person to step in to provide customer service," said Debbie Levitt, president of the eBay consulting firm As Was, and a consultant to PowerSellers. "Your customers will be so much more comfortable with you when they can communicate with you in their native tongue." They'll never have to know it's not you writing!

■ Look to your local high school or community college to find people who teach foreign languages to fill this role for you. They are usually fluent in the languages they teach, plus they also have a great understanding of the cultures behind those languages. Your business may not support a full-time employee who speaks another language yet, but when you do hire help, consider whether or not the person you hire does speak another language.

■ If, for now, you have limited need for someone who speaks another language, try sites like Freetranslation.com. Translation software can be problematic, but it can also help you out in a pinch. This Web site provides free translation tools that you can try out for yourself before you need to use them. Another popular translation site is Babel Fish at AltaVista.com. "The translations can be comical," notes Andy Mowery, "but you get the point. It allows me to communicate."

■ If you use these translation sites, you'll be happier if you've kept your language simple in your listings and e-mails. Your customer may also be using translation software, and using simple language will decrease the chances of misunderstandings.

■ ■ ■

)) LET YOUR CUSTOMERS BE YOUR CONSULTANTS

As we mentioned above, international buyers tend to come back to the sellers they've had good experiences with. Once you've established yourself with an international buyer, ask her to help you out. Tell her you are trying to do a better job serving customers in her country and ask her to take a look at your auction listings, policies, and e-mails to help you better target her specific market.

PowerSeller Adam Hersh has had excellent experience with this method of expanding his business into the German market. "The rules are different for that economy. How people pay is different," he told us. He says that he learned those differences because his customers taught him. They either yelled at him for making mistakes or showed him how to do things differently. In time, he developed a set of practices that allowed him to operate comfortably in the German market.

LET'S GET TO WORK...

- Ask your international customers which shipping methods they find to be most efficient. Ask them to help you understand the customs issues of their specific countries.

- Use your customers as a resource and ask them to critique your listings to see how you can make them more user-friendly to their markets. Ask them also to help you with your About Me page.

- Ask your customers about practices that can reward or entice other customers from their own countries. Is there the equivalent of a frequent buyer program, for example?

- Perhaps your customers can help you determine what products might sell well in their countries. Ask them if there are particular items that they have trouble locating locally. Also ask about fads in their countries, to gather further clues about what might sell.

- Find out if there are some native complimentary phrases or terms you could include in your feedback ratings for international customers. How much nicer it would be for you to use a pleasant local greeting to thank your customer for her business.

- Ask your customers about holidays and vacation times in their countries. That will help you plan your strategy for international sales throughout the year.

■ ■ ■

WHAT YOU DON'T KNOW CAN'T HELP YOU: HIRE YOUR OWN CONSULTANT

If you feel like you've learned all you can from your customers, you may want to consider hiring a consultant. Adam Hersh began working with a German consultant once he felt he'd reached a limit to what he could learn from his customers. "I hired a consultant when I wanted to take my business to the next level," explained Adam. It's taken him a lot of work, but now many of his interactions with his German customers are automated.

Debbie Levitt of As Was works in the United States, but she is an advocate of finding consultants to work with you no matter which market you are trying to expand. "We may be working with an Australian seller to help him sell in the United States," she said, "but international sales go in all ways." According to Debbie, a local consultant will be able to help you create a whole look for your international eBay business that will reflect the values and tastes of the overseas market you are attempting to appeal to. She recommends you consider every part of your operation from the perspective of the overseas customer if you want to branch out into international sales. We highlight some of the points she suggests you consider below.

LET'S GET TO WORK...

- Take a look at your listing template. Designs that may work for Americans or English speakers may not work for people in other countries. Buyers there may have different things they find attractive or unattractive so there may be other ways of effectively listing your items.

- Match your eBay store and your About Me page. Again, the look and flow of these may need to be altered to appeal to the sensibilities of overseas customers.

- Your listing strategy may be different. The consultant will know some of the best ways and times to list your auctions in order to capture the audience in a particular country. She can also help you research and identify good markets and help you figure out what your average selling prices may likely be.

- You may have your consultant help you create invoices in her own language. That will really show your international customers how much you respect them.

- Your consultant can help you create a promotional flyer to include in your international shipments. You may find that a particular type of brochure will appeal to these customers, or maybe you'll want to consider business cards in their language. A consultant will know what is culturally appropriate.

- You may be able to establish a customer service program with your consultant to take care of your customers in her market. She might be able to handle e-mail, instant messaging, or even phone calls. Customers who see you address them in their own language may expect that level of service throughout all of your communications.

■ ■ ■

IMPROVE YOUR INTERNATIONAL SALES EXPERIENCE WITH MYSTOREMAPS

MyStoreMaps is a new and clever tool offered by the firm MyStoreCredit. Based in North Carolina, this company has been offering eBay-related marketing tools and services since 2003. Through the MyStoreMaps service, a map is included in all of your auctions that will reveal, in real time, the various international locations of customers you've served. This little map can go a long way toward reassuring your international customers that you know how to serve the needs of their markets. Figure 8.1 shows a sample map from an auction listing from Australian PowerSeller Phil Leahy. As a potential buyer you choose locations Phil has shipped his items to for North America, Europe, and the rest of the world. "If you want to show you are committed to offshore selling, I highly recommend the maps. Customers, especially 'newbies,' who are worried about the seller's ability to deliver to their country or region are made confident by this tool," said Phil.

FIGURE 8.1: MyStoreMaps shows international customers exactly where you've shipped your items and how many sales you've completed in each location.

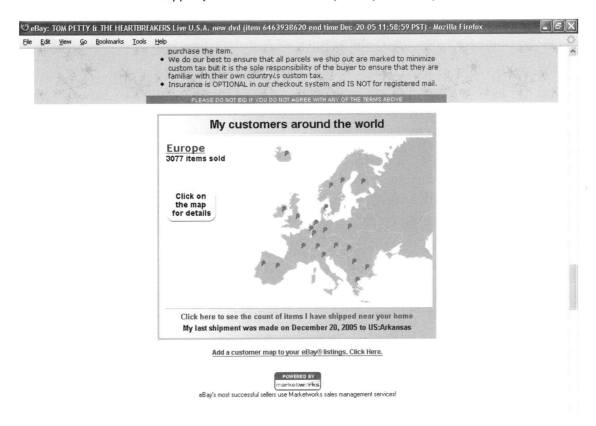

When you sign up to include the maps in your listings, you can designate which of these maps you'd like to include. From the time you sign up, all the statistics are listed automatically within your map. You can also choose to input the historical data you already have for various countries so that you can present the most accurate information possible to your customers. For $69.95 you can have the map(s) included in up to 7,500 of your eBay listings for one year. If you need coverage for additional auctions, you can add them in increments of 7,500 for an additional $29.95 for each incremental step. For the price of the service, you will also receive a monthly e-mail report showing your total sales, your international sales, and your repeat sales.

LET'S GET TO WORK...

- You can include your international shipping, payment, and return policies right on each of your maps. That way your international customers can see your business practices at the same time they view your international sales history.

- Because of its graphical nature, your customers don't have to have to speak English to see how you operate internationally. This is just one more way for you to overcome your language barriers with overseas customers.

- MyStoreMaps can help you locate international partners. As you look for international sellers to partner with, you will become a more attractive business partner to those who can see your international sales history so readily.

- MyStoreCredit offers an affiliate program to allow you to help it market its product. As you've seen, affiliate programs are useful ways to grow your revenues. If you like their product, consider including an affiliate button for them in your listings.

- You will receive your first month's service free as a trial. If you decide any time within the first year that you are unhappy with the map service, MyStoreCredit will refund your money. You really have very little to lose by giving this a try.

■ ■ ■

CREATE DIFFERENT IDs FOR INTERNATIONAL SALES

You may very well find that you want to branch out with one or more entirely different user IDs for your international sales. Some of the most successful international sellers we know have found this to be a viable option. Australian PowerSeller Phil Leahy of philsales1 uses that ID for his Australian sales. He uses philsales2 to identify his sales in the United Kingdom. "It's the same product," he explained, "but it allows me to tailor my listings to each market."

Your consultant will be able to help you choose the right user name for the countries in which you want to expand. "It's a matter of branding," noted Debbie Levitt. "Your consultant will know if you need to adapt your name, and which name would appeal to customers in your target country if you do need to choose another one." Targeting an international audience with a relevant user name is just one more way you can approach the international market with respect for and sensitivity to the culture in which you wish to operate. Working with a consultant will ensure that you don't accidentally create a user name that would be rude, insulting, or just ineffective.

LET'S GET TO WORK...

- Use your alternate user names to offer your listings in the currency of the country that you are targeting. Phil Leahy's Australian listings are listed in Australian dollar amounts. His U.K. listings are in pounds, and his North American listings are in U.S. dollars. That way he doesn't make his customers do the work of figuring out just exactly how much each item costs.

- By dedicating a different user name for each international market you pursue, you can simplify your shipping, payment, and return options. There will be no need to list every contingency for each market. You can simply include the information that's relevant to the market in which you are listing.

- When you tailor your user names, you will be able to shape sales and special offerings for different segments of your business. Over time you'll know which items are most likely to sell for the highest prices in which markets. Then you can gear your entire listing to serving those markets.

- Having separate user names will also help you when you're sourcing your products. You'll easily be able to track which items are selling well in which markets. "That's how I've had some of my best sales," says Tony of wegotthebeats.com. "I got

$600 for a CD that was a hit in Japan but a flop in the U.S. I found it in a clearance bin for $1. I never would have known to purchase that CD if I hadn't done my research on eBay. I had never heard of the artist or producers. I would have passed by it like so many hundreds of other Americans passed by it before."

■ ■ ■

FILL OUT CUSTOMS FORMS FOR FUN AND PROFIT!

No, your authors haven't gone mad. Among the PowerSellers who spoke with us and actively pursued international sales, one theme resounded. International sales can be more challenging. International shipping requires a bit of extra trouble.

Similarly, customs forms can be time-consuming and annoying. But once you have a few of them under your belt, there's no need to be intimidated by the process. The rewards for expanding your business are potentially just too important to turn away the vast majority of humanity as potential customers to your business.

Most sellers who do international sales find their own methods for dealing with the extra steps required to process orders and ship them internationally. The more you can streamline everything you do, the more you maximize your profits. Time is money, and anything you can do to reduce the time it takes to process an order, whether it's domestic or international, will be time you can better spend researching, listing, or selling products. PowerSellers claim that, with time, international order fulfillment can be as routine and smooth as the domestic kind.

LET'S GET TO WORK...

- Have your customs forms filled out as completely as possible before the item is ready to ship. Don't get caught standing at the post office with your package ready to go while you complete the form.

- If you ship items less than four pounds, you can use the simplified green form. For items that weigh more, you'll need the longer form. Either way, keep a supply of both types at home so that you can have them ready to go when you need them. "If you pre-fill much of the information on those green customs forms, such as your return address and signature, then it makes shipping an international package almost as quick as a U.S. package when the time comes," says a PowerSeller from the Southeast. "I do this every once in a while in the evening when I'm watching television."

- If you'll be shipping items of a uniform size, you can go one step further. "I have bubble mailers with the customs forms pre-filled, stuck on, with an airmail sticker, and stamped 'fragile' all ready to go," he says.

- Consider automating your process. Look into automation programs such as ShipWorks from Interapptive.com (see Chapter 7 for more on ShipWorks). This tool allows you to automatically print completed U.S. Postal Service customs forms for international shipments. You can complete the forms with a series of mouse clicks and print them all ready to go.

■ ■ ■

Adam Hersh

Adam Hersh came to eBay as a college student in 1998. His plan was to look the site over as eBay was about to become a public company. He thought it was intriguing, so he looked around his apartment for things to sell. He quickly sold off some of his belongings.

You can **Make Money** on **eBay**

Learn How with Expert **Adam Hersh**

He started selling more and more, and word spread on campus that he was making money by selling stuff he didn't want. Since college kids always need money, friends started asking him to do the same for them. He quickly became everyone's best friend, because he was acting as a trading assistant without charging his friends for his work. Then someone he didn't know called to make the request. He asked to take a piece of the profit from the sale, and that's when he stepped into the world of the professional trading assistant. Of course, when he sold this item (a pair of tires), the trading assistant program had not yet been launched!

Today, at the ripe old age of 27, Adam of AdamHershAuctions is one of the biggest sellers on the site and the number one poster and print seller. Not only does he list over 100,000 auctions per month, but he also sells on Overstock, Yahoo!, shopping.com, bizrate, and shopzilla. He is also an eBay consultant to others who want to get started, and he has consulted with the South Korean government to help it explore the potential of eBay.

He has 16 employees in his Florida warehouse and 7 people who work for him in his New York offices. He is more dedicated to international sales than many of the big sellers on eBay. He has created his own presence on eBay Germany with all of his listings there in German. As we write this, Adam has begun working with a German consultant to expand and develop his German presence.

Adam routinely shops on eBay both for items for personal use and for inventory to supplement his business. He has seen the site evolve over the years. In spite of his tender age he had this to say about life on eBay: "It's not the olden days where anything would sell. Now it's survival of the fittest. Those who pay attention to their businesses, study their businesses, study their numbers do well."

In addition to running his amazing e-commerce business, Adam enjoys holding charity auctions. He has run a series of auctions for the New York City Public Library. Working in conjunction with local restaurants in the city, they gained a great deal of exposure and raised $30,000 for the library. He has also done charity auctions for Big Brothers/Big Sisters. When you ask Adam about life on eBay, he responds enthusiastically, "It's so much fun!"

CHAPTER 9

Your Online Store and So Much More

If your plan is to build an e-commerce business, you're going to need a store. Operating your own store is a much more efficient way for you to sell on eBay, and it is essential if you decide to venture out beyond the comfortable confines of eBay and onto the Internet. We'll be sharing a lot of incisive and valuable information about selling on other venues in Chapter 10, but for now let's explore the issues of having a store both on eBay and on the Web. We didn't speak with a single top eBay seller who doesn't operate an online store, and that's no surprise.

Your eBay store allows you to keep your inventory available for sale for much longer periods of time than your auction listings. You can list items to stay active until they're sold. Listing fees for putting inventory into your store are less. Although rate hikes have increased final value fees and monthly store fees, eBay stores are still a good value. You may be asking yourself why you'd plan to stick with eBay in view of its increased fees, when you can pay another company to host your own Web store. Lots of PowerSellers have asked themselves that question. But the fact is you lose a great deal of marketing exposure by moving off eBay. Once you venture onto the Web, you will have to be far more involved in driving traffic to your site. You won't have a partner with millions of shoppers already looking for what you sell.

Now that doesn't mean you shouldn't venture onto the Web. Many PowerSellers *do* take that next step. It only means don't rush to get there. Let your business and brand grow and gain strength on eBay. You'll know when the time is right to take the next step. You'll have the customer base, the experience, and the marketing savvy to make the most of the move if you allow yourself to first grow your business on eBay.

In 2005 eBay introduced ProStores to help you do just that. eBay executives noticed that some successful sellers were moving off the site in favor of the Web, and they introduced ProStores as a way to help eBay sellers broaden their horizons without leaving eBay behind. The idea was a solid one, but unfortunately, the ProStores product, as it is currently presented, is not popular at all among the top eBay sellers most likely ready for this next step. Almost without exception, the PowerSellers we spoke with claimed that ProStores lacked the functionality and the flexibility they'd need to make it a good match for their businesses. They also reported to us that although ProStores was very simple to set up, it was not easy to change, making it laborious for them to make alterations to their stores, once they were established. Some of the sellers also noted that ProStores was expensive. Their feelings were that if they had to spend that much money to create their Web stores, they might as well be working with an established third-party solutions provider.

In this chapter, we'll be looking at the options these solutions providers offer. We'll also explore the possibility of your creating a Web store without them. But first, let's take a look at how you will use your store as an integral part of your whole e-commerce business. You will start with a modest eBay store, expand as needed, and then eventually, perhaps you'll venture out to the Web. Step by step, our network of PowerSellers and other industry experts provide the advice you need to make that happen.

)) YOUR BUSINESS NAME REALLY MATTERS

You probably chose your eBay user ID a long time ago. Maybe you chose something close to your e-mail address. Maybe you went with some familiar, comfortable nickname or phrase that means a great deal to you. You may even love your user ID. But, whether or not that ID is a good name for your business remains to be seen. As you contemplate creating a store, you'll want to first take a good hard look at that ID and think of it not only as the name of your store and business but also as the brand your company will use. You will want your user ID to be the same as your store name, because that will make it easier for more shoppers to find you. Don't worry about having to change your name and the effect that this will have on your current sales. Almost to a person, PowerSellers told us that changing their name had little effect on their sales, even when they had feedback ratings in the thousands.

As long as we're getting your store underway, now's the time to make your choice of a business name a great one. As you remember in Chapter 4, we talked about marketing your business by creating your brand. Your store will be an integral part of the brand, so make it count. This time create a name that you can stick with. Choose one that can be used as a Web site, because if you do expand onto the Web, you'll want to be able to own the name on there as well. Be sure your domain name is still available to you on the Web before you commit yourself to that name on eBay, and then be sure to register it so no one else can scoop you on it!

LET'S GET TO WORK...

■ Consultant Deb Levitt recommends choosing a name that is not commonly misspelled by the general public. For example, although you may think *genr8trs* would be a cute name for someone who sells generators, will that also be a name someone else will easily remember? Also, don't use dashes or nonalphanumeric characters in your name. People often forget where they get placed in the words, and even a simple mistake will make it so you don't pop up in a key word search.

■ PowerSeller David Yaskulka recommends that you make the name of your store and your user ID something simple to remember. As you remember, he and his wife operate blueberryboutique. Now, he claims that he chose a name that is slightly too long. But, on the other hand, not only is it easy to remember, but it also conjures a pleasant image of a little shop where you could stop by and purchase men's dress shirts. It's easy for satisfied customers to recommend blueberryboutique to their friends rather than to say they purchased that shirt from some guy on eBay. You never know where inspiration for a great name will come from either. In David's case, he lives on Blueberry Lane!

■ Consider how your name might coincide with a logo. Your goal is to create an entire brand, so although your business name may never be as familiar to people as "Kleenex" or "Xerox," you'll want to choose a name that can complement your symbol. For example, by now you're familiar with PowerSellers Andy and Deb Mowery who operate debnroo. It's short, simple, and goes along just perfectly with the two cats they use in their listings, store, and About Me page. With their tails affectionately intertwined, these little cartoons suggest a peaceful and happy shopping experience, and the people who buy home, garden, and pet supplies from debnroo, are bound to recognize that sense in their branding.

■ ■ ■

YOUR LISTINGS DON'T MATTER AS MUCH AS YOUR STORE

When you begin selling on eBay, your listings are everything. You work hard to produce the cleanest, sharpest, best listings possible. You work on templates that make your listings attractive, and you agonize over every detail of timing, pricing, and length. That's just as it should be. The listings you create will build your business, your feedback, and your experience. Once you stand ready to move from modest seller to PowerSeller, you'll learn that your listings aren't as important to your business as you once thought. You'll move from using them to generate revenue on their own to using them as advertising to drive traffic to your store. Your store will become the hub of your e-commerce business. (Note: This is not to say that if you have an especially rare item to sell, or even a hot commodity item, that you should stop listing them on the core site, even once you have your store humming along. Those kinds of listings will get a lot of attention there.)

"Your Web site should be the center of your multichannel strategy," says David of blueberryboutique. Other PowerSellers are also concentrating their efforts on their own Web sites. Jody of beachcombers! has a Web site that she actively promotes through search engine optimization techniques, as we saw in Chapter 4. But Deb Levitt is wary about advising people to jump too quickly away from eBay. "I think that depends mostly on the marketing and advertising budget of the seller," she notes. "If you don't have the money to spend on advertising, then you should spend what money you do have where the buyers already are. That'd be eBay." Whether you concentrate on your Web store or your eBay store, eventually you'll come to view your listings as the method you use to get your customers into your virtual store, and not as the main revenue generators of your business.

■ Consider taking a loss on some of your listings to boost traffic to your store. Andy of debnroo described to us some auctions he recently ran to generate store traffic. He had a selection of KitchenAid mixers. At the time, *KitchenAid* was the third most popular key word searchers used in eBay's Home category. The mixers are heavy to ship, and Andy wasn't selling them well through his store inventory. Instead, he listed them in auction listings that began at $1 with a reserve of 10 percent off his wholesale cost. Now his customers were likely to get a great price on the KitchenAid mixers so many buyers were looking for. Although Andy technically lost money on many of the mixers he sold, his sales in his store were 200 percent better than they were for the same period a year earlier. The traffic his listings created, through links to his store, was worth sacrificing some profit on his mixers.

■ Because of eBay's increased store fees, it's become more difficult to offer bargains through your eBay store, according to Andy. That means that your customers need more incentive to go to your store where they can find a steady and simple source for the products you sell. Use your auctions as a means to drive customers to your store, but then make sure your store inventory, your policies, and your presentation make it a destination your customers will return to. You won't be ready to sacrifice your listings until your store is up and running efficiently.

■ ■ ■

YOUR STORE SHOULD PLEASE YOUR CUSTOMER, NOT YOU

Once you get your customer into your store, everything about that store should be designed to please your customer, make shopping with you easy, and provide all the information necessary to make your customer want your product and buy it, at that moment. You want to eliminate anything that will be likely to make your customer click out of the store, because once that happens, that customer is on the way to another buyer. So your store has to be professional, pleasing, easy to use, and attractive.

"Make sure the items for sale are the stars of the show," advises Deb Levitt. "Everything else either enhances that or works against it. MIDI (sound) files can work against it, so can pictures of dancing bears. It doesn't tell the buyer anything they didn't already know." Following Deb's suggestions will ensure that you focus your store to concentrate on what your customer needs and wants to make an immediate buying decision. "Anything that helps you stand out is worth it," she added. To that end, PowerSeller Christina of wiccan well offers pages of information about metaphysical issues her customers would find interesting. Figure 9.1 shows her store's home page with hyperlinks for the different subjects she's written about across the top of the page. Now she has the opportunity to pique her customers' interest, and perhaps keep them in the store longer than they'd planned, appreciating her services as much as her products.

· ·

FIGURE 9.1: Wiccan Well is a PowerSeller who offers a good education along with a well-organized store.

■ Jody of beachcombers! has worked hard to make her store everything her customers could want in an online shopping destination. Figure 9.2 shows her store's home page. Notice that her store name, Beachcombers Bazaar, ties in well with her user ID. It won't be difficult for her customers to find her the next time they want to shop.

FIGURE 9.2: PowerSeller beachcombers! has an attractive and dynamic store home page. Notice how well the name of the store ties in with the seller's user ID.

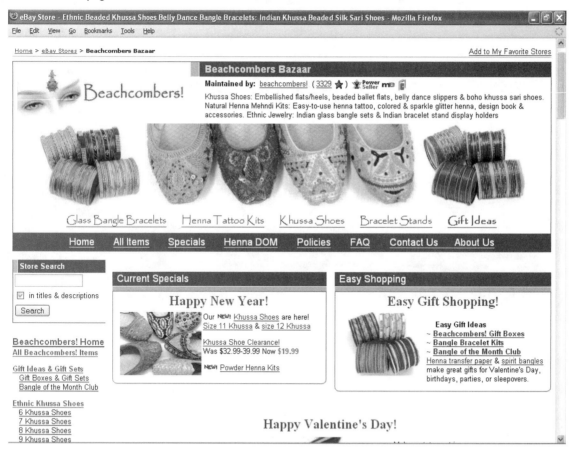

■ The store is branded, and the brand is featured in the store's header. A shopper can see immediately that this store owner is a professional seller. Jody has clearly displayed the products she offers for sale. Not only are the products Jody offers clearly featured, but so are the current specials and the gift department she created to simplify shopping.

◼ As you scroll down the page, shown in Figure 9.3, you can see that Jody offers a no-risk return policy clearly featured on the left side of the page. A customer can feel certain that he is shopping with a professional. As an added customer service feature, Jody includes a toll-free telephone number, making it easy for the customer to ask any remaining questions without the need to fuss with e-mail. Jody doesn't want someone to click his way out of the store now that she has that person interested. She also uses this space to welcome international customers to her store.

• •

FIGURE 9.3: Everything a customer might need to know about this seller's policies and practices is readily available on this easy-to-navigate page.

- Finally, near the bottom of the page you can see a mention of Jody's Preferred Clients program. This is how she creates a customer list for e-mail and promotional materials. Since signing up is strictly voluntary, she knows only interested customers will participate. Now she has a base group of people who will be the first to know about her specials and promotions. She's turned a casual shopper into a loyal customer.

■ ■ ■

DESIGN YOUR TEMPLATES TO KEEP PEOPLE IN YOUR STORE

Once you have the customer interested, do everything in your power to keep that customer in your store. As you build a storefront appearance that will be attractive and efficient, remember to account for everything a customer might need to continue shopping with you. As you saw in the above examples, Jody has done a great job of offering her customers every reassurance that they've found a professional seller, but she's found ways to go beyond that and spotlight her products and services clearly and attractively.

If a customer has any interest at all in buying the types of products she sells, Jody has made it almost impossible for that customer to leave without making a purchase. Her customers may never realize how successfully she's directed them to buy an item, but that's even better. She gets what she needs, they get what they want, and everyone is happy. You can use her examples to see just exactly how you can also design your templates so that your customers have no excuses to leave empty-handed. What's more, she does that in every auction listing, before a customer ever actually enters the store itself. Let's take a clear look at a typical auction listing so that you can see just how effectively Jody turns a shopper into a buyer. Figure 9.4 will serve as an excellent example.

LET'S GET TO WORK...

- Using a typical listing for khussa shoes, shown in Figure 9.4, Jody highlights the features of her store. Prominently displayed next to the item listed is the current feature item being promoted in the store. That feature will change regularly, but the link is always there.

. . . .

FIGURE 9.4: A typical listing for beachcombers! khussa shoes shows just how effectively this PowerSeller has designed templates that get her customers into her store and encourages sales.

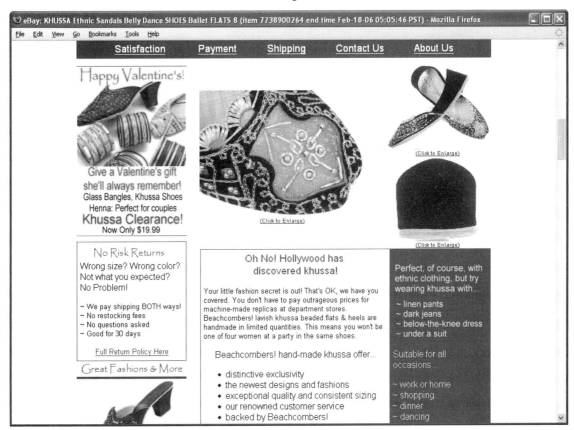

- Along the left of the listing are pictures that link to the different departments of her store. Because she's using only pictures, not words, there is no risk of key word spamming that would result if she listed the words "glass bangles" or "henna" in her listings for shoes. As a customer is shopping for shoes, she can also see what other products Jody offers in her store. Then, with the click of a mouse she can jump over to Jody's store to browse for even more of Jody's wares.

- Jody even has a listing on the right-hand side of the page to show the sizes these shoes are available in. "We don't want someone to say, 'This is not my size' and go back into the eBay search to find their size, potentially from another seller," explains Jody. If Jody doesn't happen to have a particular size in that exact shoe, the link is going to take a customer to other choices in her size. So you see, once Jody has an interested customer, the templates in her listings and store will do everything possible to see to it that she also has a sale.

■ ■ ■

MAKE YOUR STORE PART OF A VIRTUAL MALL

If you opened a business in a local mall, you'd work with other merchants to coordinate your advertising, marketing, and promotional activities. You'd feature items that complemented each other's offerings for holidays and special events. You'd even direct customers to your neighbors when they were looking for something that you didn't stock, but your neighbor did. You'd regularly meet with your neighbors and know what issues and challenges they were facing and how they were planning to cope with them. In other words, you'd be a member of a community of sellers who could all improve their businesses by working together. Just because you operate in a virtual environment doesn't mean that you can't do the same thing.

Of course, you won't be able to be quite as casual about it as you could be if you routinely met your fellow businesspeople in the mall or on Main Street, but that doesn't have to keep you from forming partnerships with other sellers, both on eBay and in other parts of the online world. Once you do, you'll be able to enter into relationships with them that will benefit both parties. We talked in Chapter 8 about creating cross-border partnerships to simplify international shipping and customs, but that philosophy can also work well within the borders of your own country too.

LET'S GET TO WORK...

■ "Drop-shipping for other sellers is actually a good idea," says Andy of debnroo. "We have a couple of sellers who are on and off eBay and who send orders to us for fulfillment on a regular basis. They are mostly selling products we already stock from their own Web sites." This type of partnership allows you to profit from the marketing and sales efforts of other sellers. It expands the amount of product you move through your operation without you having to expand your selling efforts.

- Randall Pinson of rocket-auctions agrees with Andy. "I have also formed partnerships with other online retail companies where they sell my product, and I fulfill the orders, or drop-ship to their customers. This system has worked well for my company as we don't have to manage the customer service end of the transaction."

- "One way to think about this," continues Andy, "is that your warehousing is really a separate business and profit center. If you've already committed to a warehouse, or are thinking of this, it is a feasible way of hedging your investment."

- Andy warns, however, that you shouldn't let working as a drop-shipper distract you from your core business. "The downside: You have to work with and coordinate with a number of other sellers, all with their own ordering systems, procedures, and idiosyncrasies," he notes. So give it a try, but don't let it overwhelm you.

■ ■ ■

TAKE THE EXPRESS WAY TO BOOST YOUR EBAY SALES!

eBay is *the* place to buy that one-of-a-kind item, but what if a buyer is looking for a commodity item, where one is pretty much the same as the next? Further, what if she needs that item immediately (say a power surge protector for her computer setup)? If you're an experienced eBay user, you might think to see if there's a good Buy It Now deal. But if you were a relative newcomer to the world of e-commerce you'd be more likely to buy your item from a more traditional online store such as Amazon.

eBay realized it's been missing out on sales of this type and responded to the challenge with eBay Express, which as we write this has just gotten underway. We're betting eBay Express will eventually be huge, as eBay starts to put some real marketing muscle behind it. When eBay Express was announced David Yaskulka, marketing committee chair for the Professional eBay Sellers Alliance , predicted it "will be eBay's best recent move to attract new customers." debnroo went even further calling eBay Express "absolutely the most important change to eBay in years."

eBay Express is technically a separate Web site with its own URL (www.express.ebay.com), but with many links and cross-marketing to eBay itself. It is geared to new items, and every item is available immediately for a fixed price—no waiting for auctions to end. Also, only sellers with a minimum of 100 feedbacks and a rating of 98 percent positive can list on eBay Express, so buyers can rest assured they're dealing only with experienced sellers.

eBay, of course, is hoping that once these new customers get comfortable with eBay Express, they'll also give eBay at large a try. As sellers it will be your job to first rope them in via eBay Express auctions and then move them to your eBay store, where they become *your* customers, and not just eBay's.

LET'S GET TO WORK...

- If you already have an eBay store and already sell fixed-price items, get your eBay Express marketing plan in place and soon! If you meet the seller feedback criteria, your listings of this type will automatically appear on eBay Express. So ready or not, those eBay Express customers will be headed your way.

- Jody of beachcombers! advises that you include many links back to your store or auction items in your eBay Express listings. Now that you have the attention of these new buyers, don't waste the opportunity to make a new customer.

- Branding on eBay Express is as important as ever, since as beachcombers! also told us, you want buyers to come back to *you* specifically, not eBay in general. All the advice we've been giving you about the importance of a logo and a consistent (and professional) look and feel is very important here as you seek to convert Express customers to your customers.

- eBay Express will also appeal to your current eBay customers who are looking to buy commodity items at fixed prices, so be sure to market to them as well through whatever means (for example newsletters, e-mails, or ads) you're using now.

- Selling on eBay Express may require you to get used to less stringent "buyer qualification" standards than you have in place now. Huh? eBay requires eBay Express sellers to set their PayPal settings so PayPal users with unconfirmed addresses are not prohibited from shopping with them. Some sellers are concerned that this may make eBay Express too attractive to scammers who could buy expensive items, have them shipped to unconfirmed addresses, and then file PayPal disputes. One option you have is to decide on a case-by-case basis if you will ship to someone with an unconfirmed address, by asking such buyers to first check with you.

■ ■ ■

REACH MILLIONS OF GOOGLE SEARCHERS FOR FREE WITH GOOGLE BASE

Google Base is a separate area within Google where you can upload just about any type of information you'd like—recipes, job listings, articles, and yes, product descriptions—at no charge. The descriptions can include hyperlinks to your eBay store, for example, where a potential buyer can then go to actually buy the described item.

Before Google Base you had to pay to harness Google's tremendous popularity (hundreds of millions of searches are completed on Google every month). As we described in Chapter 4, Google's AdWords service enables you to create ads that appear automatically whenever someone types the key words you designate into the Google search box. How often and just where among all the ads *your* ad appears depends on what you're willing to pay per click. Many sellers find Google AdWords very effective. If you're selling through a Web store, it's a way to reach millions of buyers whom you wouldn't be able to reach otherwise. Plus, they see your ad when they are specifically searching for information related to your products, so you're reaching them when they are potentially in a mood to buy.

All this was great, but it cost real money and not every seller had the marketing budget for an AdWords campaign. Google Base, on the other hand, drives traffic to your store or auction listings at no charge! That's because any information you upload to Google Base will show up as part of "regular" Google searches. It's no wonder that eBay seller listings appeared within hours of Google Base going live, and within days tens of thousands of listings had been uploaded. Within that same brief time period QuickDrop International, a leading chain of eBay drop-off stores, reported that Google Base listings were driving thousands of potential buyers to their eBay listings. As we suggested in an article we wrote for *AuctionBytes*, given all this traffic, why wouldn't a seller upload his listings to Google Base as a way to drive more traffic to eBay listings, an eBay store, or a Web store? Figure 9.5 shows the Google Base home page.

· ·

FIGURE 9.5: Google Base allows eBay sellers, and anyone else, to post free product descriptions that include hyperlinks to their stores and eBay auctions.

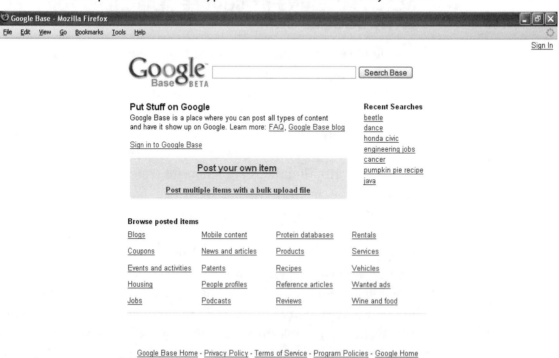

LET'S GET TO WORK...

- Creating a listing is simple and quick. If you have a lot of listings ready to go, you can upload them en masse to Google Base via its bulk-listing feature. What's more, Google Base also accepts daily data feeds so you can easily keep all those listings up to date.

- If you work through an auction management services company, such as ChannelAdvisor, it can help you painlessly port over your existing listings to Google Base. You don't work with one of these companies yet? No problem. There's information right on the site about how you can do this yourself.

- See Figure 9.6 for an example of a Google Base listing that includes a hyperlink to an eBay store from where the item can be purchased. The store in this case is moms2moms.

FIGURE 9.6: This example of a Google Base listing shows the promotional and marketing advantages the database can provide an eBay store owner.

- Note that as an added plus, your Google Base listings may also appear on Froogle, Google Local, and Google.com, giving you added exposure for your trouble.

- Monitor your Google Base listings and the traffic they generate carefully. As we are writing this, Google has yet to implement security safeguards, and at least one PowerSeller has found that another company had copied his entire product feed, including images and product descriptions, and then linked everything to its own site! Another thorny issue we pointed out in *AuctionBytes* is vetting. eBay has its feedback system of course, but ads appearing on Google Base could be from "anonymous" sellers. "Without vetting," debnroo told us, "reputable sellers could be lost in a sea of frauds."

■ ■ ■

EXPAND YOUR CHECKOUT OPTIONS WITH PAYPAL'S VIRTUAL TERMINAL

PayPal now offers a suite of products for the small- to medium-sized business called PayPal Website Payments Pro. One of these offerings, the Virtual Terminal, is perfect for the eBay seller who wants to build up his store's clientele. With Virtual Terminal, you can accept credit card payments over the phone, by fax, or through the mail, whether or not the party paying is a PayPal member. "For those starting a new business, it's the perfect solution," says Andy of debnroo. Andy noted that there are simply no cost comparisons possible between using Virtual Terminal and establishing a merchant account to process credit cards. Virtual Terminal costs $20 per month.

One concern about instituting Virtual Terminal is the potential for fee avoidance when a customer calls on the phone to complete a purchase. eBay has traditionally been very sensitive to fee avoidance issues, and that's understandable. The Final Value Fees that sellers pay when a transaction is complete are a major source of revenue for the company. When a transaction takes place over the phone, it's outside of the eBay System. But Virtual Terminal doesn't seem to be causing any alarms to sound. For one thing, processing a phone order can be a little more time-consuming than having your customer pay for your item through the eBay site. That phone call can likely come in just as you're in the middle of working on something else. Andy often answers the customer service question and then offers the customer the option of paying over the phone. However, Andy notes that if the customer is comfortable making the purchase online, he actually encourages her to go back to the site and pay through eBay. This lets Andy get back to whatever he was doing when the call came in. "People who are using Virtual Terminal to avoid eBay fees are also going to exhibit other behaviors that will catch them," he noted.

LET'S GET TO WORK...

- Institute Virtual Terminal as early as possible when you're building your business. It's much harder to go back and redesign your payment options once your business has matured. Do it as you build so that you won't have to rebuild to accommodate it.

- Use Virtual Terminal as part of your total eBay accounting system. Because it is tied entirely to the eBay system, it shows up on PayPal like all your other payments. That makes accounting much easier than if you were to go with a merchant account. Your Virtual Terminal payments become nothing more intimidating than an additional line item on your accounting records.

- Be sure to advertise that you accept Virtual Terminal in all your advertising, auction listings, and store pages. You want your customers to know this is an additional level of service you are prepared to offer. For those customers who are reluctant to input credit card information on the Internet, you may just have found the additional boost they need to make the purchase with you. Also, Virtual Terminal is good for first-time buyers who don't yet have a PayPal account or who think they'll only be buying through eBay occasionally.

- You can also use Virtual Terminal to process in-person sales. If you sell at trade shows or other offline venues, you'll be able to accept credit card payments in person for the same low fee you're already paying for your eBay sales.

■ ■ ■

YOUR WEB STORE: MAYBE YOU CAN DO IT YOURSELF

When the time comes for you to venture off eBay for the most part, and pursue your own Web store, perhaps you'll be able to tackle the design and building of that Web site for yourself. If you have designed and created Web sites before, you'll have a head start, and fortunately, plenty of businesses are out there willing to be your partners as you expand. One PowerSeller, Mike Martyka, decided to venture out on the Web for himself after reading an article about ShopPal and the services this company offers to budding Web entrepreneurs. He had already built several Web sites using Front Page and ProStores. He soon launched solidcolorneckties.com, shown in Figure 9.7, to complement his eBay store solidcolorneckties. He said that his startup costs were about $200 and it took him about six months to get his site looking the way he wanted it to look. Because Mike sells about 200 items, his monthly fees to ShopPal for running his site are only $19.95. Fees increase once a seller offers more than 500 items.

Another company, Miva, offers Miva Merchant, which also allows you to set up and operate your own Web site. PowerSeller consultant Deb Levitt notes, Miva offers shopping cart software "that's been around for years." Now the company will also help you set up a Web store. It offers support for everything from importing your inventory to search engine optimization to e-mail outreach for advertising to your customers. The Miva Merchant 5 software module starts at $995. Contact Miva at www.mivacentral.com for more specific pricing information.

While here and in the next few pages we explain the value of moving away from eBay and creating your own Web store, many Internet retailers still maintain some kind of eBay presence. That's because they use eBay to enhance sales on their off-eBay Web stores, and vice versa. You can do the same by making it clear on your Web site that you also sell on eBay. Some surfers who find your site through a Web search and are eBay savvy will go straight to eBay and check your feedback. This way, sellers can take advantage of their good eBay reputation and port it to the rest of cyberspace. This will distinguish your store from the many other stores out there that pop up in a typical Google search. Also, you should probably accept PayPal through your Web store. Shoppers who have PayPal accounts trust that system and can shop your Web site without entering personal information.

. . . .
FIGURE 9.7: solidcolorneckties.com, a ShopPal Web store.

LET'S GET TO WORK...

- Remember that moving off eBay means you will be responsible for marketing your own business. You won't have an automatic stream of potential customers in your neighborhood anymore. So be prepared to add promoting your site to the tasks you have to manage, and be sure you're willing to give it the time and energy required. "My site's up, the world will come to me," Mike Martyka thought when he first launched his Web store. He found this wasn't so and soon realized that he wasn't promoting his site the way he should be.

■ Explore Google AdWords. Although ShopPal offer help in getting your store into search engines, Mike found that his business really took off once he started using Google AdWords. Mike reported in an article for *AuctionBytes* that within a few days of using AdWords, he had more orders coming into his business than he'd had in the previous three months combined.

■ Be sure you are working with a company that can offer you reliable service. According to Mike, ShopPal had almost no downtime at all in the first year he was operating his business with it. He also reports excellent service from the company's support team. These are two important factors to consider if you're thinking of going it on your own.

■ ■ ■

)) CLEARLY DEFINE YOUR PROBLEMS BEFORE SEARCHING FOR A SOLUTION

As an alternative to building your own Web store, you may be tempted to go with one of the more common third-party providers who offer complete solutions for setting up a Web store and helping you operate it. Marketworks and ChannelAdvisor are the two most prominent companies in this field. You will find they both offer a full suite of services from designing the look of your store to handling your checkout procedures to managing your inventory. You will also find that each company has its camp of loyal supporters and more than a few vociferous detractors. There is no such thing as a single service provider that can offer you a turnkey system that will be simple and affordable, no matter what your business requirements are.

Considering those business requirements will be strictly up to you. Both of these companies design their products with the majority of their customers in mind, but the majority of their customers may not have the same needs that you do. "You can't wait until 80 percent of their customers have the same need as you do," notes

Andy Mowery. If, for example, you sell items that ship in oversized boxes, you may not necessarily be able to use their shipping calculator, and they may not be able to accommodate the calculator you currently use. In shopping for a third-party solutions provider, you will constantly be balancing your business needs against the products that provider can offer you. If you don't clearly understand your own challenges and where your operation is headed, you're not ready to work with a provider to design your next venture, especially when that venture is as important as expanding your business to new venues.

LET'S GET TO WORK...

- When you sign on with a third-party provider, you will pay a setup fee plus regular monthly charges. Those monthly charges will vary depending on the number of transactions you handle. Many of the services offered are à la carte. Be sure you're clear about what your monthly fees will buy you, and be sure you've reached a point in your business development when your operation can afford those additional monthly fees.

- On the other hand, those additional fees may very well bring you enough new revenue to make you look back and say that this was the best decision you made in years. Michael Kolman of parrothead88 told us, "We use Marketworks for auction management and to automate feedback. Marketworks has changed eBay as much as PayPal has. It's why sellers can now sell 3,000 items a day." parrothead88 no longer has to spend time answering e-mail and launching auctions. To Michael, it's all about time, and the time he saves makes using Marketworks cost-effective.

- Be sure your solutions provider can help you move from one venue to another. "You need to be able to track where customers are coming from regardless of the channel," says David of blueberryboutique, who uses ChannelAdvisor for his Web store, shown in Figure 9.8. Handling "end-to-end automation across channels and across processes" is a must. Streamlining becomes even more important when you're talking about the same inventory being made available through more than a few sales channels. Consolidated reporting is extremely important, so be sure your provider can give you that.

· ·

FIGURE 9.8: Blueberryboutique.net has been created and managed using ChannelAdvisor as a third-party solutions provider.

■ Use the discussion boards devoted to the provider you're considering both on eBay and on the Web sites for each of the companies. Note what issues other users are currently dealing with, but also watch for the tone of the discussions. You'll quickly see if the people are frustrated or satisfied, and that will help you see what life is like on a day-to-day basis for those who are already using the products.

■ ■ ■

RELIABILITY, FEATURES, AND FINALLY PRICE SHOULD DRIVE YOUR DECISION

Most of us consider price first when we go shopping. We determine how much we can afford to spend, and then we go out searching for a product that will be within our price range. Andy of debnroo advises against this common practice when you're considering third-party solutions providers. "We've been a month away from going out on the Web for the last two years," Andy observes. The problem is that he hasn't found a company that can satisfy all of the requirements of his shipping needs while at the same time providing him with the reliability he needs to entrust his business to it. Andy noted that some of the very small providers he spoke with were able to meet his specific needs, but when it came to reliability, they were just too small to ensure that they could consistently operate without system stoppages.

Beyond reliability, insist on a full set of features. "We all have unique business needs that have unique requirements," remarks Andy. Don't settle for a system that meets some of your needs, but not all of them. Look also for a provider with a proven record of adapting to eBay's changes. eBay so frequently rolls out new features that you simply can't afford to wait months for your solutions provider to catch up. Finally, consider price, which in the long run is the least important part of this triad that also includes reliability and features.

LET'S GET TO WORK...

- Reliability is more important than anything and should come first when evaluating a provider. "If reliability isn't there, the ultimate cost will be so much more than you can save by going with a lower price," says Andy. "The damage to your account will be irrevocable if it's repeated regularly."

- You will find all kinds of companies who will be willing to offer you all types of features. When the sale is up for grabs, promises are easy to make. But insist on reliability demonstrations based on the experiences of others. If they can't provide you with a list of their customers who can verify reliability over a period of time, keep shopping. Here's one shopping experience where you don't want to be the test case.

■ Make pricing negotiations the last thing you work on with any provider, and remember, a price quote is nothing more than a suggestion. "Treat that first price like you were a tourist in a marketplace at a Mexican resort," says Andy. That first price quote should be a place to start. Remember, these companies are selling products. You wouldn't buy a house without attempting to negotiate, so don't take the first price offered without trying to negotiate for a better one.

■ ■ ■

Jody Rogers and Asad Bangash

Just a few years ago, Jody and Asad were both working at car dealerships in Ohio, when they first started playing around with eBay. Jody credits Asad with showing her what great potential was to be found on the site. He offered to sell some spare parts for the owner of the dealership, and

Jody saw right away that here was a new opportunity for earning income. Having just lost her health insurance coverage, the timing was perfect. The couple started the way most eBay sellers do; selling items found at garage sales and thrift stores, but then they found their own particular niche. In asking themselves the question, "What can we bring to eBay that others cannot?" they found the perfect answer.

Asad's family is Pakistani, and his mom was returning to Pakistan for a family wedding. The couple gave her some seed money and asked her to purchase a variety of ethnic products they could test out for sale on eBay. They tried a little bit of everything. First they started to sell salwar kameez (Pakistani ladies' garments). These beautiful outfits were good sellers, but the couple came across some challenges. For one thing, each listing required extensive measurements to ensure that the garment would actually fit the customer properly. Listings were laborious and very time-consuming. Next was an issue of quality. Jody had decided very early in her eBay career that she only wanted to sell high-quality products. Showing quality of fabric and craftsmanship proved to be difficult on eBay, and she found herself competing with other sellers who were selling poor-quality items for much lower prices.

Eventually, Jody and Asad decided on a series of products that features handmade khussa shoes, glass bangles, and henna tattoo products, among other accessories. To find a supplier of shoes, Jody and Asad actually identified and developed a working relationship with an individual shoemaker in Pakistan who works with the couple via the phone, e-mail, fax, and live chat to design each pattern of shoes. Only a couple dozen pairs of each style are ever produced to keep the look fresh and exclusive. With each pair of shoes, Jody sends along instructions for properly "breaking in" the shoes to ensure a comfortable fit.

When they started just a few years ago, Jody claims she knew little about online commerce. Now she can hold her own in any conversation about search engine optimization, third-party solutions providers, and maximizing your eBay presence. She is extraordinarily successful at creating a captivating look and feel for her business. As you can see by looking back at Figure 9.2, Jody and Asad's eBay store has a distinctive look. The couple chose Marketworks to integrate their eBay business with their Web store shown in Figure 9.9. It complements the look of the Beachcombers Bazaar eBay store, and the look of the beachcombers! eBay auctions too. Customers have no doubt when they visit these three sites that they are shopping with an e-commerce business, and not just someone who has some listings on eBay.

FIGURE 9.9: Jody and Asad's Web store, shopbeach-combers.com, complements the look of their eBay store and all their listings.

One thing Jody and Asad didn't have to learn through e-commerce, was customer service. From the beginning the couple has offered a no-risk, money back guarantee. They even offer to cover shipping in both directions. They also know how to be great neighbors. They are very active on the eBay boards and are more than willing to help educate and inform less savvy eBay sellers. When eBay suddenly changed the logo for identifying sellers' stores from a tag to a door, Jody and Asad began a marketing campaign to help educate users about the change. The Doors2Stores program became so successful that as of this writing, more than 300 eBay members participate with over 33,000 listings that show up together in title and description store searches.

CHAPTER 10

An eBay Professional Beyond the Borders

As we start this final chapter of the book, we hope you've come to see yourself as a professional eBay seller. As you've worked your way through the chapters, you've gained a lot of great advice about everything from finding your product sources, to creating your listings, to developing and promoting your own business brand on eBay and the Internet at large. You have a great start on your life as a professional e-commerce seller, not just a person who sells stuff on eBay. Now that you're thinking of yourself in this light, let's look at how you can take that new you and make the most of your experience and knowledge. It's time to take your e-commerce experience and expertise out of the realm of eBay and even a Web store. It's time to venture beyond those borders.

If your mom is anything like ours, you heard many times over, "Don't put all your eggs in one basket." We also heard, "Stop that before you poke someone's eye out," but that's not terribly relevant to the discussion we're having here. Not putting all your business eggs in one basket isn't just a cliché—it's a strategy PowerSellers feel is essential. "The day we started selling on eBay," remembers Drew of whitemountaintrading, "I was nervous that all of our products were sold only on eBay. From the first sale I made, I started building my own customer database. I never planned for eBay to be 100 percent of my business." That was more than seven years ago, but Drew thought from the very beginning of building a business that would span several platforms, leaving him less vulnerable to the vagaries of any one venue and maximizing his products' exposure to as many potential customers as possible. We'll share with you some ways to start branching your business out away from 100 percent dependency on eBay and your Web store alone. That will include looking around for other places online to sell and also looking for retail opportunities in the real world, too.

But it isn't just looking around for the next great marketplace that can lead you to a successful and multifaceted e-commerce business. There are other ways for you to turn your eBay life into a profit center. By the time you have a thriving eBay business, you will have learned a great deal about eBay, online auction sites, and e-commerce in general. This information and knowledge will have become a commodity valuable enough for you to profit from. You'll find yourself among an educated minority. Sure, just about everyone knows about eBay. But there are still millions of people who have items they'd like to sell and no confidence in their own ability to sell them on eBay. Some may be happy to pay you to do that for them. You'll also find lots of people who already buy on eBay and would like to sell also, but feel they need some help making that leap. Still others may be selling pretty successfully, but need an expert's input to take their businesses from hobby to livelihood. (Of course, we know a couple of great books that might help with that!) For all of these groups of people, you can provide services—services that people will be very willing to pay you for.

As we move through this chapter, we'll take a look at other online destinations for you to set up shop. We'll look at whether you'll want to consider a brick-and-mortar operation to go along with your e-commerce business. We'll look at how you can market your skill, knowledge, and expertise to those who are less experienced. Not everyone will feel comfortable pursuing all of the things we'll look at here. For example, some of the online destinations will be more relevant for one type of product than for another. Some people will never be comfortable teaching others about eBay. And some sellers may just decide their products and operations are serving them just fine, and they're best off devoting their efforts to good ol' eBay. Whatever you decide to do with your e-commerce business, we want you to leave this book feeling that we've outlined all of your possibilities and helped you define their potential for your business.

» EXPLORE FREE SITES: YOU HAVE NOTHING TO LOSE

No other online destination will offer you the target audience you'll find on eBay. Where else will you find a potential market of 200 million shoppers? But on the other hand, other sites do have their own value, and you'll want to explore other options as you spread your e-commerce wings. With that in mind, why not consider working with a few sites that don't charge you anything to list your items? When the listings are free, you can feel pretty good about exploring the world beyond eBay. You'll see soon enough whether free listings are paying off for you.

In Chapter 9, we told you about Google Base. That's just one example of a destination to promote your business online for free (and now, as the payment processing functionality is rolled out, actually sell products too). We'll show you some other sites that will allow you to complete transactions as well as advertise products. We feel obligated to add one caveat in our discussion about moving off of eBay. Do it with a very clear eye on what it's costing your business, not so much in money as in attention and energy. Remember, your first obligation is to the core eBay business you're building. Anything that supports and augments that is good. Anything that keeps you from success on eBay should be reexamined and perhaps jettisoned!

LET'S GET TO WORK...

■ First among the free online sites is Yahoo Auctions. In its favor, Yahoo! has a proven brand name and a huge user base. More than 400 million unique users worldwide visit Yahoo! monthly. On Yahoo Auctions, a part of Yahoo Shopping, you will find tens of thousands of listings already there, so it is a viable marketplace. Recently, listings on Yahoo Auctions became totally free. There are no charges or fees for any of the services available to sellers. PowerSeller David Yaskulka supports Yahoo! for the simple fact that it costs nothing to list and sell there. But the site also includes paid ads on every page. The page your listing is on will come complete with a list of ads from Yahoo!'s sponsored searches. These ads, in our opinion, reduce the quality of the browsing experience for buyers. See for yourself in Figure 10.1. (Interestingly, as we write this, eBay and Yahoo! have announced a comarketing relationship, so those Yahoo! ads may very well be on eBay pages too. You may want to keep an eye out for how they affect the eBay shopping experience.)

■ You probably know that Froogle is one of the best sites for comparison shopping. There's a link to it right from Google's homepage, so you can't beat it for exposure. It's not a site where transactions take place, but eBay will send Froogle your eBay store listings, and Froogle will post them for free. (Froogle does not accept individual eBay auction listings, just store listings.) While eBay sends Froogle a product "feed" for its stores that have Buy It Now items, you do have to make a file of your listings available to be downloaded. Store owners should go to http://pages.ebay.com/help/sell/contextual/export-listings.html for more information. If you have your own store outside of eBay, you'll need to send Froogle a product feed yourself. Click on the Information for Merchants link at the bottom of the main Froogle page to get started. For now, we think you should list on both Google Base and Froogle. It remains to be seen what becomes of Froogle as Google Base continues to roll out the ability to accept payments, but listing here is free and easy, so why not take advantage of it?

FIGURE 10.1: A typical Yahoo Auctions listing includes a series of ads from Yahoo!'s sponsored search feature.

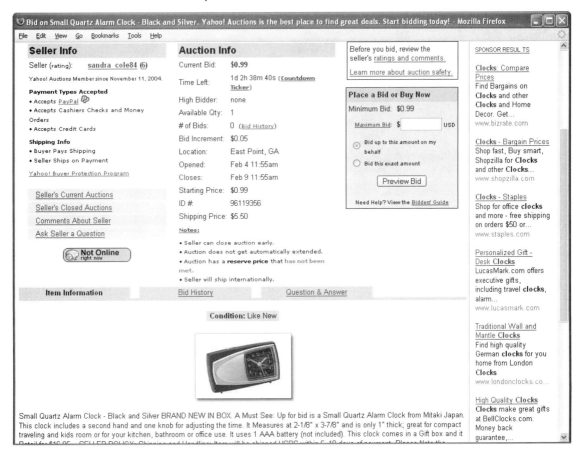

- Ioffer.com claims it's not an auction site, "It's better!" According to *AuctionBytes* it's very popular, and the online newsletter has given it a positive review. It costs nothing to list your items there, but there are final value fees when you make a sale. You can list on a fixed-price or best-offer basis. It's reminiscent of eBay in that you can establish a store, and the site includes discussion areas. One of the best things about Ioffer.com is the Mr. Grabber tool. This will allow you to "bring over" to Ioffer.com, your eBay feedback rating, your listings, and any listings you may have on Yahoo!, Bidville, Overstock, and Sell.com. Visit Ioffer.com, shown in Figure 10.2, for more complete information and current final value fees.

FIGURE 10.2: Ioffer.com charges nothing for you to list your items. You can export your eBay listings and feedback rating to the site.

» EXPLORE EBAY'S TOP COMPETITORS

We'd like to be able to tell you that PowerSellers are flocking to eBay's main competitors, Amazon and Overstock and finding overwhelming success. Many of the PowerSellers we spoke with were enthusiastic about the potential of these other venues. Many of them have also scaled back some of that enthusiasm in the face of reality. But most sellers acknowledge that they simply must look for venues outside of eBay. "Rising fees have forced me to focus on selling smarter," says Bob Sachs, "to keep costs in line, and to begin selling on other sites as well, if only to keep up with my competitors." So, despite your loyalty to eBay, and we share that loyalty, you simply must evaluate your alternatives.

These sites provide opportunities that will only improve with time. As it is, they are excellent destinations for the right product line. For example, you'd think that for independent merchants, selling books on Amazon would be like trying to sell snow at the North Pole, but we've found it's actually a better venue for used books than eBay is. It could just be the critical mass of book buyers who come to shop on Amazon, but we've found success there selling titles that simply did not move on eBay. Based on our discussions with other sellers, our experience is not unique. So, once again, the importance of understanding your product line and your customer base is reinforced.

LET'S GET TO WORK...

■ Know what Amazon sells before you decide what to list. Unless you are willing to compete on price (and if you're selling used items you can do that, since Amazon itself is not in that market), it's best if you're not going head to head against Amazon. So before you list your new items on the site, make sure it doesn't already carry your product. Drew Friedman of whitemountaintrading had excellent success with a toolbox he sells on eBay. He listed it on Amazon and found it didn't move at all. Research turned up the fact that Amazon is a direct customer to the manufacturer who makes the toolbox. It's just not possible for Drew to undersell them on this item, so he no longer even tries. Now his Amazon listings include only items that don't compete directly with the online giant.

■ If at first you don't succeed, don't give up either. The online market is expanding and evolving at rocket speed. If you find that you try other major venues and don't get the results you were hoping for, don't give up too easily and retreat. Consider Overstock, for example. It's obvious that Overstock feels it is in this business for the long haul, as it works hard to advertise and promote its site to drive buyers to it. When we checked, Overstock had 200,000 auctions listed and approximately 800,000 buyers and sellers. If you don't find the critical mass you'd like there now, try it again in another six months. The entire landscape may be different by then.

■ ■ ■

❯❯ TAKE YOUR NICHE AND LOOK BEYOND EBAY

If you've settled on a niche market, you are likely to be able to find Internet auction sites devoted to your product area. These can be small and specific, but they're also likely to attract other people who genuinely share your interest. You can use these outlets to sell, but you can also use them to buy. You may find these can be a source of product for you to turn around and sell to the larger eBay market. Or you can consider these sites an excellent source for market research. Once you enter a community of devotees, it's likely you can see what's hot and what's selling to this niche market.

As just one example, Heritage Auctions is an online auction house that sells both online and off. Among other items, it specializes in comic books. You will find the site (at http://www.heritage-galleries.com/) includes a database of every comic ever sold through a Heritage auction. If you have a comic to sell, you can trace its value over time by studying the selling price of comparable comics going back for years. There are no fees for accessing this database.

LET'S GET TO WORK...

■ For handmade crafts and art objects, try Etsy.com. Shown in Figure 10.3, Etsy is an innovative venue for all things handmade. You can create your own Etsy store. You'll pay just $.10 for each listing and a commission on sold items of 3.5 percent. Your customers can even pay you through PayPal. You certainly won't find the traffic on Etsy that you will on eBay, but you'll find a fun shopping experience and a targeted audience. You can actually shop by color on the site, and it's lots of fun to play around, just to see what you can find. Plus, you'll know that the shoppers are all interested in handcrafted items, otherwise they would never have found the site in the first place!

FIGURE 10.3: The Etsy home page is your entry point to a unique and fun shopping experience.

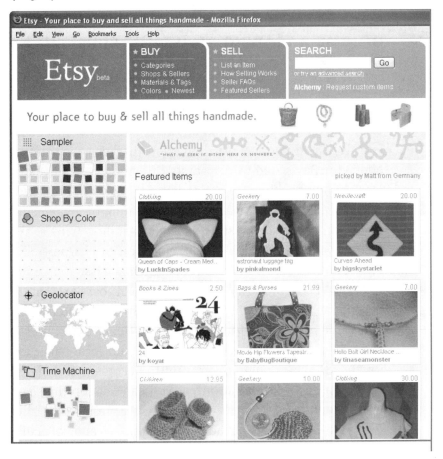

- If you really know your market, you can use these small sites to find product you can resell on eBay. Because they attract a much smaller audience, bargains do come up. We bought a Golden Age comic through a Heritage auction that we later sold on eBay for a considerable profit. There were just more people willing to compete for it on eBay, and that was certainly good news for us.

- Targeting your audience through these small niche sites can help you even when you can't actually sell on the niche site you find. For example, UFLIPIT.com is for college students only. You won't be able to buy or sell there, unless you're starting your eBay career before you graduate, as some PowerSellers actually have. Remember Adam Hersh? But if you sell products that appeal to this audience, you can certainly browse around and see how your target market is selling your product to each other. That's bound you help you make your listings more competitive.

■ ■ ■

BECOME A TRADING ASSISTANT? SURE, BUT NOT LIKE YOU'D THINK

Becoming a trading assistant is one way for you to branch out and add a revenue stream to your business. It's not hard to qualify for eBay's trading assistant program, and once you do, you'll find eBay is a dedicated partner in helping you market your services. To be added to eBay's Trading Assistants Directory, you must have sold at least 10 items within the previous three months. You have to have a feedback score of at least 100 with a rating of 97 percent positive feedbacks, and you must be in good standing with eBay, having paid all your eBay bills. That's it. Now you can harness all the tools eBay offers to help you with your new business. You can list yourself within the Directory by your physical location, and then add descriptors that highlight your services, specialty interests, and fees. You can download and use eBay promotional flyers, and there are some press materials you can submit to your local paper for publicity, too. So why wouldn't you want to become a trading assistant?

You probably will, but only if you can take on the sales of others without taking away from the core business you're already trying to build. If you are already selling antiques and collectibles, then sure, why not take on other peoples' antiques and collectibles? If, however, you're trying to build your business with new, commodity items, taking on the castoffs of others may detract from the business plan you've devised. Every time you sign on to sell something for someone else, you've taken it upon yourself to learn enough about the item to know how to feature it and market it effectively on eBay. That means research, research, and more research. You may have to do some research before you even sign an agreement, because you'll have to determine if the item is valuable enough for you to accept for consignment. If not, you'll be doing all the work necessary to create a single auction for an item you're not familiar with for a very modest return. You can't sustain a solid business flow when you are not being adequately compensated for your time. Plus, it doesn't do your business reputation any good if you take on consignments and end up disappointing your consignee. That kind of word spreads fast. So how should you consider becoming a trading assistant? Glad you asked.

▮ LET'S GET TO WORK...

- ▩ Specialize. PowerSellers Bob Buchanan and Greg Scheuer of avforsale became eBay sellers in order to sell off the inventory of an audiovisual rental/production business where both men worked. In the late 1990s the company moved from Georgia to California, and both men lost their jobs. Their final task was to liquidate a warehouse full of inventory that no one seemed to want. Both men had played around on eBay, but neither had any experience with the site. What they did have was expertise. They'd been in the industry for more than 20 years, and they knew the equipment and the people who used it. So they did very well for their former employer by selling the inventory on eBay. Now they have 130 different industry suppliers, 15 employees, and a thriving business. So if you have some special area of expertise, by all means market yourself to that industry.

- ▩ Go after the whales, not the guppies. If you're going to sign on to sell items for others, why not shoot for the businesses in your area rather than the people who are cleaning out Grandma's attic? Offer your services to the commercial players. Take on their end-of-season items or their returns. That way, you are still likely to be able to list multiple auctions for the same item, writing the listing once and selling it more than once. PowerSeller Paul Fletcher of dealtree and his business partner Gary Heath started their eBay business after being laid off from Buy.com in 2001. They specialized in big box returns. Today they operate two warehouses, employ dozens of people, and have developed their own proprietary auction management software. "Most of our inventory comes from large manufacturers, retailers, and dealers," Paul told us. "We're looking for large volume."

■ Still other PowerSellers offer their expertise to liquidate entire estates. Lynne Baron of Baronart deals in fine pieces of artwork. She works to liquidate the holdings of wealthy art collectors. Likewise, generalent's Harvey Levine and Marcia Cooper sell the contents of peoples' homes. Some of the items they sell on eBay, but they've also developed other outlets for the ones they know won't do well in online auctions.

■　■　■

ADD SOMETHING ELSE IF YOU WANT AN INDEPENDENT DROP-OFF STORE

Some of the PowerSellers who worked with us operated their own drop-off stores. We also spoke with those who'd purchased franchise operations (see Chapter 1 for more), but it's the independent owners who brought an interesting and new perspective to the drop-off store phenomenon. The sellers who took this step already had thriving eBay businesses. They didn't build their presence on eBay by operating a drop-off store; they took their eBay businesses and moved them into the bricks-and-mortar world. In each case, the drop-off part of their business was a new revenue stream, not the means of supporting their entire enterprise.

PowerSeller Drew Friedman was in the process of opening a drop-off location at the time of this writing, but he'd taken an interesting approach to the new enterprise. He had just finished negotiating a contract with the U.S. Postal Service to provide limited supplies and services to postal customers at his retail location. Drew will be authorized to sell stamps and provide metered postal services. Several times a day, a U.S. Postal Service truck will pick up the items he posts, and his eBay packages too. The U.S. Postal Service will provide all of the signage and promotional materials. It also provides all necessary materials and equipment, and it will pay for any work necessary to get the operation up and running. The postal part of Drew's store will require 100 to 200 square feet, and Drew has rented a 1,000-square-foot location. That leaves the remaining 700 to 800 square feet for Drew's own operation. His customers will purchase their postal services at the same price they'd pay at the post office, and Drew earns a commission for every sale he makes.

To further maximize his services to his customers, Drew will offer shipping supplies and provide shipping services for those who need help packaging items. He is considering setting up a copy center for those customers who need a quick photocopy of something before they mail it. He will stock his store with some of the same items he sells on eBay, and he will also accept consignments for others. With his retail store in place, Drew hopes to be able to expand his product line and sell more actively on Amazon as well as eBay. He's found that some suppliers won't work with him because he doesn't have a retail store. Now that he has a thriving eBay business, he can support the store he needs to branch out his inventory to be ever more successful on Amazon and in the e-commerce world in general. "My goal isn't to expand my eBay business; it's to expand my family's business," explained Drew.

LET'S GET TO WORK...

- Consider an independent drop-off store rather than a franchise. "We want our drop-off store to be gravy for our business," explains Drew. "If I went with a franchise, I'd have to depend on that part of my business." The overhead built into a franchise makes it challenging to earn enough money with consignments to support the overhead.

- Couple your drop-off store with other services and supplies you can offer. Drew's route to a drop-off store was through the U.S. Postal Service. Although it currently has about 5,500 independent postal units in operation, not everyone will be able to take this route to a brick-and-mortar business, but you may have other things you can offer to potential customers. If you have consulting skills, programming skills, or Web design experience, you may be able to put together enough different revenue streams to support the overhead of a retail location.

- Consider the numbers. "The figures for the holiday season for 2005 indicate that 5 percent of shoppers purchased items online," notes Drew. "But that means that 95 percent of shoppers didn't. I want to find a way to reach that population too." Drew further reminded us that although he's enjoyed building his eBay business, it was never his intention to have *only* an eBay business. We suspect his mom also mentioned the "all your eggs in one basket" thing!

- Your drop-off store may help create balance in your life. Although those sellers who operate drop-off stores work long hours, they also report that it's gratifying to be able to close the door and physically end their workdays. The temptation to "take care of one more detail" can be overwhelming to an eBay entrepreneur, especially one who works from home. It can be a challenge to make oneself stop when that next e-mail could result in a good sale. Having a drop-off store with a lock on the door and a regular closing time can help you stop, if you sometimes find you can't quite stop yourself.

■ ■ ■

RECOGNIZE THAT EBAY MAY BE WRONG FOR YOUR SALE

Okay, we all love eBay. And we know it's true that everything eventually turns up on eBay, from the wacky to the commonplace, to the rare. RVs, cars, real estate, fine jewelry, you name it, and someone has probably tried to sell it on eBay. But to succeed and, especially to do right by clients who may trust you to do your best for them, it's important for you to be able to recognize when you need to find another marketplace beyond eBay. This may not be terribly important to you if you structure your whole business around brand-new, commodity items. But, if you decide to add being a trading assistant to your résumé, or if you plan to open a drop-off store, or if you handle antiques and/or collectibles, you have to be able to offer your customers and yourself the best place to sell what you find, and that's simply *not* always eBay.

Lynne Baron of baronart came to eBay more than seven years ago to sell fine paintings. At the time, she remembers that critics were skeptical that she could sell valuable paintings on the site. But she built a thriving business as an art dealer on eBay and now uses other outlets for much of her business. "I have put a cap on eBay sales of individual works," she told us. "We try to limit them to $3,000." Lynne noted that paintings selling for more than that require listing fees that just make eBay too expensive to be her best sales outlet. For the more expensive works, and some of them bring $50,000 and more, she sells them on her own Web site, through her extensive file of past customers, or at offline auctions and galleries.

▮ LET'S GET TO WORK...

▣ You probably never thought you'd see eBay and Sotheby's in the same sentence, but PowerSellers told us that they turn to the famous auctioneers when they come across the right item. "We do sell through private auction galleries like Sotheby's," said Harvey Levine and Marcia Cooper. "We get some things from clients that we know won't do well on eBay, so we use the auction galleries when they're having special sales." If you live near New York or London, you can arrange to go into Sotheby's for a valuation of your items. But if that's not practical, don't despair. Sotheby's has made it possible for you to work with them through the mail. You'll find complete information on the Sotheby's Web site shown in Figure 10.4.

▣ To get a feel for the world of live auctions, visit eBay's Live Auctions at liveauctions.ebay.com, shown in Figure 10.5. Here you can actually watch auctions as they happen in some of the world's most prominent auction houses. You can see what types of items are brought there to be sold and how much those items are selling for. Watching some of these items will help you develop a sense of what is better sold through venues other than eBay. Keep track of what auctions are coming up and browse the catalogs to educate yourself about the categories of items handled. These include jewelry, antiques, real estate, and fine art, just to name a few.

• •

FIGURE 10.4: Famous auction gallery Sotheby's has a Web site to help you work with its auctioneers and valuation experts even if you can't visit the offices in person.

■ Don't forget to keep good records of your own customer base. Every sale you make gives you the potential for another sale. If you've completed a successful sale in an area of jewelry, collectibles, or antiques, for example, you have a customer who may just want more of what you find.

FIGURE 10.5: Visit eBay's Live Auction area to learn who the movers and shakers are in the rarefied world of great auction houses.

BOOST YOUR BUSINESS BY EDUCATING OTHERS

We can say from personal experience that the world at large is hungry for information about how to take the eBay hobby and turn it into a thriving business. We regularly offer free seminars on the subject of building your eBay business through public library systems. We have never given a seminar that didn't have a standing-room-only crowd. Our local library had to offer the seminar twice, and both times the event drew the largest audience on record for an adult program. Sure, we were offering the seminar for free, but the fact that we can consistently attract that many people to come out to the library on cold winter nights speaks to the demand for information about eBay.

Not everyone is comfortable in the role of teacher or public speaker. We are certain that teaching requires a skill set and abilities that not everyone has, but if you do have those, you can supplement your eBay income tremendously by becoming a certified eBay educator. In fact, some of the educators are so busy, with classes to teach nearly every day, it's a wonder they are able to maintain their PowerSeller status. Yet they do. They realize that this real-world experience is what makes them invaluable as instructors.

eBay has a thriving and comprehensive program for those people who would like to become certified as eBay educators. (Figure 10.6 shows the eBay Education Specialist Program site at http://pages.ebay.com/esp/.)

To become an eBay educator, you need to complete the $149 curriculum for the beginner's course, "The Basics of Selling on eBay." The course materials include an instruction manual, a student's manual, and the eBay University CD. Complete your course and eBay will send you a certificate and the official "Education Specialist" logo. You will then be eligible to access your individual Instructor Site, where you'll find classroom materials and professionally designed templates for business cards, ads, and flyers, which should really help you launch your new venture.

LET'S GET TO WORK...

- Use your entry in the Education Specialist Directory to market yourself on eBay. Your directory write-up allows you to toot your own horn and promote your own particular areas of expertise. Aside from giving you a space to provide your own biography, your students get to rate your performance. Do a good job, and you will receive a five-star review, which means that 90 to 100 percent of the feedback from your students is positive.

- Use the directory to assess how competitive the field is for education specialists in your area. You can search the directory by state, telephone area code, and Zip Code. If you have a lot of competition, consider how many local and community colleges are available to you. This is often where these courses are held.

· ·

FIGURE 10.6: The eBay Education Specialist site covers everything you need to know to become a certified eBay educator.

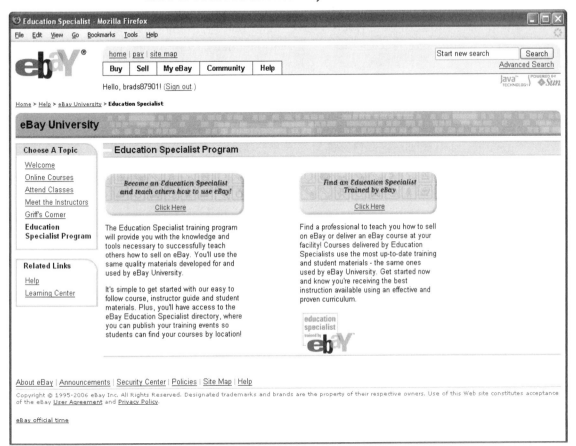

Your students may also become your customers. Some of those students are going to be so interested in eBay that they'll hire you on a private basis as a consultant to help them grow their businesses. Others may decide that they aren't going to pursue a professional life on eBay, and then you can offer them your services as a trading assistant.

■ ■ ■

Here, eBay PowerSeller, trading assistant, and education specialist, stephintexas provides advice to those considering branching out from their eBay businesses.

The majority of my annual income is generated by my eBay training on the private and collegiate levels. I have found that my trading assistant and consulting referrals have increased, exponentially, from former students and clients. The two revenue streams are a natural fit for me, and I rarely have time to sell my own items any more, which is great, because I'm not spending lots of time trying to source product.

It goes without saying that additional eBay services translate into additional revenue streams, and that's always a good thing. It really helps to become certified as an eBay education specialist; however, there are so many instructors now, that one must be very diligent and creative in marketing his or her classes.

A seasoned seller can easily become a trading assistant, and eBay has many wonderful marketing tools to help build a successful business. Trading assistants need to specialize in certain items and stick to what they know to be successful. It is critical to stay abreast of the current marketplace and educate yourself as to what the competition is doing. This research needs to be done on a regular basis, and a Web site is always helpful, and the About Me page is a great way to advertise your services.

GET PAID FOR CONSULTING WITH OTHERS WHO WANT TO DO WHAT YOU HAVE DONE

Once you've created a thriving eBay business, you'll be in the position to help other people who want to do the same. Of course, part of your success will have been built on the help and support you receive and give to the eBay community at large. We're counting on you to be valuable contributors to the boards and groups that reside on eBay, giving back to the community that sustained you as you grew. But, beyond that community, you'll find others who want the life and business you've created and will be willing to pay you for your services in helping them to get it. eBay PowerSellers get noticed, both on the site and off, and that leads to phone calls from people asking them for help. "We don't do any marketing, and my clients tend to either be found through online inquiries, eBay, or the media," said PowerSeller and consultant, Andy of debnroo.

So clients will find you through your own success, but you can also carve out a niche for yourself by offering your services in specific areas. David Yaskulka of blueberryboutique also operates Blueberry Consulting. As you saw in Chapter 1, David is a big proponent of strategic philanthropy. He has created a consultancy to help others find ways to use their eBay expertise to raise money for good causes and improve their own profitability at the same time. As we write this, David is working with his largest client, MissionFish, to grow the use of cause marketing on eBay. MissionFish has allowed small- and medium-sized businesses on eBay to attract the attention of large charitable groups like the Red Cross, the Nature Conservancy, and the Make a Wish Foundation. The MissionFish partnership allows the smaller businesses to compete with large corporations for recognition from these well-established charities, adding name recognition and credibility to their brand names.

LET'S GET TO WORK...

- Strategic philanthropy isn't the only way David has used his consulting skills. He also consults with less experienced sellers about launching an eBay business, developing listing templates, and using automation tools. He also offers services in other related areas such as staff training and brand development.

- Look for what you can specifically offer to your clients. David was a natural consultant for combining charitable giving with successful eBay selling. He'd been a strong advocate for cause marketing and philanthropy before he became a successful eBay seller, so that was a great blend for him. You may have more experience in the creative parts of the task, or you may have background in human resources, or systems design, or product sourcing. Every successful seller on eBay had a pre-eBay life.

What did you bring to the market that you can turn into a new revenue stream?

■ Because you'll become an expert in your area of eBay, you can provide your consulting services to your customers as well as to other would-be sellers. Bob Buchanan and Greg Scheuer of avforsale provide consultancy for both their buying customers and their consignment customers. In their industry, products become obsolete very quickly, "The resale pricing curve for our products is a pretty straight line down," explained Bob. "It only holds value until the latest version from the manufacturer, and then it drops. Six months can make a big difference." Because these two know their products, industry, and customers so well, they can approach them with news of pending changes and help them see when the time is right for them to sell their items at the highest price possible. This saves their customers from ruinous losses on obsolete products and provides a great service for the buyer who doesn't need the latest manufacturers' offering. A consultancy, in this case, was born into the structure of the business these two built.

■ ■ ■

Debbie and David Yaskulka

Meet a PowerSeller

Debbie and David Yaskulka have achieved a remarkable spot on eBay. They attained Platinum PowerSeller status and are the number one category leader in the area of men's shirts and ties. Blueberry Boutique also sells sunglasses, suits, belts, and underwear. They carry designer names including Armani, Burberry, Gucci, Piattelli, Versace, and Zegna. All of these items are offered on eBay at 40 to 80 percent discounts. Although Debbie and David enjoy remarkable success, what's truly astounding about this couple is that they've reached this success in fewer than four years of operating their business!

As so many eBay sellers will tell you, they started on eBay more or less as an experiment. Debbie had been dabbling on the site for about a year, when she began thinking about a part-time job that would allow her to spend more time with the couple's young children. They bought a digital camera that had a 30-day warranty, figuring if they didn't like what happened in the next 30 days, they could recoup their $200 investment. To start with, they sold things from their closets, which gave them an eclectic inventory that included Mary Kay cosmetics, outgrown clothing, and whatever else they didn't want. When their closets were cleaned, they were fortunate to find a wholesale lot of luxury neckwear right on eBay. At the time, that was a great category for growth. Although Blueberry Boutique still occupies the number one spot, it now has more than 4,000 competitors!

Today the Yaskulkas both work for the business. They employ six part-time workers and are among the most well-respected and beloved members of the Professional eBay Sellers Alliance (PESA). David has served as the marketing chair for the organization. Of course, marketing and volunteering have been David's passion far longer than eBay has. Before coming to eBay, he worked in marketing for both nonprofit and for-profit companies. David calls himself a cause-marketing and philanthropic advocate (see Chapter 1 for more information). Not only does contributing a portion of your proceeds to a worthy cause make you a better citizen of the planet, but sales figures support that it also increases your profits, too. It's a way to help you "do well" while you also "do good"!

When you gather with a group of PESA members, it doesn't take long for David's name to come up in conversation. It's usually followed by one of several statements. "I don't know how he gets it all done!" "I don't know what we'd do without him." These are just a couple we heard at a recent PESA summit. But David and Debbie are driven by a passion for marketing, for philanthropy, and for great customer service. That's why they can proudly claim some of the best repeat business numbers in their category. Their customer service statement reads: "We absolutely guarantee your satisfaction! We are committed to taking care of you if you are not pleased for any reason." We get the feeling, through their exceptional business practices and their dedication to charitable giving that Debbie and David are helping to take care of us all.

APPENDIX A

eBay's Top Sellers Ranked by Feedback Numbers

W e've come full circle. In Chapter 1 we mentioned the Nortica 500 list, a monthly compilation of eBay's top sellers as ranked by their overall feedback numbers. We are providing that list here so you can see for yourself who eBay's most successful sellers are and research how they operate their eBay businesses. The current month's list is available on the Internet at www.nortica.com/user-area/ebay500_34.asp.

If you access the list online, you can take advantage of the hyperlinked user IDs. Click on an ID, and you're taken to a new page where you'll see that seller's ranking over the last couple of years. If you click on the user ID from that new page, you'll go to the seller's eBay Member Profile page. From there you can review their feedback comments and go quickly to their current auctions.

RANK	ID	FEEDBACK	YEAR STARTED	RANK	ID	FEEDBACK	YEAR STARTED
1	everydaysource	314614	2000	20	foto-walser	147148	2000
2	eforcity	283084	2000	21	bargaincell	145166	2001
3	accstation	272560	2001	22	the_sharper_image	143095	1999
4	jayandmarie	268988	1999	23	greatdeals00	141045	2000
5	glacierbaydvd	268192	1999	24	ebestdeal4u	140375	2001
6	itrimming	266014	2000	25	alibris	139621	1998
7	mancon2	234868	2001	26	copro-online	139084	2001
8	moviemarz	230278	2004	27	totalcampus.com	137894	1998
9	justdeals.com	210016	1997	28	papier11	137643	1999
10	mr.mobile	191802	1999	29	patan01	136583	1999
11	skshop	187120	1999	30	okluge_de	136209	2001
12	buyessex	183057	2000	31	soundcitybeaches	135632	2001
13	casacaiman	179839	2002	32	foto-kontor	129604	2002
14	onando	179598	2001	33	dynamic-auction	128425	2001
15	grapevinehill	177608	1999	34	greatbuybooks	127665	2004
16	memoryworld1	174182	1999	35	restaurant.com	127660	2001
17	abebooks-half	166977	2001	36	bargainland-liquidation	124891	1999
18	daniks-world	160736	2000	37	airbrushtower_de	124073	1999
19	pugster888	148456	2002	38	cametaauctions	122320	2001

Nortica eBay 500 (as of February 2006)
(Copyright © 2006 Novato Technology. All rights reserved.)

RANK	ID	FEEDBACK	YEAR STARTED	RANK	ID	FEEDBACK	YEAR STARTED
39	olly_trading!	121446	2002	72	www.1aautomotive.com	93383	1999
40	hoots-loot	121141	1998	73	cofystoreuk	90962	2003
41	gothamcityonline	121016	1999	74	partyman1	90484	1998
42	mombocom	120804	2003	75	solfire2	89711	2001
43	save-it-smart_de	120284	2000	76	rikkyboy69	89552	2001
44	play_it	119896	2001	77	extras4nz	89323	2003
45	symmic	119185	1999	78	cellow-online	88935	2000
46	megabuys.com	118990	1998	79	jewelryauctioneer	88878	1999
47	egameuniverse	118546	1999	80	designerathletic	88491	2003
48	xcceries	118124	2001	81	elephantbooks-half	87622	2000
49	sell2all	115148	1999	82	handy-foto-pc-de	87213	1999
50	celiko-store	115013	2001	83	fantastic_shopping	86852	2002
51	adamhersh	113953	1998	84	inflatablemadness	86752	2002
52	allshewants	113893	1999	85	jayhawkks	85798	1998
53	procarparts.com	113443	2001	86	inno-online	85144	1999
54	bargaindepot04	110228	2002	87	bookcloseouts	84666	2000
55	rockbottomgolf	109877	1998	88	47st.photo	84517	2000
56	findingking	109788	2001	89	fairpricemedien	84305	2003
57	addtronic	109422	2002	90	pcpartusa	83943	2001
58	kmak333	104761	1999	91	bargainbuyers621	83896	2000
59	*123trading*	102719	2004	92	www.csl-computer.com	83805	1999
60	emilyandlily	102498	2003	93	booksxpress	83054	2000
61	buddentown	100160	2002	94	brentscard	82845	1998
62	playdeluxe_de	99748	2003	95	maxstore_de	82195	2001
63	crazyprices-half	98782	2001	96	lhobo	81663	1998
64	gowingstore	97169	2004	97	ryanmcc	81656	1998
65	digitalwebtronics	97069	2004	98	iss-shop	81599	2001
66	edmwholesalers	96799	2003	99	w.o.m	81000	2001
67	toysbabyfacemarkt	96637	2003	100	kfzteile24-de	80833	2001
68	yescomusa	96372	2002	101	inetdvd	80737	1999
69	customerone	95692	1999	102	goldngems1	80600	1999
70	videoplanet	95286	2000	103	indoo_half	80045	2001
71	swedemom	95147	1999	104	pda-heaven	79596	2003

■ Nortica eBay 500 (as of February 2006) (continued)

RANK	ID	FEEDBACK	YEAR STARTED	RANK	ID	FEEDBACK	YEAR STARTED
105	auctionbrokersaustralia	79118	2000	138	herko_de	70260	1999
106	phoenixtradingcompany	78290	2001	139	der-grosshaendler	70071	2001
107	techmedia-shop	78242	1999	140	ctideals	70049	2001
108	weisse-villa	78034	2003	141	player004	70041	2000
109	1busyman	78009	1998	142	cali-tel	69793	2002
110	hpcb-online	77073	1999	143	cofan222	69519	1998
111	moviemagicusa	76900	1999	144	www.adko.de	69407	1999
112	potis-half	76857	2002	145	retrofacts	69206	2001
113	yang32096	76843	2001	146	venize.de	68997	2000
114	bargains4less	76538	1999	147	www.cmttrading.com	68569	1998
115	shoebacca	76451	1999	148	multistore2002	67940	2002
116	williamady	76014	2002	149	www.5stardeal.com	67329	2001
117	no1-store	75552	2003	150	a1_books	67225	2004
118	jewelrybyezra	75308	2000	151	ediscountbike.com	67192	1999
119	muzic-hall	75020	2003	152	www_boardbroker_de	67066	1999
120	sim-buy	74964	2002	153	extremehut	66702	1999
121	dealtree-auctions	74452	2000	154	flashman852	66320	2004
122	carpartswholesale	73992	2004	155	smokymtnbooks	66223	2002
123	vonderpalette_de	73815	1999	156	recordsurpluschi	66204	1999
124	shopagift	73786	1999	157	kbmill2	66093	2000
125	bargainphone	72951	2002	158	e-artikel	65929	2001
126	digitaldogpound	72343	1999	159	ebr01	65913	1999
127	kg-computer_de	72342	1999	160	gsm-store	65892	1998
128	parrothead88	72173	1997	161	diageminc	65690	1998
129	globalgolfusa	72108	2002	162	dotcom-sales	65335	2000
130	beadsncharms	71951	2002	163	jewels-schmuck-design	65303	2004
131	schnaeppchen-tmcenter_de	71864	2004	164	dvdlegacy	65198	2000
132	fonport_de	70931	2002	165	jdmadera	65048	1999
133	powernetshop.de	70620	1999	166	pariser_mode	65003	2002
134	somedudesstuff	70526	2001	167	akku-king	64901	1999
135	beavinsons	70510	1998	168	cat_from_mars	64865	2002
136	fragrancealley	70467	1999	169	99volts.com	64396	1999
137	betterworldbooks	70328	2002	170	all1euro	64345	2002

Nortica eBay 500 (as of February 2006) (continued)

RANK	ID	FEEDBACK	YEAR STARTED		RANK	ID	FEEDBACK	YEAR STARTED
171	bargainbookstores	64319	2002		204	schnaeppchen-welt	60113	2000
172	akkumann01	64287	2001		205	wirelesshut	59868	2000
173	goelecsa	64197	2002		206	fitformobile-de	59572	2002
174	rgelber	64155	1998		207	abcsound	59572	2004
175	vcc113	63911	1999		208	bookmarz	59478	2004
176	henrys.com	63909	1999		209	shoetime	59462	2000
177	viccap99	63872	2000		210	digital-media-world	59162	1999
178	pdg43y	63607	1998		211	marsh-net	59156	1999
179	firqual	63549	2002		212	joeleighs	59105	1998
180	art.com	63339	1999		213	abacusink	59086	2003
181	efavormart	62923	2001		214	sfplanet	59049	1999
182	evalueville	62762	1999		215	hitmenowdotcom	58931	2000
183	simseg	62757	2001		216	gameliquidations	58837	2003
184	digidepot	62651	2001		217	stadt7	58745	1999
185	dackel-hamburg	62508	1999		218	drstevew	58577	2000
186	vge007	62328	1999		219	premium-cable	58505	2002
187	trade4less_de	62089	1999		220	waxacar	58360	2001
188	dvd-palast	62009	2003		221	sport-otto	58334	1999
189	equiteric	61883	2000		222	tommyway.com	58075	1999
190	worldsbestdeals	61720	1999		223	chinaezone	57806	2003
191	econdo_de	61492	2002		224	gogamerscom	57718	2000
192	ecellphone	61446	2002		225	blsmartcom	57523	1998
193	patrick224	61258	2000		226	budget-pc.de	57421	2001
194	wyomingben	61254	1999		227	mugsfrank	57376	1999
195	proshopwarehouse	61221	2001		228	oezcang	57334	2001
196	aaka_de	61137	1999		229	schuetz-neue-medien	57102	1999
197	consumersolutions	60887	2003		230	dd_discounters	56896	2002
198	cwgift	60791	1998		231	spoolmak	56772	1998
199	mjrsales	60761	2001		232	makotoautotrends	56567	2001
200	boing737	60732	1999		233	bestchoiceproducts	56397	2003
201	bluedrop101	60553	2002		234	kokonuts!	56372	1999
202	usbebase	60364	2004		235	computermuething	56214	2002
203	jrtradingco	60300	2000		236	moviesunlimited.com	55950	1999

Nortica eBay 500 (as of February 2006) (continued)

RANK	ID	FEEDBACK	YEAR STARTED	RANK	ID	FEEDBACK	YEAR STARTED
237	cashco1000	55947	1999	270	beadaholique	52471	1998
238	videogameswholesale	55927	2002	271	universalmusicgroup	52377	2002
239	nochbilligereinkaufen	55753	2003	272	x-part.de	52343	1999
240	directtoyou	55476	2001	273	videojam-half	52305	2000
241	seedrack	55384	2000	274	startup_software	52210	2001
242	tuningschnellversand	55374	2002	275	azsonra	52094	2003
243	megamediadepot	55353	2001	276	closeoutvideo-half	51991	2000
244	wesellart	55310	1997	277	paylessauction	51929	2002
245	bookbyte_for_textbooks	55276	1999	278	eurofuxx	51880	2001
246	aboncom	55209	1998	279	globalqualifier	51859	2000
247	exotictruck-auto	55165	2004	280	schnellelieferung*de	51842	2001
248	dans_cellular_accessories	55137	2001	281	landofjewels	51765	2002
249	omnideal-de	54947	2001	282	pda-schutzfolien	51693	2003
250	collectionstop	54868	2002	283	trendline_24zig	51655	2002
251	telko24	54816	2002	284	yesinternational	51542	2001
252	rcboyz	54685	2000	285	mydealsdirect	51509	1999
253	premiertekinc	54554	1998	286	www.silvershake.com	51126	2001
254	dauerschnaeppchen	54482	2004	287	justdeals-uk	51106	2004
255	milde4	54353	2001	288	pfandhaus-hermann	51103	1999
256	dallasgolf	54101	1999	289	netclearances	51067	2001
257	gotobidnow	53787	2002	290	animecast	50917	2000
258	omaha	53511	1998	291	oldwillknott—(great-scales!)	50485	2000
259	derbuchbaer	53487	1999	292	familyfundist	50472	2000
260	projectb_de	53467	1999	293	kriete	50418	1999
261	foto-handy-online	53314	2001	294	ez-drop	50359	2003
262	adeal.com	53247	1998	295	cyber-checkout	50287	2000
263	cheapdiecast	53168	1999	296	starbella1	50227	2003
264	ewimedia	53097	2002	297	1a-handyzubehoer	50178	2000
265	merchantoverstock	53067	2001	298	www_bbt-shop_de	50149	2001
266	sterlingtek.com	52973	1999	299	price-guard	50036	2000
267	aaccessories	52665	2001	300	edselbabe	49941	1999
268	toys-babyworld	52626	2003	301	inter-net	49939	2001
269	op2104	52472	2003	302	hpcbonline-half	49902	1999

Nortica eBay 500 (as of February 2006) (continued)

RANK	ID	FEEDBACK	YEAR STARTED	RANK	ID	FEEDBACK	YEAR STARTED
303	voeing*de	49890	2000	336	ecampus.com	47625	2001
304	smartstation	49852	2002	337	gmtobra	47527	2002
305	loreleijewelry	49815	1997	338	zzl	47454	2000
306	maxmaxshop	49791	2002	339	online-versand-grafenau	47438	2002
307	dvds123dotcom	49778	2001	340	cd-hammerpreise.de	47266	2001
308	opinionsrfun	49749	1999	341	erwinschabulke	47189	2001
309	daydeal.com	49739	2000	342	numismaticbureau	47128	1999
310	www.dealcat.de	49679	2003	343	bunches_of_books	47025	2002
311	cdplusinc	49392	2002	344	ebatt_de	47009	2002
312	vdowarehouse	49184	2002	345	marketplacebargain	46998	2001
313	hdoutlet	49176	1999	346	laser-charm	46983	2001
314	speedah	48945	2001	347	edeals	46971	2000
315	volcanogames	48928	2000	348	rcorner	46956	1999
316	chris9er	48857	2001	349	scala1	46657	1999
317	sandra0905	48804	2001	350	und-aus	46499	1999
318	mk-klema	48720	2001	351	deltatecc	46482	2002
319	seansky82	48697	2001	352	network482	46306	1999
320	mr.barlow	48634	1999	353	watchesrme	46265	1999
321	2joy-de	48615	2002	354	weisbaden	46113	1999
322	handytech24	48575	1999	355	ztradingpost	46069	2003
323	99centbookshop	48574	2003	356	universalathenaeum	46056	2002
324	twoladz	48497	2001	357	superdiscountbridal	46029	2002
325	ultrabuys	48431	2002	358	shoppingstore24	45968	2002
326	mwire	48329	1999	359	ultimatehut	45809	2001
327	doublejmusic2	48260	2000	360	dcbuys	45795	2000
328	ctgdirect.com	48048	2001	361	parrish-newbooks	45738	1999
329	mcx001	48036	2001	362	theplace	45725	1999
330	faxbook	47886	2000	363	toynk	45694	1998
331	la_tronics	47847	2003	364	xinar	45689	1998
332	numarkets	47847	1999	365	kttraders	45683	1999
333	www.peanutscharms.com	47830	1998	366	sportstown24	45675	2001
334	doulmite	47663	1998	367	buy_quick	45628	2003
335	media-distributors	47644	1997	368	postergiant	45617	1999

Nortica eBay 500 (as of February 2006) (continued)

RANK	ID	FEEDBACK	YEAR STARTED
369	stiller66aol	45570	1999
370	newtownvideo.com	45559	2001
371	cmhowell5	45551	1999
372	everydayhut	45541	2000
373	peelplus	45520	2004
374	member9ctb	45435	2000
375	dealhaven	45413	2003
376	sib-usa	45359	2002
377	watches2u_uk	45302	2002
378	uzman-import-export	45270	2002
379	nationalmusicsupply	45226	1999
380	b2cshop24	45178	2001
381	usbestdeals	45159	2004
382	wchedmond	45103	2003
383	ink-shop.de	45078	1999
384	apusauction	45054	2002
385	a1techbooks	44897	2001
386	tgm_skateboards	44889	2000
387	sprinter91801	44849	2002
388	cdsandsinglesstore	44821	2002
389	wadsey	44816	2002
390	oftimespast	44697	1998
391	dealit_de	44659	2001
392	esmy	44631	1998
393	inet-electronics	44614	2002
394	konsole2000	44500	2002
395	shippingsupply.com	44481	1997
396	genuine_oem	44426	2001
397	vanzy	44329	1998
398	versandhaus-kern-closed	44290	2001
399	daddyhog	44250	1998
400	esupplystore	44085	2000
401	cdi-wholesaler	44026	2000

RANK	ID	FEEDBACK	YEAR STARTED
402	jadgang	43951	1998
403	abacus24-7	43695	2001
404	super-cover	43639	2001
405	bluejays1	43470	1999
406	tichnak	43452	2001
407	returnbuy	43451	2000
408	posterplanet.net	43449	1997
409	gamewholesaleltd	43441	2001
410	5-stardeal	43413	1999
411	h—c	43383	2003
412	baunsal-tuning	43347	2001
413	digitaleyesdvd	43294	2002
414	connect-comp	43173	2000
415	wwcomshop	43136	1999
416	rc-company	43119	2001
417	autoaccessory4u	42931	2002
418	gsprod2	42683	2000
419	ravenb99	42659	1999
420	gogomarket	42631	2004
421	mcmccomics	42596	1997
422	doolicity	42545	1998
423	knallerpreis	42505	2002
424	jim.and.joyce	42485	1997
425	fullhousedvd	42447	2000
426	spartechnik	42440	2003
427	supercards	42306	1998
428	mobilestore1	42276	2000
429	barneysrubble	42240	1999
430	lowestpricemovie	42223	2002
431	gearbox-pc	42115	1999
432	pcsurplusonline.com	42075	1999
433	monoprice.com	42028	2000
434	gilbertandfrech	42004	2000

Nortica eBay 500 (as of February 2006) (continued)

RANK	ID	FEEDBACK	YEAR STARTED	RANK	ID	FEEDBACK	YEAR STARTED
435	gold-pool	41909	2002	468	extras4au	40348	2003
436	cleonejr	41895	1998	469	skinnyguy.com	40303	1999
437	buzzlghtyrby	41865	2001	470	fortunaenterprises	40291	2002
438	crazyape	41863	1999	471	dvdparty	40290	2001
439	design-outleter	41792	1999	472	eldirect	40236	2003
440	bananaroad	41756	1999	473	tylermartin1	40188	2000
441	topwertig	41639	2001	474	watchliquidators	40155	2002
442	kipndave	41629	2003	475	aleegold	39971	1998
443	parob	41604	1998	476	lars-369	39959	2001
444	computer-nation_de	41586	1999	477	penniesonthedollar!com	39959	2000
445	saversonlinesales	41517	2003	478	ramprodinc	39845	2000
446	www_memoryworld_de	41472	2002	479	vglq	39822	1998
447	tradizio	41403	2003	480	fastmemoryman	39817	2003
448	theubershop	41387	2000	481	spokanediscount	39746	2001
449	accessoryexport	41371	2003	482	masscloseouts	39742	1998
450	sib-auctions	41232	2003	483	mermaidink	39684	1997
451	hotdigital	41209	2001	484	legendmovies	39660	2001
452	bookemporium_half	41206	2001	485	npetrov	39553	2000
453	got_cellstuff	41177	2004	486	sweethome9	39550	2001
454	bw-discount_de	41045	2002	487	chris_hamill	39530	2001
455	resurs2	40927	2002	488	www-internetishop-com	39525	1999
456	plegend2001	40899	2001	489	bausihausi	39513	1999
457	great_service	40803	2001	490	schutzfolien24-de	39491	2001
458	www_replicawrestlingbelts_com	40750	1998	491	sandy810	39388	1999
459	hitmenow.com	40558	2001	492	texassizedeals	39355	2001
460	parrothead888	40552	2000	493	dvdukltd	39274	2003
461	doublebeez	40535	1999	494	www_pda-shop_net	39206	1999
462	wannsee-electronic	40498	2001	495	geiershop-2	39171	2004
463	cablesforpc	40460	2003	496	shatzee	39170	1998
464	buch-de	40445	2003	497	phoneparts24	39170	2004
465	discdiggers	40444	2002	498	mobilnet-24	39134	2003
466	innex_inc	40359	2002	499	mrpaolo69	39061	2002
467	frsvegas	40352	2003	500	electronicgiant	39002	2001

Nortica eBay 500 (as of February 2006) (continued)

APPENDIX B

eBay's Fastest Growing Sellers

T his list presents eBay's sellers ranked by the number of positive feedbacks they have received *in the past 30 days*. Even more than the Nortica 500, this list gives you an idea of which are currently eBay's most successful companies.

If you take a look at both lists, you can do some interesting comparisons. The companies with the greatest number of feedbacks (on the 500) are not necessarily growing as quickly now. For example, everydaysource, ranked number one on the 500 list, is seventh on the 200 list, and mancon2 has taken the number one spot on the 200. For updated information go to www.nortica.com/UserArea

RANK	ID	POSITIVE IN 30 DAYS	FEEDBACK	RANK	ID	POSITIVE IN 30 DAYS	FEEDBACK
1	mancon2	32896	34868	22	rocknrocks	13559	28282
2	pugster888	28879	148456	23	trading_circuit	13322	28561
3	gilbertandfrech	27166	42004	24	patan01	13251	136583
4	accstation	27154	272560	25	betterworldbooks	12284	70328
5	moviemarz	26172	230278	26	okluge_de	11910	136209
6	eforcity	24199	283084	27	schnaeppchen-tmcenter_de	11511	71864
7	everydaysource	21769	314614	28	findingking	11279	109788
8	casacaiman	20804	179839	29	gogomarket	11020	42631
9	itrimming	19802	266014	30	justdeals.com	10814	210016
10	jewels-schmuck-design	18696	65303	31	inflatablemadness	10614	86752
11	jayandmarie	18559	268988	32	superdiscountbridal	10518	46029
12	bargainland-liquidation	16925	124891	33	beadaholique	10414	52471
13	quigesnl	16856	8076	34	dynamic-auction	9977	128425
14	skshop	16796	187120	35	pfandhaus-hermann	9859	51103
15	big-food-net	16743	28911	36	schmuck-itter	9843	25112
16	dauerschnaeppchen	16655	54482	37	edmwholesalers	9688	96799
17	grapevinehill	16156	177608	38	bargaindepot04	9680	110228
18	greatbuybooks	15657	127665	39	egameuniverse	9618	118546
19	hippo_books	15500	28455	40	gothamcityonline	9616	121016
20	gowingstore	15160	97169	41	flashman852	9570	66320
21	colordrives	13633	30140	42	designerathletic	9457	88491

Nortica Fast Growing 200 (as of February 2006)

RANK	ID	POSITIVE IN 30 DAYS	FEEDBACK	RANK	ID	POSITIVE IN 30 DAYS	FEEDBACK
43	abeysale	9353	24144	76	paperbackworld	7003	34304
44	auctionbrokersaustralia	9348	79118	77	equiteric	6991	61883
45	evalueville	9318	62762	78	maxmaxshop	6974	49791
46	megabuys.com	9248	118990	79	collegebooksdirect-half	6967	14279
47	adamhersh	9229	113953	80	parrish-newbooks	6930	45738
48	jewelryauctioneer	9216	88878	81	luxus-mode	6881	28656
49	carpartswholesale	8972	73992	82	alpha-versandhandel	6837	18864
50	factorydealz	8685	19605	83	kimberly-mode	6794	7443
51	milehighcomics	8603	5782	84	pariser_mode	6782	65003
52	bargaincell	8500	145166	85	tntnorthnj	6779	20849
53	best-connect	8403	27777	86	rockbottomgolf	6769	109877
54	auktionwelt24	8376	19231	87	thaigem.com	6754	35187
55	cali-tel	8183	69793	88	kooljewelry	6611	12266
56	smokymtnbooks	8092	66223	89	skgames	6591	25879
57	b2cshop24	8067	45178	90	cofystoreuk	6545	90962
58	cellow-online	8053	88935	91	celiko-store	6544	115013
59	aacharm	7795	13804	92	discountcardz	6531	24860
60	thegadgetstop	7755	15746	93	preistaktikde	6527	24361
61	yayago-shop	7745	23131	94	bangkokgems	6464	9943
62	tmrn83	7739	4979	95	collectionstop	6454	54868
63	solfire2	7690	89711	96	ebestdeal4u	6406	140375
64	soundcitybeaches	7654	135632	97	greatdeals00	6401	141045
65	andreas-diehl	7641	37189	98	fonport_de	6348	70931
66	digitalwebtronics	7529	97069	99	bigrockmedia	6294	35582
67	fortunaenterprises	7498	40291	100	recordsurpluschi	6291	66204
68	mr.mobile	7463	191802	101	daniks-world	6288	160736
69	rcboyz	7445	54685	102	exotictruck-auto	6274	55165
70	great_service	7365	40803	103	www.silvershake.com	6160	51126
71	weisse-villa	7236	78034	104	monoprice.com	6145	42028
72	buddentown	7191	100160	105	premium-cable	6107	58505
73	memoryworld1	7117	174182	106	h—c	6078	43383
74	thebookpros	7052	36781	107	lead-zephyr	6063	29197
75	emilyandlily	7050	102498	108	lenycik	5992	26082

Nortica Fast Growing 200 (as of February 2006) (continued)

RANK	ID	POSITIVE IN 30 DAYS	FEEDBACK	RANK	ID	POSITIVE IN 30 DAYS	FEEDBACK
109	abe1819	5971	24257	142	fairpricemedien	5293	84305
110	bhexpress	5966	31364	143	moviemagicusa	5262	76900
111	handy-foto-pc-de	5963	87213	144	maxstore_de	5262	82195
112	abacusink	5922	59086	145	farmerjerry64	5209	10706
113	lets-sell!	5921	21136	146	silver_trend	5170	6512
114	nortado	5916	16298	147	globalgolfusa	5143	72108
115	addtronic	5914	109422	148	tchibo_auktionen	5142	19899
116	accessoryexport	5888	41371	149	charms.for.you	5122	13608
117	globalqualifier	5875	51859	150	dov4u	5111	14598
118	alengio*	5840	6131	151	glo_books	5091	4510
119	moviemars-uk	5818	8275	152	op2104	5088	52472
120	ecellphone	5817	61446	153	worldsbestdeals	5084	61720
121	belissio	5802	14039	154	summitimage	5049	24746
122	kg-computer_de	5785	72342	155	allshewants	5045	113893
123	biggtimesports	5728	16755	156	perfekt-style	5035	15934
124	ozauctionbroker	5727	28410	157	kbmill2	5015	66093
125	econdo_de	5701	61492	158	sim-buy	5000	74964
126	gamezforless	5689	38330	159	www-jpc-de	4955	24958
127	tradekontor24	5686	20888	160	megamediadepot	4953	55353
128	bargainbookstores	5662	64319	161	timikes_uk	4929	13229
129	*123trading*	5626	102719	162	hajunga	4923	5577
130	trade4less_de	5616	62089	163	$1clearance	4916	6303
131	goldkittys	5608	34725	164	coinsbybobby	4912	23684
132	phoenixtradingcompany	5585	78290	165	foto-kontor	4888	129604
133	perfect-magic-nails	5565	12733	166	toysbabyfachmarkt	4875	96637
134	dealtree-auctions	5545	74452	167	goelecsa	4871	64197
135	jadlamracing	5533	14931	168	thevideobarn	4855	21432
136	ez-drop	5490	50359	169	derbuchbaer	4853	53487
137	smartstation	5439	49852	170	justdeals-au	4851	19818
138	mediacrazy	5399	24097	171	cametaauctions	4846	122320
139	fantastic_shopping	5348	86852	172	playdeluxe_de	4827	99748
140	schmuckmueller	5312	3761	173	onlyjerseys	4819	12554
141	buy_quick	5309	45628	174	dd_discounters	4806	56896

Nortica Fast Growing 200 (as of February 2006) (continued)

RANK	ID	POSITIVE IN 30 DAYS	FEEDBACK
175	mjrsales	4800	60761
176	dealhaven	4766	45413
177	frugalmedia01	4765	21159
178	copro-online	4764	139084
179	bargainphone	4759	72951
180	rikkyboy69	4754	89552
181	moviedogpd	4753	12454
182	xxl-outlet	4744	20359
183	gsm-store	4739	65892
184	ylanx	4711	9892
185	electronic_kaufhaus	4696	32587
186	efavormart	4655	62923
187	kfzteile24-de	4614	80833

RANK	ID	POSITIVE IN 30 DAYS	FEEDBACK
188	fragrancealley	4612	70467
189	skapetze	4595	28254
190	online-versand-grafenau	4593	47438
191	brentscard	4550	82845
192	joeleighs	4545	59105
193	rubystamps	4531	20117
194	milde4	4512	54353
195	discountgames	4507	21935
196	numismaticbureau	4492	47128
197	tinxi_com	4491	21662
198	the_sharper_image	4466	143095
199	exgoods	4453	21904
200	indoo_half	4439	80045

Nortica Fast Growing 200 (as of February 2006) (continued)

INDEX

INDEX

ABOUT THE AUTHORS

Brad and Debra Schepp met as Rutgers College students and have been collaborators ever since. Cheerfully blending their interests in technology and popular culture, they write about cutting-edge technologies and how those technologies are changing our lives. Together they've written 11 books from *The Complete Passive Solar Home Book,* to *The Telecommuter's Handbook* to *Kidnet: The Kid's Guide to Surfing Through Cyberspace.* Their recent book, *eBay PowerSeller Secrets* (McGraw-Hill), is among the best-selling eBay books.

Their work has been featured in publications such as *Newsweek, The Chicago Tribune,* and *U.S. News and World Report.* They have both worked as writers and editors for McGraw-Hill. Brad was also editorial director for America Online's book division.

Brad and Deb have been buying and selling on eBay since 1999 and are eBay Trading Assistants. They are also associate members of The Professional eBay Sellers Alliance and regular contributors to AuctionBytes. If you have any comments or suggestions regarding this book or eBay in general, feel free to contact them through their website at http://www.bradanddeb.com/.